"Ryan Rindels and Vance Salis<del></del> study, as well as recovery, of sor<del></del> we treasure our beloved America<del></del> ...<del></del> of the faith (e.g. Edwards, Judson, Hodge, Warfield, Machen, etc.), it is also important for us to remember others who were greatly used by God to carry forth the gospel of the kingdom to the farthest reaches of the wilderness frontier. *Fathers of an Extensive Country* is a welcome exploration into the lives and pastoral ministries of Congregationalist Jonathan Fisher and Baptist Daniel Merrill. Not only is it well-written and engaging, it is also helpful and encouraging. As this generation of scholars continues to labor for historical recovery, I am grateful to Rindels and Salisbury for their commendable and heartfelt work."

Nate Pickowicz
Pastor, Harvest Bible Church, Gilmanton Iron Works, NH;
Author of *Reviving New England* and *How to Eat Your Bible*

"*Fathers of an Extensive Country* is an enlightening analysis of the theology and impact of Reverends Jonathan Fisher and Daniel Merrill of Maine. Rindels and Salisbury successfully examine the theological environment of Maine during the late eighteenth and early nineteenth centuries, while also situating Fisher and Merrill in the greater context of the evolving religious culture of the American Early Republic. Rindels and Salisbury explore the distinctions between Christians during the period of study while acutely observing that Fisher and Merrill ultimately shared a desire to spread the gospel. This work demonstrates that then, as now, theology has the power to divide and unite and can have both immediate and long-ranging impacts."

Brittany Goetting
Assistant Professor of History,
University of Pikeville

"Rindels and Salisbury carefully examine two important figures in the religious history of Evangelical Christianity in Maine. Daniel Merrill's leadership among the Baptists is an example of the positive social benefits of advocating for theological conviction while working within society to address tangible needs. This well-researched volume provides a great contribution to the history of Baptists in Maine in light of a fresh examination of primary sources. It also gives a case study for determining how churches can collaborate without violating doctrinal distinctives."

Jonathan McCormick
Associate Professor of Theological Research,
Gateway Seminary

Strengthened by the discovery of a number of new sources, this study illuminates the development of Evangelical Christianity in the early United States by juxtaposing the careers of two pastors in Downeast Maine who began as collegial Congregationalist neighbors: Jonathan Fisher (b. 1769) of Blue Hill, committed all his life to the Standing Order; and Daniel Merrill (b. 1765) of Sedgwick, fifteen miles away, who discovered credobaptism in 1803 and soon took his congregation (and much of Fisher's) into new Baptist churches in both communities. The authors argue convincingly that in the end their similarities proved more significant than their theological differences: that their common devotion to Calvinist principles, their missionary zeal, and their successful efforts to establish educational institutions for coming generations, shaped Maine's emerging religious culture so as to allow collaboration among Evangelicals in spite of doctrinal disagreement.

Michael McVaugh
Wells Professor of History (emeritus),
University of North Carolina

"Historians of the early American republic tend to overlook any co-operation between Baptists and Congregationalists in New England, a place not known for its religious toleration. But the eastern frontier of Maine was a different animal. In *Fathers of an Extensive Country*, Ryan Rindels and Vance Salisbury demonstrate how the explosive issue of baptism did not prevent two pastors in historically rival denominations from nation-shaping with those of other convictions. This is a side of the New England tradition not often told, and Rindels and Salisbury tell it well. A great read."

Obbie Tyler Todd
Pastor, Third Baptist Church Marion, IL;
Adjunct Professor of History,
New Orleans Baptist Theological Seminary

Fathers of an Extensive Country

To mom and dad, who brought me up in the discipline and instruction of the Lord; evangelicals, in the best sense of the word.

Ryan

In memory of Ronald S. Baines,
Maine Baptist pastor and historian.

Vance

"For though you have ten-thousand guides in Christ, you do not have many fathers. For I became to you a father in Christ Jesus through the gospel."

1 Corinthians 4:15

RYAN RINDELS & VANCE SALISBURY

FATHERS OF AN EXTENSIVE COUNTRY

The Lives and Ministries of
Daniel Merrill & Jonathan Fisher

H&E
Publishing

H&E Publishing, West Lorne, Ontario
www.hesedandemet.com

Front cover image: Lighthouse at Camden Maine by Fitz Henry Lane, 1851

Paperback ISBN: 978-1-77484-118-1
eBook ISBN: 978-1-77484-119-8

Contents

Preface

In his 1949 book, *Christianity and History*, Cambridge historian Herbert Butterfield (1900–1979) noted that history is a "peculiar science," as it relies as much on, "insight, sympathy and imagination" as documentary evidence. Assuming, as Butterfield did, that such terms and conditions are necessary components of the discipline, a historian must therefore, "use his imaginative sympathy, must give something of himself, to the reconstruction of an historical character."[1] The present authors concur with Butterfield's sentiment and offer no pretense of detached objectivity—an approach whose plausibility and value is questionable. Historical knowledge itself is, as David Bebbington has written, "a matter of personal engagement."[2] The lives of Jonathan Fisher and Daniel Merrill are interesting in many respects, particularly for readers curious about Maine during the Early National Period. Fisher's life has been the subject of numerous contemporary studies. Surprisingly little has been written on Merrill. This study focuses on the ecclesial aspect of Jonathan Fisher and Daniel Merrill's lives. Understandably, this entails exploration and engagement with their theology and spirituality.

Fathers of an Extensive Country draws from original primary sources, many of which were previously unpublished. Important as research may be for the purpose of scholarship, we believe that the narrative of Jonathan Fisher and Daniel Merrill's story offers contemporary readers value of an instructive nature to those who

---

[1] Herbert Butterfield, *Christianity and History* (New York: Charles Scribners, 1949), 17–18.

[2] David Bebbington, *Patterns in History: A Christian Perspective on Historical Thought* (Vancouver, Regent College Publishing, 2000), 149.

profess—or are at least open to—the Christian faith these pastors believed. As their writings attest, Jonathan Fisher and Daniel Merrill were classically evangelical, with Calvinistic emphasis on the sovereignty of God, a passion for personal conversion, and intentional activity oriented towards revival.[3] They were men, who, in the words of the late Martin Lloyd-Jones (1899–1981), realized that they were "confronted by something that is too deep for [their] methods," and thus needed "something that could go down beneath that evil power and shatter it."[4] They needed the power of God. And by their own testimony, if only for a brief time, they received it.

The Bible teaches that human nature remains fundamentally unchanged through the centuries. If this is true, then contemporary audiences can learn from Fisher and Merrill's sermons, books, and example not only knowledge, but wisdom. Cross-denominational cooperation, diffusing of conflict, and even rigorous methods for discipleship—these are a few things they did well. Granted, the world is dramatically different today than it was in the early nineteenth century. This poses a challenge to transposing some aspects of their ministry into a modern key. Nevertheless, two centuries of distance is not an unbridgeable span.

Understandably, there are methodological concerns in making prescriptive conclusions from historical content. Can an author be both historian and preacher without corrupting both? In an essay discussing the "providential" interpretation of history, Andrew Atherstone argues that there is place for "confessional" and "professional" works of history.[5] While this book does not give

---

[3] Alec Ryrie's comments about Protestants in general as a people who possess, "a certain generic restlessness, an itchy instability" are apropos. See *Protestants: The Radicals Who Made the Modern World* (London: William Collins, 2017), 4–5.

[4] Martin Lloyd-Jones, *Revival* 5th ed. (Wheaton, IL: Crossway, 1997), 19. The book was the product of a series of lectures Jones gave in 1959.

[5] Andrew Atherstone, "Hagiography and History." Cited in Nathan A. Finn, *History: A Student's Guide* (Wheaton, IL: Crossway, 2016), 79.

providential explanations for the course of events (except where Fisher and Merrill make explicit claims themselves), we believe in providence on the basis of our Christian confession. We do not presume to adequately understand, much less explain, the full and final meaning of their lives for the same theological reasons. Whether we balance the professional-confessional tension will be for the reader to judge.

This book divides into five chapters. The introduction provides historical context for Congregational and Baptist churches in New England beginning in the seventeenth century. Chapter one is a biographical overview of Jonathan Fisher's life; chapter two is devoted to that of Daniel Merrill. Chapter three focuses on Daniel Merrill's reasons for embracing believer's baptism and conversely, Jonathan Fisher's rationale in defending pedobaptism. Chapter four explores the nature of Fisher and Merrill's cooperation before and after Merrill's decision to become a Baptist. Included are the challenges each pastor faced, the extent to which they successfully worked together, and inherent limitations to their fellowship. The concluding chapter offers guidance for contemporary readers, particularly those in pastoral ministry. The events and experiences of these two New England pastors, their convictions and passions included, have the potential to illumine our own age, whether by example or as warning.

Introduction

In 1804, Congregationalist pastor Daniel Merrill faced a difficult decision. Through rigorous study of the Bible and extended reflection, he had come to the conclusion that infant baptism had no warrant in Scripture. Like many converts to a Baptist identity before and after him, Merrill did not consider questions of the proper mode and subject of baptism as theologically-tangential to the Christian faith. When and how a person was baptized mattered. To err in this regard was grievous; the consequences for such actions profound. Daniel Merrill knew that becoming a Baptist would transform his ministry, but the outcome of this transformation lay in an unknown future. Understandably, there were disconcerting questions that would need answers. For example, did baptism of infants, by its very practice, disqualify a gathered body of worshippers from the very appellation "church"? And if the New Testament pattern—as provided in the Acts of the Apostles—describes demonstrable, personal faith as preceding baptism, is infant baptism therefore invalid? Surely, no church can exist if its members are in fact, *unbaptized*. Additionally, what would this shift mean for a future relationship to Congregationalism? Daniel Merrill was no sectarian. As a member of the Hancock Association of Congregational ministers, he devoted time and money to evangelizing the frontier regions of Maine. He did not want to dispense with this aspect of his pastorate.[1]

---

[1] Calvin Montague Clark, *History of the Congregational Churches in Maine, Volume 2: History of the Individual Churches 1600-1626* (Portland, ME: The Congregational Christian Conference of Maine, 1935), 381: "The next ... Association to be formed was the Hancock ... The versatile and eccentric Jonathan Fisher had begun his more than forty years' pastorate at Blue Hill ... The organization of the Association, as already noted, was at Sedgwick, and it may easily be surmised that the leader in the

Balancing newfound ecclesial convictions with biblical exhortations that Christ's body be unified (John 17:21) has been, historically speaking, one of Protestantism's greatest weaknesses. Yet for all its admirable dimensions, contemporary ecumenicism struggles to account for cases like Daniel Merrill's. Why, after all, could Sedgwick's pastor not simply baptize persons who professed faith in Christ while accommodating those whose consciences did not compel them to be baptized as adults? This path would plausibly diminish the risk of offending the Congregationalist majority, and preserve the existing fruitful cooperation with pastors such as Jonathan Fisher. But maintaining the status quo is exactly what Daniel Merrill's conscience would not allow. Granted, Merrill was not alone in his shift to Baptist views. The majority of his Sedgwick congregation were not only convinced by their minister's arguments, but many would become zealous Baptists themselves, as would a number of Fisher's congregation in Bluehill. Like all growing movements, the passion and energy that brought in converts simultaneously made new enemies. Baptists in New England may have lacked cultural prestige, but they could no longer be suppressed or ignored.

Daniel Merrill and Jonathan Fisher's story is perhaps most interesting because it takes into account the limits of cooperation when two denominations hold firmly to their respective theological positions. Rare is the occasion in which two traditions make concessions to the other, accepting a kind of idealized theological middle ground for the sake of unity. Even in instances where it does happen, the respective parties are not equally satisfied with the arrangement. Furthermore, such compromises are often prompted by concerns about viability. A dying church, for example, that merges with a stronger one for the purposes of survival is

---

movement for organization was the independent and enterprising pastor of that church, Daniel Merrill."

6

compelled to make compromises. For ascendant denominations, doctrinal distinctives are what usually constitute their very strength and vitality. As a Congregationalist-turned-Baptist, Daniel Merrill was ascendant. He would thus have to reimagine and reorient his ministry in the same community that knew of his old identity. The same would be true of Jonathan Fisher, a Congregationalist pastor who would have to navigate the sobering realities of a growing Baptist presence in Maine without waging denominational warfare or violating his own conscience.

Baptist and Congregationalist beginnings

Baptist historians and theologians have an ongoing debate about the very meaning, and consequent boundaries of the denominator "Baptist." Is a Baptist defined by their adherence to credobaptism, the belief that only persons who can profess faith in Christ and provide evidence of repentance, as opposed to the sprinkling of—or in the case of the Orthodox tradition, immersing—infants? Or is a Baptist defined by polity, notably the conviction that a local church should be led by members of the congregation? Most Baptists in the past four centuries have affirmed both components as necessary. But the very fact that congregational governance is a sufficient marker, that a figure no less than John Bunyan (1628–1688) is embraced as a Baptist despite allowing pedobaptists to be members of his church, shows how proximal these two Protestant traditions are.[2] The step from one into the other is short indeed.

Congregationalists and Baptists emerged from Puritans dissatisfied with lack of reform within the Church of England in the

---

[2] See Joseph D. Ban, "Was John Bunyan a Baptist?: A Case Study in Historiography" *Baptist Quarterly* 30.8 (1984): 367–376. Bunyan wrote, *Water Baptism no Bar to Communion* in 1673 as part of a pamphlet war with the Particular Baptist pastor and theologian William Kiffin (1616–1701). Cf. Steve Weaver, "When Biography Shapes Ecclesiology: Bunyan, Kiffin, and the Open-Communion Debate," *The Journal of Baptist Studies* 9 (2018): 31–54.

1580's.[3] By strict chronology, churches of congregational polity in America can be traced to the Separatists that settled at Plymouth in 1620. It was, however, the immigrants that settled at Massachusetts Bay in 1630, and led by governor and layman John Winthrop (1588-1648), that took the mantle of ecclesial leadership in New England.[4] In the same decade that saw the settlement and growth of Massachusetts Bay, several Puritans in England founded an independent congregational church, Calvinistic in theology and with Separatist leanings. Led by Henry Jacob (1615-1691), John Lathrop (1584-1633), and Henry Jessey (1603-1663), the "JLJ church," whose origins can be traced to the early 1630's, had some members who were rebaptized as early as 1633.[5] By 1638, several persons left the JLJ Church to join a group led by John Spilsbury, who explicitly rejected infant baptism and required that its members be baptized as believers. Distinguished by their doctrine of a "particular redemption" (typically called *limited atonement* today), they were identified as Particular Baptists. By the mid-1640's there were seven known Particular Baptist churches in London, by 1660, these churches numbered 130 across England, Wales, and Ireland.[6]

In America, notable figures of Puritan origin who became Baptists included Roger Williams (1638/39), John Clarke (1651), and Harvard's second president, Henry Dunster (1609-1659) in 1653/54. A Baptist church, led by Thomas Goold was founded in

---

[3] We are aware that General Baptists led by John Smyth and Thomas Helwys predated Calvinistic English Baptists by two decades. However, their descendants were less numerous and the majority became unorthodox by the late seventeenth century. Some General Baptists settled in America, but most Baptists, like Daniel Merrill, came out of New Light Congregationalism.

[4] During the 1630's, around 20,000 immigrants came from England settled at Massachusetts Bay. See Robert Handy, *A History of the Churches in United States and Canada* (New York: Oxford University Press, 1977), 20.

[5] Both Lathrop and Jacob ventured to America and Lathrop died in Massachusetts.

[6] Anthony L. Chute, Nathan A. Finn, and Michael A.G. Haykin, *The Baptist Story: From English Sect to Global Movement* (Nashville, B&H, 2015), 25.

Boston in 1665. Its existence was, however, tenuous as members faced fines, imprisonment and disenfranchisement.[7] With numeric and civic advantages, Congregationalism would establish a foothold in New England by the 1630's and hold unrivaled political, cultural, and religious hegemony for nearly two centuries, often referred to as the Standing Order.[8] It is from Massachusetts, the heart of New England Congregationalism, that Jonathan Fisher and Daniel Merrill would come. The genealogy and development of these respective traditions provides insight into the social context(s) and the theological milieu from which they emerged, and where they would later serve as pastors.

Congregationalism in provincial New England

As noted, Plymouth Separatists constituted the first Congregationalist presence in New England. By 1691, however, the colony was absorbed into Massachusetts Bay, their ecclesial and theological identity as distinct from their brethren to the north was lost.[9] If roles were reversed and the Separatist had numbers similar to

---

[7] Handy, *A History*, 47.

[8] Jonathan D. Sassi devotes an entire chapter to "The Standing Order's Corporate Vision" which he characterizes as "the establishment." Sassi presents a thoughtful and objective appraisal of the role and influence of the standing order in New England during the final two decades of the eighteenth and the early nineteenth century. "Formally, establishment signifies the churches that received legal and fiscal privileges from the state. In either usage, the Congregationalists were New England's legal and traditional establishment." Jonathan D. Sassi, *A Republic of Righteousness: The Public Christianity of the Post-Revolutionary New England Clergy* (New York: Oxford University Press, 2001), 19–51. See also, Alan Taylor, "From Fathers to Friends of the People: Political Personas in the Early Republic," *Journal of the Early Republic* 11, No. 4, (Winter, 1991): 465–491; Taylor, Alan. *Liberty Men and Great Proprietors: The Revolutionary Settlement on the Maine Frontier, 1760-1820* (University of North Carolina Press, 1990), 131.

[9] Winthrop Hudson, *Religion in America: An historical account of the development of American Religious Life*, 2nd ed. (New York: Charles Scribner's, 1973), 37. Hudson observes that in the New World, the central issue that divided Separatists from non-Separatist Congregationalists–whether or not the parish churches of England should be viewed as true churches—"was not of great significance, for they had to establish churches of their own. Thus, they became joint representatives of what was to be a single denomination."

Massachusetts Bay, New England may have developed differently. In England, theologians such as William Ames (1576–1633) and Henry Jacob, the LJL church's original pastor, argued strongly against the Separatist position.[10] For contemporary readers in religiously pluralistic contexts, the nature of the disagreements between Separatists and non-Separatist Congregationalists appears negligible, but the seventeenth century was not an age of theological indifference. The following assessment by New Englander Nathaniel Ward, written in 1647, captures a sentiment common at the time.

He that is willing to tolerate any Religion, or discrepant way of Religion, besides his own, unless it be in matters merely indifferent, either doubts of his own, or is not sincere in it.[11]

Ward's striking comments notwithstanding, the wider picture does provide some balance. Included among the pastors who immigrated to New England in 1633 were John Cotton (1584–1652), Thomas Hooker (1586–1647), and Samuel Stone, all capable and erudite pastors. In reply to Roger Williams' *The Bloudy Tenent of Persecution* (1644), which argued that religious liberty was necessary for genuine Christianity to flourish, Cotton penned *The Bloudy Tenent, Washed and Made White in the Bloud of the Lamb* (1647), a treatise that defended the prevailing alliance of church and state. Cotton and Williams believed in the exclusivity of the gospel, and both desired that it flourish, but disagreed on what arrangement would be most conducive to this end.[12] Charles

---

[10] Handy, *A History*, 22.

[11] Nathaniel Ward, *The Simple Cobbler of Aggawam in America*, 4th ed. (London, 1647), 8.

[12] John G. Turner's comments provide insight. "Williams did not favor protections for dissenters because he liked and respected them. Quite the contrary. Williams believed that nearly all existing churches were full of Antichrist. In a sense though, Williams's own intolerance and zeal led him to embrace religious liberty." See *They*

Hambrick Stowe comments that although history has favored Williams, "Cotton's position that personal faith and public are interconnected has also persisted in America."[13] In *The Keyes of the Kingdome of Heaven* (1644) and *The Way of Congregational Churches Cleared* (1648), Cotton proposed church polity on the basis of believers "making public confession of their faith before the Lord, and their brethren."[14] It was from Cotton's own preaching that Anne Hutchinson (1591-1643) embraced a spiritualism that led her to denounce what she believed was arid, religious formalism. She would consequently be banished to Rhode Island on the basis of supposed antinomianism.

As the above example attests, emphasis on the conversion of individual souls—an encounter with the living Christ—stood in inescapable tension to state-supported denominational uniformity. The test of spiritual experience, so vital to pastors like John Cotton, was, in the words of Susan Hardman Moore, New England's "startling innovation."[15] Sustaining a community that emphasized the need for personal conversion on the one hand, while proscribing the options for its citizens, became nearly impossible to maintain without conceding to demands. Seeds with the potential to sprout dissent continued to be sown in sermons, tracts, and books. And yet unlike a majority of mystic and spiritualist movements, an educated clergy remained a priority for these Puritans.

Adherence to the Reformed theological tradition combined with a high regard for a learned ministry, led non-Separatist

---

Knew They Were Pilgrims: Plymouth Colony and the Contest for Religious Liberty (New Haven: Yale University Press, 2020), 153.

[13] Charles Hambrick Stowe, "'Christ the Fountain of Life' by John Cotton" in *The Devoted Life: An Introduction to the Puritan Classics*, eds., Kelly Kapic and Randall Gleason (Downer's Grove, IL: Apollos, 2004), 69.

[14] Stowe, "Christ the Foundation of Life," 69.

[15] Susan Hardman Moore, *Pilgrims: New World Settler and the Call of Home* (New Haven: Yale University Press, 2007), 5.

Congregationalists to establish an academic institution for training pastors, Harvard college, in 1636. In *New England's Firstfruits* (1643), the authors wrote,

> After God had carried us safe to New England and we had builded our houses, provided necessaries for our livelihood, reared convenient places for God's worship, and settled the civil government, one of the next things we long for, and looked after was to advance learning and perpetuate it to posterity, dreading to leave an illiterate ministry to the churches when our present ministers shall be dust.[16]

The concluding line is significant, for it presages conflict between Harvard's vision of the pastorate and the values of later sects, the majority of which did not place primacy on formal, institutional instruction.[17] The rapid growth of New England's population required that new ministers be sufficiently trained and then be assigned in new communities. As would be the case of the Bluehill Congregational church in the late eighteenth century, demand on the Maine frontier exceeded supply. Isolation made it nearly impossible to educate ministers at a pace necessary to accommodate the eastward expansion.[18] With their ecclesial flexibility and primacy on "calling" over academic credentials, Methodists and Baptists, beginning in the late eighteenth century would exploit this weakness, reaping large numbers of converts.[19] One-

---

[16] Hudson, *Religion in America*, 38.

[17] Priscilla Adams comments, "In the eighteenth century, the position of minister was a demanding one which required a man of letters to officiate as legal counsel, doctor, administrator of social mores and teacher." See "Jonathan Fisher" in *Versatility Yankee Style*, The Farnsworth Museum (Rockland, Maine: Courier-Gazette, Inc., 1977).

[18] During this period, population in the district of Maine increased more than ten times. Taylor, *Liberty Men and Great Proprietors*, 135.

[19] John Dillenberger and Claude Welch, *Protestant Christianity: Interpreted through its Development* (New York: Charles Scribner's, 1954), 148. Jonathan Fisher did believe some men qualified for ordination though they lacked formal education. Thus, he presided over the ordination of Ebenezer Eaton as an evangelist in July of 1823. See

hundred-and-thirty new Baptist churches were established between 1772 and 1820.[20] Yet the weakening and stagnation of Congregationalism, particularly at the beginning of Fisher and Merrill's pastorate, could be as much attributed to internal as external factors.

As Sydney Ahlstrom argued, potential for theological liberalism was inherent in the Puritan vision of the church. He cites a 1629 church covenant from Salem in which the members agreed to "walk together in his waies, according as he is pleased to reveale himself unto us in his Blessed word of truth." In addition to doctrinal minimalism, Ahlstrom observes a tradition that placed great value on reason.[21] The same New England soil which produced a Jonathan Edwards could also bring forth a Charles Chauncy (1705-1787). A later slide towards Unitarianism—Chauncy was the first notable Congregationalist to do so—though it did not necessarily follow from a voluntarist ecclesiology, is unsurprising. What does come as a modest surprise is the firm orthodoxy Jonathan Fisher held despite being trained at Harvard in 1790's. As early as 1740, evangelist George Whitefield criticized the school for the "bad books" popular among students and tutors.[22] By the time Fisher was a student, Harvard offered a diluted classical curriculum with little Latin and less Greek. Young men were not required to read classic works of seventeenth-century Reformed orthodoxy or even the writings of Jonathan Edwards.[23] As his facility with classical languages and texts and familiarity

Richard S. Carter "A Puritan Encounter with the Nineteenth Century: The Mind and Ministry of Jonathan Fisher." (Unpublished doctoral thesis. Gordon-Conwell Theological Seminary. South Hamilton, MA, 2004), 7.

[20] Hudson, *Religion in America*, 73.

[21] Sydney Ahlstrom, *A Religious History of the American People* (New Haven, CT: Yale University Press, 1973) 390.

[22] George Whitefield, *George Whitefield's Journals (1737-1741)*, October 5, 1740, ed. William V. David (Edinburgh : Banner of Truth Trust, 1986), 144.

[23] Gary Dorrien, *The Making of American Liberal Theology: Imagining Progressive Religion 1805-1900* (Louisville: Westminster John Knox, 2001), 11.

with Reformed divines and Jonathan Edwards indicate, Fisher supplemented his learning.

At the conclusion of the eighteenth-century, three distinct parties vied for denominational leadership. The theological heirs of Edwards and the New Divinity school took on the label, "Consistent Calvinists." Moderate anti-revivalists identified as, "Old Calvinists." Those of a rationalist bent, represented by the faculty of Harvard and a majority of the churches of eastern Massachusetts, were deemed "liberal," though as Gary Dorrien notes, theirs was a conservative version of Unitarianism.[24] William Ellery Channing (1780-1843), who led his Congregationalist church in Boston into Unitarianism, eventually becoming its most persuasive and fashionable apologist, claimed in an 1815 letter written to Samuel C. Thatcher that, "I will venture to assert, that there is not on earth a body of men who possess less of the spirit of proselytism, than the ministers of this town and vicinity."[25] The statement captures a disposition that stood in sharp contrast to the evangelistic ethos of Merrill and Fisher, local missionaries in their own right—and self-consciously so.

Liberal Congregationalist churches such as Channing's would embrace Unitarianism, notably en masse around 1815.[26] The Old Calvinists would split, some into Unitarianism, and a conservative contingent would adopt the revivalist wing. Resistance to progressive trends came from the leadership of Jedidiah Morse (1761-1826).[27] The *Panopolist*, a journal that sought to represent orthodox Calvinism, and Andover Theological Seminary were notable fruits that emerged from conservatives. A contingent of students

---

[24] Dorrien, *The Making of American Liberal Theology*, xxii.

[25] Dorrien, *Making of American Liberal Theology*, 26.

[26] Hudson, *Religion in America*, 120. For the history of Unitarianism see E.M. Wilbur, *A History of Unitarianism in Transylvania, England, and America* (Cambridge, MA: 1952). Henry Ware (1745-1815)'s appointment to the Hollis professorship of divinity in 1805 marked a definitive liberal shift.

[27] Handy, *A History*, 198.

at Williams College participated in the so-called "Haystack Prayer Meeting" which led to the sending of Congregationalist missionaries and founding of influential missionary agencies. Interestingly, the legendary missionary couple Adoniram and Anne Judson—the former being an Andover graduate—were commissioned as Congregationalists but became convinced Baptists once in Asia.

Fisher fit squarely in the Consistent Calvinist camp and maintained these theological commitments throughout his life as the following words, written to his son, Josiah in 1837, make clear,

> The doctrines of divine foreordination, entire human depravity; predestination, or eternal election, free justification, and the perseverance of the saints, are precious to me notwithstanding all that in these days is said against them.[28]

Fisher and other Consistent Calvinists paid a heavy price in terms of loss of cultural influence. By the late 1820's there were 135 Unitarian churches in Massachusetts, close to one hundred of those came off Congregational rolls. Perhaps most significantly, Congregationalism's most prestigious churches, including twenty of the twenty-five original churches in Massachusetts became Unitarian.[29] Fisher and Merrill would live long enough to see the progressive religion's rapid shift. In 1831, Ralph Waldo Emerson, raised in the first generation of Massachusetts Unitarians, was preaching that "a trust in yourself is the height, not of pride, but of piety."[30] In 1833, he inverted the classic *regula fidei*, claiming

---

[28] Kevin D. Murphy, *Jonathan Fisher of Blue Hill, Maine: Commerce, Culture, and Community on the Eastern Frontier* (Boston: University of Massachusetts Press, 2010), 228.

[29] Dorrien, *Making of American Liberal Theology*, 38.

[30] Ralph Waldo Emerson, "God in us," Blotting Book II, July 15, 1831, 3:279. Cited in Dorrien, *Making of American Liberal Theology*, 62.

that Christianity, "is a rule of life, not a rule of faith."[31] Emerson may have been an outlier in the 1830's, but sympathetic New Englanders would not be far behind. Unlike most intellectual movements, theological liberalism did not originate in the academy and then make its way into the pulpit. As Gary Dorrien has written, Henry Ward Beecher (1813–1887), the most famous American liberal preacher in the second-half of the nineteenth-century, was fond of noting that "theological conservativism was dethroned in America by pastors, not by academics."[32]

Baptists in New England

Just as there is no direct genealogical line—despite theological commonalities—from continental Anabaptism to the General Baptists in England, so one does not find descent from seventeenth-century Calvinistic Baptists in New England to the many congregations which would emerge from the fires of revival that began in the 1740's.[33] One interesting regional anomaly is the establishment of the first Baptist church in Maine at Kittery, organized by William Screven (1629–1713) in 1682. The Kittery church's leaders drafted one of the earliest Baptist covenants in America. In language reminiscent of *New England's Firstfruits*, the signers promised to observe,

> all his most holy and blessed commandtts Ordinances Institutions or Appointments, Revealed to us in his sacred word of ye ould and new Testament according to ye grace of god and light att present through grace given us, or here after he shall please to discover and make knowne to us thro his holy

---

[31] "The simplest person," in Emerson, "The Over Soul" (1841), reprinted in the *The Essays of Ralph Waldo Emerson* (Cambridge: Harvard University Press, 1987), 173.

[32] Dorrien, *Making of American Liberal Theology*, 248.

[33] In addition to Roger Williams, Henry Dunster, and Thomas Goold, John Clarke and Obadiah Holmes (1607?–1682) were baptized as believers and ministered in Rhode Island. William McLoughlin said of Baptists in America, it was, "essentially an indigenous parallel movement to that in England and not an offshoot or extension of it."

spirit according to ye same blessed word all ye Dayes of our lives.[34]

In 1695, Screven and his congregants, harassed by Massachusetts' Congregationalist authorities, moved to South Carolina where they formed the first Baptist church in the region.[35] Though Baptists in the south would be a minority for another century, the move portended the future center of the denomination. Once in Charleston, Screven served as pastor until 1708. He encouraged the congregation to select a pastor who would be "orthodox in the faith, and of blameless life, and does own the Confession put forth by our brethren in London."[36] "The Confession" was likely the *Second London Confession of Faith* (1677/1689), the most thorough exposition of Calvinistic Baptist theology. This detail is significant in light of theological shifts that occurred in the subsequent four decades.

Between the years 1700 and 1730, virtually no new Baptist churches were established in New England. Seminal to invigorating Baptist churches were George Whitefield's early preaching tours, particularly during the years 1739-1742. Baptist opinion on Whitefield was divided at the time. In 1742, for example, support for the evangelist caused a schism at the First Baptist church of Boston.[37] The most significant person converted under Whitefield, and who later left the Congregationalist establishment was Isaac Backus (1724-1806), an influential figure in American Baptist history, whose own story bears close resemblance to that of

---

[34] Bill J. Leonard, *Baptist Ways: A History* (Valley Forge, PA: Judson Press), 83–84; William G. McLoughlin, *Soul Liberty: The Baptists' Struggle in New England, 1630-1833* (Lebanon, NH: University Press of New England, 1991), 19.

[35] Sydney Ahlstrom comments on sect formation as an expression of alienation; "it is a movement of people who are spiritually, socially, economically, educationally, or other ways 'disinherited.'" See *A Religious History of the American People*, 473.

[36] O.K. Armstrong and Marjorie Armstrong, *The Baptists in America* (Garden City, NJ: Doubleday, 1979), 82. Cited in Leonard, *Baptist Ways*, 84.

[37] Chute, Finn, Haykin, *The Baptist Story*, 76.

Daniel Merrill. Backus, after reading a defense of believer's baptism by the English Baptist Samuel Wilson, became convinced, and told his congregation of his new position. Upon becoming a Baptist, there were 29 such churches in Massachusetts and Connecticut, yet by the 1790's, the same region had 86 new congregations.[38]

Like Merrill and Fisher, Backus promoted cooperation among autonomous congregations, thereby increasing their scope of influence. In 1742, the Philadelphia Association was formed, a prototype of future associational denominational organization. Bill Leonard notes that the Philadelphia Association "demonstrated the effort of early American Baptists to maintain local autonomy and congregational authority while joining in cooperative endeavors."[39] William McLoughlin observes the contrast between Roger Williams' vision of America, and that of Isaac Backus, the latter of which anticipated, "the day when Baptist ministers and evangelists would convert all Americans to antipedobaptism."[40] Backus, for example, supported the constitution of Massachusetts that required holders of office to take religious oaths, and supported regulating activities that could be lawfully done on Sundays.[41] In this sense, Backus retained the New England Puritan vision of a godly society in which church and state worked in close cooperation. Considering the dramatic increase of Baptist growth in New England, it's understandable that Backus' broader objectives appeared to be within reach. Jonathan Fisher and Daniel Merrill were born four decades after Isaac Backus, yet their ministries and experiences had parallels to the first generation of New

---

[38] Chute, Finn, Haykin, *The Baptist Story*, 76.

[39] Leonard, *Baptist Ways*, 115.

[40] William McLoughlin, *Soul Liberty Soul Liberty: Baptists' Struggle in New England 1630–1833.* (Hanover, NH: University of New England Press, 1991) 259. Backus did not believe in granting full religious liberty to Roman Catholics believing that doing so undermined democracy.

[41] Leonard, *Baptist Ways*, 124.

Light Congregationalists. They would, however, be the last generation with direct connection to the men and women converted during the first Great Awakening, and who could assume that a vast majority of the nation's residents were Protestants who fit broadly in the Reformed tradition.

Conclusion

As will be discussed, despite their obvious disagreement over baptism, Jonathan Fisher and Daniel Merrill held similar views, not only of the pastorate, but the wider culture of New England, and the state of Maine in particular. Their desires for the young American nation overlapped, and were at times, interwoven. Considering the parallels between Congregationalists and Baptists who emerged from a Puritan context, adherence to seventeenth-century orthodox Calvinism, insistence that churches should be led by members of local congregations, and the importance of regeneration, it is not surprising to see fruitful cooperation on the Maine frontier. The inevitable downside of such proximity was the potential for defections. Like most families, siblings have a proclivity to distinguish themselves in an attempt to prove their independence, by overemphasizing genuine, albeit, minor differences. And while Fisher and Merrill proved to be wise and understanding to the other's cause, the theological distinctives were weightier to their less sympathetic disciples.

1
Established:
Jonathan Fisher, pastor at Bluehill

In a 1988 essay, "Jonathan Fisher's Emblematic Mind," David Kleitz observed that, "No single figure of the Early Republic commanded more scholarly attention in 'Maine Statehood' than the Reverend Jonathan Fisher, the versatile parson of Blue Hill."[1] Fisher's multifarious giftings have prompted extensive study on facets of his life, though scholarly interest tends to focus on sociological and economic concerns rather than the pastor's theology and spirituality. Fisher would likely be disappointed that contemporary researchers are more interested in the crafts he made than the Calvinism he preached.[2] Fisher may, in part, bear some of the blame. By encoding some 3,000 sermons that were delivered over a 40-year period, the reverend saved paper at the expense of a

---

[1] Cited in Charles E. Clark, James S. Leamon, and Karen Bowden, eds., *Maine in The Early Republic* (Hanover, NH: University Press of New England, 1988), 198–213. Alice Winchester described Fisher as "a vivid personality, lively-minded, many-sided, he was the universal man of a little Maine town, more than a versatile Yankee: in a remote little Maine town he was the universal man." See Murphy, *Jonathan Fisher*, 76.

[2] A single chapter of biography cannot do full justice to Jonathan Fisher. The most definitive biography to date is Mary Ellen Chase's *Jonathan Fisher: Maine Parson, 1747–1815* (New York: The Macmillan Company, 1948). Chase characterized Fisher's theology as "a high and dry Calvinism with no unusual notes at all." Chase, *Maine Parson*, 37. Rev. Stephen Thurston provides a more sympathetic assessment, "The life of such a man exerts a powerful influence for good. I knew him well. I was once, for several months, a member of his family, and more than ten years a member of his church. I can truly say that I have never known a man who better illustrated in private life the religion which he publicly taught. His religion was deep and vital, experimental and practical. It was the element in which he lived and breathed. Whether he wrought in his field or shop, his study or pulpit, he did all to the glory of God. His reverence for God was deep, uniform, and influential." Cited in Chase, *Maine Parson*, 279.

wider future readership.[3] Such cost-cutting measures, by their very existence, provide insight into the life and times of the Maine pastor. The same man who created a sophisticated shorthand, lacked the parchment (or the capital) to compose weekly sermons. One perceives a fitting parable for Fisher's life, a mixture of the extraordinary and commonplace.

Jonathan Fisher was born on October 7, 1768 in the village of New Braintree, Massachusetts, a fifth-generation descendant of Anthony Fisher, who immigrated from England in 1637. Jonathan's father, who bore the same name, died of dysentery when serving as a Lieutenant in the continental army at Morristown, New Jersey in the autumn of 1777.[4] Katharine Avery Fisher, Jonathan's wife, was thus left with six children to support, in addition to being pregnant with a seventh.[5] After the birth of the youngest child, Samuel, the family was broken up. Jonathan's uncle, Joseph Avery agreed to raise his nephew, and would do so until Jonathan enrolled at Harvard College in 1788. The institution experienced pronounced unrest during the last decade of the century. In addition to internecine theological battles between Old and New Lights, the fervor of the French Revolution and its intellectual currents affected the student body. Harvard historian Samuel Eliot Morison provides the following summary: "The typical student of the early seventeen-nineties was an atheist in religion, an

---

[3] Richard S. Carter explains the history and development of deciphering Fisher's shorthand in "The Mind and Ministry of Jonathan Fisher," xi–xii. Cf. Raoul Smith, "The Language of Jonathan Fisher (1768–1847)," *Publication of the American Dialect Society* 72 (1985).

[4] Lieutenant Fisher was reputed to be among Washington's men who crossed the Delaware River and launched a surprise attack against Hessian soldiers at Trenton on Christmas Day, 1776. Richard Carter, "Mind and Ministry of Jonathan Fisher," 22. Carter later concluded that, after joining Washington's army, Fisher may have actually been stationed at a military prison in southern New York at the time of the attack. Richard Carter, *personal correspondence via email dated August 11, 2022.*

[5] Chase, *Maine Parson*, 6. Of the four Fisher sons, three would become ministers.

experimentalist in morals, a rebel to authority."[6] Fisher was of course, not a typical Harvard student. By his own detailed accounts, he judged himself to be unconverted until his junior year. Fisher was nevertheless a moral, pious, and diligent young man, who graduated with honors, and gave a commencement address in Physics on the subject of Jupiter's moons.[7]

Upon completion of his studies, Fisher was ordained on July 13, 1796, an event attended by four clergymen, Daniel Merrill being among them. Fisher would spend the entirety of his ministry at Bluehill, a town in Hancock County, east of the Penobscot River. Bluehill, created out of Plantation Number 5, had received a charter for a Congregational church in 1762, but could not procure a qualified pastor until Fisher took the position.[8] Congregationalist churches at the time maintained high educational standards, regardless of the communities where they ministered. Fisher's decision to minister at rural Bluehill was unusual, as sophisticated and urbane New England pastors were typically assigned a parish in cities or towns rather than the frontier. Given the opportunity to serve at Ashby in eastern Massachusetts, Fisher declined the offer. The decision incidentally cost him the possibility of marriage to Betsy Heath of Brookline, who was unwilling to be a pastor's wife on the Maine frontier. Despite various hardships, Fisher never regretted the decision, observing that

---

[6] Samuel Eliot Morison, *Three Centuries of Harvard* (Cambridge, MA: Harvard University Press, 1936), 185.

[7] Carter, "Mind and Ministry of Jonathan Fisher," 84.

[8] Originally one word, Bluehill would become Blue Hill. Early town records record the name Bluehill, Blue hill and, occasionally, Blue Hill by various scribes in the minutes of town meetings. Neighboring Sedgwick comprised what are now the towns of Sedgwick, Brooklin (Port Watson), and Brooksville, as well as other neighborhoods or villages such as Sargentville. Nearby Union River would become Ellsworth and Buckstown or Buckston, Bucksport.

over the years, the Ashby church moved in a theologically-unorthodox direction—a drift that Fisher himself firmly resisted.[9]

Bluehill provided ample opportunity for Fisher to exhibit his broad skillset, notably architecture, surveying, and farming.[10] The frontier region was, however, dominated by working-class citizens whose Republican sentiments eventually clashed with the staunchly-Federalist parson. Fisher lived during a time where emergent sects such as Baptists and Methodists were expanding across the American landscape. The Puritan vision of the Congregationalist pastor as a town's principal spiritual and civic leader—one that held for nearly two centuries, and of which Fisher considered himself an heir—was waning. New ecclesial alternatives combined with a growing populism placed him in an unenviable position of competition with other Protestant churches. Critics, for example, cited Fisher's unimpressive preaching.[11] Member defections to Baptist congregations entailed dissatisfaction with their former pastor's doctrine. The conclusion that Fisher's pastorate could have more closely resembled his ideal if he was born even a generation earlier is not far-fetched. Social and intellectual trends would test the fortitude of Fisher's Calvinist theology. Pastoral commitment to a single community, however, provides

---

[9] Carter "Mind and Ministry of Jonathan Fisher," 9. The following excerpt from a letter by Fisher's friend and classmate Levi Hedge reveals the plausible pull Fisher felt to serve in Massachusetts: "It is unquestionably a laudable employment to spread the gospel in the wilderness but would you not do more service to society and more good to the causes of religion were you to plant yourself at Ashby?" Cited in Carter, "The Mind and Ministry of Jonathan Fisher," 94.

[10] For a description of these pursuits see Esther Wood, *Deep Roots* (Camden, Maine: Yankee Books, 1990), 155.

[11] Swan Pomeroy's well-known description of Fisher's as having a voice that "being destitute of an ear for music, his emphasis was sometimes misplaced and intonations inappropriate." Cited in *The Annals of the American Pulpit; or Commemorative Notices of Distinguished American Clergymen of Various Denominations, from the Early Settlement of the Country to the Close of the Year Eighteen Fifty-Five. With Historical Introductions*, ed. William B. Sprague (New York: Robert Carter and Bros., 1857), 2:349.

strong evidence that providence for him was no idle term, but a theological and existential reality.

The Spirituality of Jonathan Fisher

Fisher left posterity with extensive access into the details of his interior life. In addition to sermons, correspondence, and an auto-biography, diary entries are crucial for understanding his spirituality. Richard Carter notes that there are three sources of interwoven autobiographical narratives: "spiritual concerns," "temporal concerns," and "Sketches." Fisher began his spiritual concerns diary in 1787, a year he believed to have had a potential conversion.[12] Fisher's torturous journey towards personal salvation had recognizable theological contours, typical of persons immersed in Scripture, and reared in the Puritan milieu.[13] Probing accounts feature unconfessed sins and frustration at the inability to change. Indicative of a sensitive conscience, Fisher identified card playing and idleness among sins committed in early adolescence. In one instance, he drank alcohol to excess, a lapse that was unique and never repeated. Fisher did overeat, a vice he battled throughout his life. Even with firm resolve not to gratify the flesh—Fisher claimed to have "avoided particular intimacy with the other sex"—he cites lust and consequent self-gratification as a chief transgression.[14] As for the state of his soul, Jonathan lamented to

---

[12] "Sketches from the Life of the Rev. Jonathan Fisher, pastor of the Congregational Church in Bluehill, Maine, interspersed with extracts from his journal written by himself" (*Sketches*), 1812, trans. Edith Weren (handwritten manuscript), Blue Hill Library, Blue Hill, Maine. Richard Carter, "Mind and Ministry of Jonathan Fisher," xi. Carter describes the timeline and process of translation and transcription.

[13] Fisher's diary entries express confession of guilt, despair at the prospect of damnation, fear that God is not loved for his own sake. Finally, a breakthrough comes, with noted resolve to follow Christ wholeheartedly.

[14] Fisher did attribute the awakening of lusts to the unchaste conversation of a servant girl. An extended, years-long battle with masturbation—obliquely called a "secret sin"—was the subject of guilt and much anguish. For wider understandings of masturbation in Fisher's time, see Kevin D. Murphy, *Jonathan Fisher of Blue Hill,*

his brother Stephen that he was, "too little affected by this solemn and awful transaction (e.g., the death of Christ)."[15] In a positive turn, Fisher identified the hearing of a Mohawk convert preach on Matthew 7:13–14 at Westhampton in the spring of 1787 as a formative event in his path to conversion three years later.

It should be noted that in addition to the overall tenor, Fisher's reading prior to his conversion paralleled that of an earlier generation of evangelicals. He read William Law's *A Serious Call to a Devout and Holy Life*, a classic devotional work that was instrumental in the conversion of evangelicalism's first generation.[16] In a diary entry from October 31, 1789 Fisher wrote: "Reading the life of Mr. Joseph Allan, who was settled in the ministry in the 21st year of his age, and was eminent for his piety and godliness." Being the same age at the time, Fisher comments, "I was ashamed and angry with myself, that I had made no better improvement of the privileges, with which I have been favored." In 1795, he records being strongly moved after completing Jonathan Edwards' *Diary of David Brainerd.*[17]

Rigorous self-assessment, common among evangelicals at the time, can strike an errant chord to modern ears. In form and content, however, Fisher was moving through an intentional process.[18] He recorded the following diary entry on March 1, 1789,

---

Maine: Commerce, Culture, and Community on the Eastern Frontier (Boston: University of Massachusetts Press, 2010) 223–224.

[15] Chase, *Maine Parson*, 44.

[16] Chase, *Maine Parson*, 61. Fisher cites reading Williamson's, *The Afflicted Man's Companion* and *Paul and Virginia*, a novel by Jacques-Henri Bernardin de Saint Pierre. Cf. Roger M. Payne, *The Self and the Sacred: Conversion and Autobiography in Early American Protestantism* (Knoxville: University of Tennessee Press, 1998).

[17] 20 September, 1795. Fisher would also read John Owen's *On Indwelling Sin* in 1799.

[18] Mary Ellen Chase considered Fisher's self-assessment and disposition as "morbid and unhealthful," but as Bruce Hindmarsh had argued, spiritual autobiographies, including diaries, were a kind of genre used by Puritans and early evangelicals which, "served chiefly as a means of disciplined self-examination and a way of focusing religious affections. Its picture is therefore not only a man at his prayer, but also, more often than not, of a man in confessional." See *John Newton and The English Evangelical*

Lord's Day—Oh that the fulness of God may deliver me from my iniquities. I am alas a slave to the devil. If God have thoughts of mercy concerning me, happy for me, how or what can express the wretchedness of my situation.[19]

Remarkably, subsequent entries echo sentiments of similar severity. During these years, Fisher composed poems which exhibited notable tenets of orthodox Calvinism. The necessity of Christ's death and God's sovereign choice to graciously pardon recur frequently. Fisher likewise interpreted physical ailments such as migraines as spiritual chastisements. In July of 1790, he faced the last internal hurdle to making public profession of faith—his fitness to partake of the Lord's Supper. Reflecting on the Apostle Paul's warning that the church at Corinth refrain from taking the Eucharist if they did not "discern the body," Fisher asked: "Have I knowledge to discern the Lord's body? A speculative knowledge perhaps ... But I have reason to fear that I am destitute of experiential knowledge!"[20] With his will seemingly stuck in a state of equilibrium, Fisher experienced a breakthrough similar to that of Andrew Fuller (1754-1815), who entrusted his soul to Christ after relinquishing attempts to prove spiritual worthiness. Fisher's entry is worth quoting at length:

Last night in my sleep, while imaginations wandered in my dreams, I thought myself employed in a school—that one of my scholars went, without liberty, into a room contiguous to the school room and being several times called refused to come. After telling him the consequences and being no longer willing to suffer his obstinance, I went to him with a rod and was on the point of giving him a severe correction,

Tradition (Grand Rapids: Eerdmans, 1996), 22. Cf., *The Evangelical Conversion Narrative: Spiritual Autobiography in Early Modern England* (Oxford: Oxford University Press, 2005).

[19] Carter, "Mind and Ministry of Jonathan Fisher," 51.

[20] Carter, "Mind and Ministry of Jonathan Fisher," 72.

but I awoke. I reflected thus; Have I not sinfully departed from God? Has he not repeatedly called me to return? He has called me again and again, has called me in mildness and had called me in anger; he has pleasantly described the consequences of my delays, which are truly dreadful. Still I refuse to come. Do I deserve the punishment? Do I not deserve the rod? Conscience may answer—still God is waiting.[21]

Jonathan Fisher answered the call, and made his profession of faith public on August 8, 1790.

Later in life, Fisher interpreted his strenuous path to conversion as misguided on some points. In 1815, he reflected that, "Much in my own strength, soon breaking my resolution and falling again ... I did not look sufficiently to the pardoning blood and justifiable righteousness of God so, instead of advancing in sanctification, my progress for several years was that of a backslider."[22] As for conversion's salvific goal—for himself or potentially in others—Fisher never doubted its present, or future realities. Thus, the spiritual condition of church and family members, as well as residents in Maine, remained a central pastoral concern. Only six years from retirement in 1831, he recorded in his diary a visit by, "four daughters, 3 sons-in-law, 2 grandsons and 3 granddaughters." He commented that of the 13, "seven are professors [e.g., converted]. Bless be God that he has favored us!"[23] Fisher's pattern of trekking long distances—at times between ten and

---

[21] Jonathan Fisher, diary entry from August of 1790. Jonathan Fisher Memorial. Cited in Carter, "Mind and Ministry of Jonathan Fisher," 74.

[22] Jonathan Fisher, *Sketches*, 4/1815. Fisher would call his excessive, human-centered striving "I-government."

[23] Jonathan Fisher, diary entry from 8/31/1832. In a letter to a relative named Ralph Day, Fisher wrote, "I hope, dear Cousin, that you know by happy experience what it is to be born again; that you have seen the evil and perverseness of the natural heart; that you have sincerely repented, and rested your soul by faith on the merit of Christ." Fisher to Ralph Day, 4 January 1837, Jonathan Fisher House, Blue Hill, Maine.

twenty miles—to catechize persons of all ages testifies to an evangelical vision in which the spiritual state of his congregants occupied a central place.

As for theology proper, Fisher fits within the Reformed tradition as expressed in *Savoy Declaration of Faith*. Fisher was not a professional theologian. His concerns were pastoral and apologetic rather than speculative, motivated by a confidence that the received doctrines should be guarded and preserved, not emended. Examining Fisher in the context of New England's intellectual class—which was moving swiftly away from traditional Calvinism—provides insight into the tensions and cross-pressures he faced. In an undated entry from Harvard, Fisher reflected on the nature of theology and its relation to physical science, affirming a traditional scholastic view that each discipline has a proper end, the study of God occupying the highest place:

> when we approach divinity, this, like a mountain, swells before us, while those, like the hillocks, vanish behind. … Law and Physic are blessing to us in this life; Divinity informs us, that we shall live hereafter. It tells us that we are the creature of an infinite, an eternal Creator; that there is a principle within us, that will survive the waste of time.[24]

Considering the scientific achievements of the age as well as his own grasp of physics, mathematics and astronomy, Fisher's comments are important. Belief in the efficacy of science led him to be inoculated for smallpox in 1793, a risky procedure at the time, and one that almost cost Fisher his life. Upon recovery, however, he commented that, "It is lawful and even part of wisdom to subject ourselves to small dangers to avoid greater ones."[25]

---

[24] Carter, "Mind and Ministry of Jonathan Fisher," 45.

[25] Carter, "Mind and Ministry of Jonathan Fisher," 46. Jonathan Edwards died in 1758 after subjecting himself to an experimental smallpox vaccination.

Belief that the totality of human needs could be sated by modern science, thereby making theology obsolete, was an increasingly popular viewpoint. The Unitarian Joseph Priestly (1733–1804), a polymath with whom Fisher was familiar, wrote at the turn of the century that in the near future:

> Nature, including both its materials and its laws, will be more at our command; men will make their situation in this world abundantly more easy and comfortable, they will prolong their existence in it and grow daily more happy. ... Thus whatever the beginning of the world the end will be glorious and paradisical beyond that our imagination can now conceive.[26]

In perspective, Fisher maintained a comparative balance between the facile optimism of Priestly, and the pessimism that characterized some corners of evangelicalism.

Anti-Trinitarianism characterized the Harvard faculty from the early nineteenth century onwards. This in turn, affected the Congregational churches associated with the institution. Fisher, however, maintained a robust belief in the Triune God from his time at Harvard, as evident in "Thanksgiving to the Trinity," an ode he composed in 1792.[27] Fisher's writings indicate an acceptance of dogmatic boundaries on rational inquiry, a position whose popularity was waning during the era. In the aforementioned poem, Fisher asks rhetorically how the effects of sin could

---

[26] Cited in Reinhold Niebuhr, *The Irony of American History* (Chicago: University of Chicago Press, 2008), chapter 3. President Willard encouraged Fisher to read an essay by Priestly in 1792. In addition to theological and pedagogical subjects, Priestly was a fellow of the Royal Society and is credited with discovering oxygen, along with nine other gases as well as the carbon cycle.

[27] 29 of November, 1792. Jonathan Fisher House.

be cured and posits the answer: "In a manner too sublime for feeble reason to comprehend ..."[28]

In engagement with Arminians, particularly Methodist preachers, Fisher faced objections to Calvinism that relied on a simple, commonsense understanding of theology that resonated with frontier hearers. In early 1803, Fisher recorded a series of debates, held in the home of Nathan Parker, a respected member of the Bluehill Congregational church, with the Methodist itinerant Alfred Metcalf. Metcalf proposed to a listening audience several familiar theological positions such as repentance necessarily preceding faith, and that a genuine convert can commit apostasy. Predictably, the Methodist preacher's doctrines clashed with Fisher's Calvinism at various junctures, the crux of their disagreement being the nature and limits of human freedom. Metcalf drew a crowd, though Fisher appears to have won the first debate. His comments, "I feel conscious of having aimed to vindicate the truth and cheerfully submit the event to God," suggests he believed he had.[29] Subsequent discussions touched on the nature of evil, and whether the actions of reprobate persons were free, and worthy of guilt. Fisher's intellect, aided by his education, provided an advantage in the protracted debate. Reflecting on the events in 1825, Fisher commented that "after this [debate] we had but rarely a Methodist discourse in the place for 15 or 20 years."[30]

Fisher's interaction with Methodist preachers is, incidentally enough, a fitting place to discuss his eschatology. Fisher was a post-millennialist who believed a figurative thousand-year period would feature a spiritualized future reign of Christ on earth. New England theologians since Cotton Mather speculated as to when this period would commence. Jonathan Edwards in particular

---

[28] Jonathan Fisher, AMsS notebook, Jonathan Fisher House. Undated. Cited in Carter, "Mind and Ministry of Jonathan Fisher," 45.

[29] Carter, "Mind and Ministry of Jonathan Fisher," 193.

[30] Jonathan Fisher, *Sketches*, 3 July 1825.

believed the revivals of the 1740's marked it beginning. In a letter written to J.S. Popkin in 1800, Fisher claimed that although the "complete overthrow of the antichrist" would not happen for two centuries, assault on the church would intensify in the intervening epoch. He expressed concern that many persons "destitute of vital religion" would, "fall away to the Wesleyan Methodists." Though conceding the possibility that some preachers were "men of grace," Fisher had no doubt that the Methodists were, "deeply involved in error."[31]

As will be discussed later, all denominations were beneficiaries of revival that occurred during the first decade of the nineteenth century. Notwithstanding these gains, Congregationalists, Methodists, and Baptists would lose adherents to various expressions of unorthodoxy. The Shakers and Latter-Day Saints would emerge from Methodist circles, providing some vindication for his concerns. With two centuries of hindsight, it was in fact, New England Congregationalism that was moving away from the faith of its fathers on a scale larger than the Methodists or the Baptists. In an 1828 address, "Likeness to God," William Ellery Channing (1780–1842), considered the father of American Unitarianism, asked how a person obtains knowledge of God's existence and attributes. He answered,

> we derive them from our own souls, ... the divine attributes are first developed in ourselves, and thence transformed to our Creator. The idea of God, sublime and awful as it is, is the idea of our own spiritual nature, purified and enlarged to infinity. In ourselves are the elements of the Divinity.[32]

---

[31] Jonathan Fisher to J.S. Popkin, 23 February 1800. JFH. Edwards posited the year 2,000 as the culmination of the Millennium. It is highly likely that Fisher drew from Jonathan Edwards on this point.

[32] William Ellery Channing, "Likeness to God: Discourse at the Ordination of the Rev. F. A. Farley, in *The Works of William E. Channing, DD.* (Boston: American Unitarian Association, 1899), 293.

Channing, who began his ministry as a Congregationalist pastor, gradually adopted a theology with pantheistic overtones. He was not alone. And yet even admirers such as Ralph Waldo Emerson did not believe Channing went far enough. By contrast, Fisher insisted on enforcing confessional standards. For Congregationalist churches that aspired to a future with theologically-recognizable contours—much less continuity with historic Christianity—time would vindicate the concerns of Bluehill's pastor.

Fisher's published works—six total—were contextual and apologetic. Universalism and Arminianism were not abstract theological options, but formidable threats to the salvation of his neighbors. Even Fisher's defense of pedobaptism, which will be discussed in chapter three, is a response to an emergent Baptist presence on the frontier. Thus, "experimental and practical" is a fitting description of Fisher's spirituality. Resolute adherence to Trinitarian orthodoxy and confessional Calvinism at a time of Unitarian ascendance is consistent with Fisher's self-understanding as frontier missionary rather than speculative theologian.[33] Fisher's post-millennial eschatology, though it had few qualms identifying historical referents or dates, did not occupy a place of prominence in his public ministry. Like Jonathan Edwards, John Wesley, and Andrew Fuller, intense introspection preceded a definitive conversion experience. If interpretation in subsequent years admitted of excessive reliance on spiritual worthiness, Fisher never wavered on the veracity of conversion and its end: salvation through faith in Christ.

---

[33] Murphy *Jonathan Fisher*, 226: "Whereas other ministers on the Eastern Frontier, roughly Fisher's contemporaries, somewhat moderated their Calvinist theological positions in order to prevent other sects from usurping their parishioners and eroding their authority, the parson of Blue Hill was religiously inflexible; whereas the pastors of the handful of other Hancock County churches established prior to 1805 made their theology more 'fashionable' (as Fisher put it), Blue Hill's pastor resolutely refused to do so."

Marriage and Family

Ordination and marriage were interwoven and coterminous events in Fisher's life. His marriage to Dolly Battle (1770–1853) would span five decades, and though he made frequent reference to her in his diaries, she remains an opaque figure. Notifying the Bluehill congregation of his intent to wed, Fisher provided the following commentary in early 1796: "Providence seems offering me one for a companion who; though she has very few external allurements, appears to be compensated with admirable qualities of heart." Despite Fisher's detached, and arguably unflattering description of Dolly, the Fishers appear to have had a happy marriage amidst an arduous, if active, life.[34] She would bear nine children between 1798 and 1812, seven of which would live to adulthood. The Fishers lost two sons, the first, Samuel, died in 1812, only two weeks after his birth. Jonathan, the eldest after Samuel, perished from "lung fever" in 1815. Jonathan Jr.'s death was especially hard on his father, though he took great solace in the spiritual condition of his soul. On the day of his son's death, he wrote, "I conversed with my son with much satisfaction upon the solemn subject of death and eternity. Blessed be God, he expressed a calmness in the expectation of near approaching death, expressed his astonishment at the riches of redeeming love, and exhibited a calm confidence in the savior."[35]

One son, Willard, who lacked intellectual gifts, matured at a slower pace than his parents had hoped. He experienced conversion in his twenties and married later in life. Willard did assist his parents in maintaining their farm. Thus, his presence at home proved beneficial. Josiah, the eldest surviving son, followed

---

[34] Fisher may likely have had moralistic and didactic objectives as the echoes of 1 Peter 3:2–4 suggest. Peculiarly, he commented at other times on her lack of physical beauty, though in a context of praise for inward and spiritual virtues.

[35] Chase, *Maine Parson*, 146. Chase notes that Jonathan Sr.'s concern with his son's spiritual condition proved presumptive as a letter composed to his siblings, indicated a vibrant faith and concern for their salvation.

Jonathan into ministry. Converted in his late teens, Josiah showed the intellectual promise lacking in Willard. Josiah's decision to enter Bowdoin College instead of Bangor Theological Seminary in 1824 disappointed Jonathan, who played a vital role in its creation and support. In his diary he wrote, "I can hardly bear up under this. For my own son to go to another institution would seem to speak a language unfavorable to the seminary in Bangor, and in this I find my heart is much bound up."[36] Sufficiently concerned with the theological direction of New England Congregationalism to found a new school, Fisher, understandably, preferred that his son be educated at an institution of which he made heavy investment.

Dorothea Fisher, born early in 1810, certainly pleased her father when she married Robert Crossette of New Salem MA, a member of the 1830 graduating class of Bangor Theological Seminary. They served the Congregational Church at Dennysville Maine for 12 years and bore Father Fisher a grandson and namesake, Jonathan Fisher Crossette, who would serve as a missionary to China upon his graduation from Lane Seminary in Ohio. Robert Crossette went on to pastor Congregational churches in New Hampshire, Massachusetts, New Jersey, and Pennsylvania. In 1868, the couple moved to College Hill Ohio for health reasons and are both buried in Cincinnati,[37] where Robert spent his final

---

[36] Chase, *Maine Parson*, 158. For details regarding the life and ministry of Josiah Fisher, see *Historical Memorial: Presbyterian Church of Succasunna, N.J. 1765-1895*. (Dover: Press of the Iron Era, 1895), 26–29. R.G.F. Candage provides a brief genealogy and biographical sketches of the Fisher family, their spouses, and children in *Historical Sketches of Bluehill, Maine* (Ellsworth: Hancock County Publishing Company, 1905), 64–65.

[37] Rev. W.A. Bosworth remembered Robert Crossette, "If I mistake not, Mr. Crossette's ministry, like that of Barnabas at Antioch, was, to an unusual degree, a fruitful one. During his first pastorate at Dennysville, Maine, his labors were attended with four powerful revivals... This church was his first and best love, and to it he devoted many of the choicest years of his life. He was always very efficient in revivals, and was frequently called upon to assist neighboring pastors... I have this impression of him strongly fixed upon my mind: that he was, especially in the days of his prime, a

years supplying the pulpit at a Presbyterian church there. Two of their daughters married clergymen—Rev. Charles D. Curtis and Rev. H. Dinsmore.

Rev. Hosea Kittredge, a native of Mount Desert Maine and graduate of Amherst College, was a boarder in the Fisher home and preceptor of the Bluehill Academy for a time. He married Nancy Fisher and they gave the Fishers seven grandchildren. Many Congregational ministers of that era performed their vocational ministries in Presbyterian pulpits, missions, and institutions as part of the 1801 Plan of Union between the denominations, uniting to evangelize the western frontier. Hosea Kittredge followed in the footsteps of Jonathan Fisher, but in a westward direction, and proved to be an effective Presbyterian pastor, administrator, and denominational leader in Michigan.

Dolly and Jonathan would lose one daughter, Sally, the last remaining child to predecease their parents, at the age of twenty-four. Apart from the grief of giving birth to a stillborn son and dying of a subsequent secondary infection, Sally's story is tragic on account of a brief and troubled marriage.[38] Joshua Wood, a young man who served as deacon in Fisher's church and who was personally educated by the pastor, wed Sally in 1823. Only eight months later, however, Fisher recorded trouble with his son-in-law. By July of 1824, Joshua had abruptly departed Bluehill, leaving a pregnant Sally behind. In September, he returned and took Sally with him to a new residence. Several weeks later, Joshua departed for Georgia, citing poor health.[39] He never returned. News

---

man of much spiritual power, 'full of the Holy Ghost and of faith.'" *A Discourse Delivered at the Funeral of Rev. Robert Crossette, in the Presbyterian Church, College Hill, Ohio June 27, 1872* (Cincinnati: Robert Clarke & Co., 1872), 6–8.

[38] "How soon from the womb to the tomb/My first-born dear infant is fled/The blossom just came to the bloom/'Tis smitten, and withered, and dead." Cited in Chase, *Maine Parson*, 161.

[39] Chase, *Maine Parson*, 160.

of his death on January 6, 1825 in Savannah, Georgia is recorded in Fisher's diary.

Wood's reckless behavior, which members of the Fisher family could not explain, led Fisher to conclude that some form of mental illness overwhelmed the young man. At Joshua's funeral in Bluehill, the pastor offered a sympathetic assessment of his departed son-in-law,

> [S]oon after he had closed his education, a latent disorder began to prey with increasing rapacity upon his vitals. WE saw him sink under it; we saw the effect upon his mind as upon his body. ... As a last expedient for restoration of health, he journeyed to a distant clime, but it was too late. We trust that he was so far upright in the sense of our text that his end was peace and that he is already with the spirit of his consort, who took flight before him. We mourn their early departure.[40]

The gravity of the losses incurred by the Fishers can be difficult to grasp in a time when modern medicine has rendered infant mortality and death from infections such as Pneumonia rare in young persons. Life did not stop—could not stop—for Fisher and the surviving members of his household. It is remarkable, therefore, that their home was filled with guests for virtually the entirety of Jonathan and Dolly's marriage. In addition to his own children, the Fishers housed and educated distant relatives. Fisher mentions two young boys who were an unusual source of frustration as they engaged in various forms of mischief. It should be mentioned that the Fishers' hospitality was coupled with Yankee industry. Able-bodied guests who stayed at the Fisher residence labored at various domestic tasks from weaving to

---

[40] Chase, *Maine Parson*, 162.

harvesting crops. The couple thus wisely managed the influx of guests in a manner that required a broad division of labor.

Education

Despite comparative dilution from what was taught in the seventeenth century, Fisher's education at Harvard fit in the classical western tradition.[41] He read primary source texts including Homer, Xenophon, and Plato in Greek. In Latin, the list included Sallust, Terrence, Horace and Livy. Fisher would educate younger men in a tutorial role, requiring recitation of Latin texts, sometimes for hours on end. In his reading and translation of the Hebrew Bible, we find a convergence of academic and devotional streams. Fisher customarily arose early, often by 5 A.M., and after preparing the breakfast table for his household, spent an hour meditating on the text.[42] The result of his study would be a Hebrew lexicon, which, although it was unfinished and thus unpublished, constituted an ambitious achievement.[43] As noted, Fisher possessed unusual acumen in mathematics. In his *Sketches*, he reflected that while studying at Harvard, the subject "was particularly pleasing to me."[44] Living in a context that demanded application for practical problems such as building houses and roads, Fisher did not have the privilege of engaging exclusively in theoretical and speculative mathematics. His sketches, blueprints, and notebooks testify to his competence.

---

[41] See Samuel Eliot Morison, *Three Centuries of Harvard*. (Cambridge, MA: Harvard University Press, 1936).

[42] At the time Fisher recorded his morning routine in the diaries, the household numbered around a dozen, including boarders. Jane Bianco, *A Wondrous Journey: Jonathan Fisher & the Making of Scripture Animals* (Rockland: Farnsworth Art Museum, 2014), 44.

[43] Fisher jettisoned the project after an English translation of Wilhelm Gesenius' *Hebrew-Chaldee Lexicon to the Old Testament* was published in 1824. See Chase, *Maine Parson*, 130, 212–213.

[44] Fisher was particularly fond of Isaac Newton, penning on ode to the mathematician in 1791.

Much to his disappointment, Fisher's written works were rejected by most publishers. *Scripture Animals*, a book with original woodcut illustrations for which he is most famous, did not bring a profit during his lifetime. In fact, the author functioned as the text's chief salesman, soliciting potential consumers door-to-door. Fisher combined his journalistic, poetic and theological talents by writing "broadsides," inexpensive, single-page commentaries on an "event, tale, political opinion, or dream that seemed relevant to the moment."[45] On more than one occasion, Fisher witnessed a criminal execution, which he duly recorded in vivid detail.[46] Fisher's broadsides resembled an earlier genre, the Execution Sermon, in which a pastor would draw spiritual lessons from the condemned criminal for the public.

In the example of Seth Eliott, a man convicted of murdering his child and who was set to hang in February 1825, Fisher faced a familiar doctrinal foe: Universalism. Eliott told Fisher that his hope lay in the prospect that all humans would be saved without exception. Aware of contemporary appeal and eager to warn his audience, Fisher wrote the following lines,

That ancient lie, the universal scheme,
Still lulls ten thousands in a fatal dream,
Persuades its votaries they may live at ease,
Indulge in sin, their fleshly nature please,
Slight God and duty, Christ and truth deny,
And then at death to heaven and glory fly,
Thus I could it were, and did; but no
God's holy word does not allow it so. [47]

---

[45] William J. Gilmore-Lehne, *Reading Becomes a Necessity of Life: Material and Cultural Life in Rural New England, 1780–1835* (Knoxville: University of Tennessee Press, 1992), 192. Fisher composed not only verse, but also illustrations for his own broadsides.

[46] In addition to his presence at executions, Fisher regularly visited the state prison in Boston. See Richard Carter, "Mind and Ministry of Jonathan Fisher," 295.

[47] Jonathan Fisher, *Sketches*.

The doctrine of universal salvation, like Unitarianism, came in both simplistic and sophisticated forms. The confidence of Seth Eliot concerning his spiritual destiny would likely appear audacious to an audience informed of his crimes. Fisher shrewdly seized the opportunity.

A Harvard-educated pastor who chose to minister in eastern Massachusetts could have devoted a majority of his time to academic study. New Divinity theologian and Congregationalist pastor Nathanael Emmons (1745-1840), a contemporary of Fisher, made clear to the church where he served, a resolve, "to devote my whole time to the sacred work, without encumbering myself with the cares and concern of the world." Emmons once refused to replace a fallen bar on a fence lest it lead him down the road to worldly affairs.[48] Fisher's interests were sufficiently broad as to make a ministry that resembled that of Nathaniel Emmons unlikely. Nevertheless, he was a serious student, as the time devoted to producing a Hebrew lexicon proved.

Though he kept fastidious records for most of his adult life, some entries over a twenty-year period between 1815 and 1835 became disorganized or lost until recently. But, written correspondence during the time is devoted almost exclusively to what he called "our infant theological Seminary" which was established at Bangor.[49] Fisher would attend biannual meetings for its Board of Trustees, by his own estimate a "pleasant walk" of thirty-five miles. Originally called the Maine Charity School, it later adopted the title Bangor Theological Seminary. Fisher's understanding of the institution's purpose can be discerned in his reference to it as the "school of the prophets."[50] The Maine Charity School opened in 1816 with six students. Modeled after the "Dissenting

---

[48] Ahlstrom, *A Religious History of the American People*, 411.

[49] The first half of the nineteenth century witnessed the rapid growth of education in America with 516 colleges and universities being founded before the Civil War.

[50] Chase, *Maine Parson*, 195-196.

Colleges" in England, it required two years in classical curriculum prior to entering theological study.[51]

Though a proud Harvard alumnus—his son Willard was named after Joseph Willard, Harvard's president from 1781 to 1804—Fisher disagreed with the Arminian and Unitarian direction of the school.[52] His assistance in founding Bangor Theological Seminary sought to instruct Congregationalist ministers in the Calvinism of an earlier Harvard.[53] Apart from personal investment in the school, Fisher's disapproval that Josiah chose Bowdoin College over Bangor reveals the seriousness with which he believed doctrine formed the substance of an institution, and how quickly an institution can drift theologically. If Fisher imparted the majority of his academic knowledge to young men preparing for the ministry, he did value the education of women, devoting energy to establishing schools. All five daughters would

---

[51] Chase, *Maine Parson*, 197.

[52] Samuel Eliot Morison comments that after the death of President Willard in 1804, "Orthodox Calvinists of the true Puritan tradition now become open enemies at Harvard ... and pious families of the rural district of New England ... impelled their sons elsewhere." See *Three Centuries of Harvard*, 164-191. Cf. Conrad Wright, *The Beginnings of Unitarianism in America* (Boston: Beacon Press, 1957).

[53] Calvin Montague Clark, *History of Bangor Theological Seminary* (Boston: The Pilgrim Press, 1916), 18-19. Clark penned this history at the Centennial of the Bangor Theological Seminary to "present a readable narrative" and "furnish as full and accurate as possible a book for reference to the sources from which the history has been compiled ... from original sources" (vii). He writes, "Tradition is divided as to the person to whom credit should be given for the first suggestion of such an institution for Maine. One account ascribes it to Rev. John Sawyer ... Another account ascribes the suggestion to Mrs. Kiah Bayley." In a note on page 19, Clark provided another tradition: "The Rev. Arthur Smith ... formerly pastor of the Baptist Church in Sedgwick, ME, is of the opinion that not only the first suggestion, but also the partial realisation, of such an institution for Maine should be credited to Rev. Daniel Merrill, pastor of the Congregational church in Sedgwick, as early as 1802. He was instrumental in forming a 'Society for Promoting Theological Education' at or just before that date, which seems to have done something in the way of educating young men, and to which many of those who later espoused the seminary at Bangor contributed." See also, Clark, *History of the Congregational Churches in Maine*, 2:381.

attend Bluehill Academy, which their father helped found in 1803.[54] Fisher's diaries record at least one biography that he read aloud to the family, providing a glimpse into the substance of leisure activity in which the family bonded.[55]

"A glorious spiritual harvest": the Hancock revival

Fisher's experience of revival came at the beginning of his ministry, a period loosely coincident with the Second Great Awakening.[56] Three months after arriving at Bluehill, Fisher visited the aged reverend Peter Powers (1729–1799) of Deer Isle, the only other Harvard graduate in Hancock County, and one-time Old Light who became a New Light under the influence of Jonathan Edwards.[57] After spending several days with the veteran pastor, Fisher recorded the following,

> 1797—March 20–24—The former part of the week I spent in a visit at Peter Powers at Deer Isle. With him I had many pleasant communications which I hope will be to my spiritual good. At the proposal of Mr. Powers a day of fasting and prayer was agreed upon for the outpouring of the spirit

---

[54] Chase, *Maine Parson*, 151. Women were given an education, primarily for the purpose of teaching at local grammar schools. Fisher's daughters were educated in Castine or Bucksport beginning at fourteen or fifteen years of age. Literacy rates among New England women were the highest in the world, exceeding literacy in many developed countries even to the present.

[55] Jonathan Fisher, *The Diaries of Jonathan Fisher: July 1795–January 1835,* Typescript (https://digitalmaine.com/blue_hill_documents accessed May 25, 2022).

[56] The "New Light Stir" which began in 1774 and continued for a decade, led to expansion and growth of orthodox evangelicals such as the Baptists and Methodists as well as heretical sects such as Universalists and the Shakers. See Marini, "Religious Revolution in the District of Maine 1780-1820," in *Maine in the Early Republic*, Charles E. Clark, James S. Leamon & Karen Bowden, eds. (Hanover, NH: University of New England Press, 1988), 118.

[57] Congregationalist missionaries on the frontier were almost exclusively of the New Light persuasion, most being educated at Yale and Dartmouth. See Calvin Montague Clark, *The Congregational Churches in Maine. Volume 2: History of the Individual Churches 1600-1826* (Portland, ME: The Congregational Christian Conference of Maine, 1935), 103–106, 301–302, 312–315, 319–326.

to be observed in rotation thro' 4 towns, beginning with Deer Isle. May God smile upon the purpose!

As Richard Carter notes, Fisher's diary entries subsequent to the meeting with Powers were, "noticeably more upbeat, focused on the power and grace of God instead of failure and woe."[58] In a language similar to that of John Wesley's Aldersgate conversion, the young pastor lamented, "I struggled in soul to receive Christ by an appropriate faith; that I might not call him a savior, but also my savior. I trust I was enabled to do this in some measure."[59] Fisher experienced peace, recording an April 18 journal entry that he, "enjoyed much pleasure in meditating on the way of Christ." Before another week elapsed, a woman in his congregation experienced conversion. Fisher claimed to possess "considerable enlargement" in his preaching and spiritual fruit was not absent. By May, another woman in the congregation claimed conversion. In July, another two persons followed suit.[60]

Peter Powers' counsel to hold a regional prayer meeting did not go unheeded. Fisher joined several pastors of the Hancock Association at Sedgwick in September 1797. The Association's chief purpose was, "to endeavor to advance the glory of God in general, and the cause of Christianity in particular, by engaging in social prayer and instructive conversation."[61] An additional function was examination of ministerial candidates for ordination. Fisher continued to see congregants come to salvation, witnessing firsthand what would later be called the "Hancock revival,"

---

[58] Carter, "Mind and Ministry of Jonathan Fisher," 113.

[59] Carter, "Mind and Ministry of Jonathan Fisher," 113.

[60] Carter, "Mind and Ministry of Jonathan Fisher," 115. Daniel Merrill, who was also mentored by reverend Powers, traces his earliest experience of revival to the year 1791.

[61] Jonathan Fisher, "Records of the Hancock Association," 21 September 1797, Bluehill Congregational Church, Blue Hill, Maine. See Carter, "Mind and Ministry of Jonathan Fisher," 116. The association met four to eight times a year between the years 1797–1804.

which lasted from approximately 1798-1802. In correspondence to Betsy Smith, neé Heath, Fisher spoke of "reformation" and a "glorious season of grace" in the northeastern counties, a period of which he preached up to three times a week to upwards of one hundred people. He counted sixty persons who testified of experiencing personal conversion in Bluehill alone.[62] Persons in the community experienced unusual phenomena including possible angelic or demonic manifestations. Fisher recorded such events in detail, weighing possible causes, without succumbing to either skepticism or credulity.

Though it did not attain the renown—and subsequent scrutiny—of the revival at Cane Ridge, Kentucky in 1801, external evidence comports with Fisher's accounts. In Hancock County, between the years 1800 and 1820, Methodist churches grew from none to six, Congregationalist churches from six to nine, and Separate Baptist churches from one to a staggering twenty-one.[63] Correspondence during this period indicates that Fisher remained consistent in appropriating his Calvinism to interpret the nature and effects of revival. Sensing the tension between the hearers' recognition of helplessness—"our hearts are like a rock, they will not let us come"—Fisher does not deny, but comments that by such humiliation, they have been driven by the Spirit of God "till every other refuge failing them, they have fled to God. Their hard hearts have melted before all. They have closed with his salvation and have been able to say, 'Jesus thou art mine!'"[64] Fisher

---

[62] Jonathan Fisher, Letter to Betsy Heath, 2 June 1799.

[63] Kevin D. Murphy, *Jonathan Fisher*, 112. Daniel Merrill's revival experiences were coterminous with those of Fisher. Merrill identifies the years 1798, 1799, and 1802 as times of "great reformation." Methodists dated a revival in the Penobscot region that began in 1797. See also, Taylor, *Liberty Men and Great Proprietors*, 123-153.

[64] Fisher to Betsy Heath, 2 June 1799: "Those not elected have no bar put in the way of their salvation, but their own disinclination to embrace the offers of mercy. Our part is to do what God requires and that will prove our election." Cited in Gaylord Crosette Hall, *Supplement to the Biographical Sketch Of The Rev. Jonathan Fisher of Blue Hill, Maine* (New York: Gaylord C. Hall, 1946), 4. Cf. a line from "A moral *cannot*,

provided the following summary of the revival, a simple, patently evangelical assessment: "The Holy Spirit displayed his power. The church became earnest in prayer, and sinners were brought to bow to their Savior."[65] Evidence confirms this judgment.[66] By the year 1803, the Bluehill congregation had increased fivefold from the original 17 persons who signed the church covenant in 1797.

Unbeknownst to Fisher, these early revival experiences would not be equaled in any subsequent period at Bluehill. By the year 1804, the flames of spiritual vitality had waned. In a vein reminiscent of the mature Jonathan Edwards, Fisher expressed concern that the Bluehill congregation had grown languid and indifferent. In a sermon preached from the Song of Songs 5:3 on November 4, 1804, Fisher provided a classical allegorical interpretation of the text, asking where the marital passion of Christ's spiritual bride had gone: "It is fled—How cold and listless are our visits with respect to things truly spiritual! How have we been stumbling and what stumbling blocks we laid before the wicked."[67]

Years later, writing to his son Josiah, Fisher stated bluntly: "revivals where there is much excitement, do not seem to wear

---

does prevent/that all to heaven are not fully bent/But, God inclines to take the blissful way/just whom he will, and those alone obey." Cited in "Evening Contemplation #10" in *Castine Journal* (Castine, Maine) 15 May 1799. "Moral cannot" is an allusion to Jonathan Edwards' moral inability, an important conceptual category in *Freedom of the Will*.

[65] Carter, "Mind and Ministry of Jonathan Fisher," 138.

[66] A diary entry from March 15, 1803 reads: "P.M. carried Mrs. F. to Mr, E. Osgood's. Made a visit there. In the evening attended conference at Mr. George Stevens'—full conference. Some solemn eagerness. Mrs. Eliz. Parker professes a glimpse of hope. Andrew Wood, Bill Johnson and Robert Douglass under considerable impression. Blessed be God for his wonderful work!" Cited in *The Diaries of Jonathan Fisher*, 149.

[67] 1804 November 4 Blue Hill Library. Songs of Songs 5:3 (ESV) reads, "*I had put off my garment; how could I put it on? I had bathed my feet; how could I soil them?*" Membership patterns reflect this trend. After 1805, no new members were added to the congregation for over a decade. In addition to Fisher's maintenance of strict standards for membership, in 1806, no less than 28 members left the church, being dissatisfied with their baptism.

well."[68] These comments notwithstanding, Fisher's longing for an outpouring of God's Spirit did not cease. Two decades after the Hancock revival, he recorded in his diary that a "concert prayer" was held at his residence in October of 1818. Reverend Peter Powers' counsel that a young Fisher use right means for a desired end did not go unheeded. If Fisher's subsequent experiences did not match the fervor of 1800–1804, there is evidence that he was looking past the horizon of his own lifetime. The following diary entry reads,

However ineffectual my labors may be (at present) I have encouragement to labor diligently in the ministry; and if I be diligent and faithful, no doubt I shall see a reformation among my people, but I shall be made to see that the work is the Lord's.[69]

That Fisher made these comments in early 1799, prior to the Hancock revival, rather than at the end of his tenure at Bluehill suggests that he sincerely believed the contents.

Evangelical Activism

Fisher's ministry exhibited the activism that David Bebbington placed among the four cardinal points of evangelicalism.[70]

---

[68] Murphy, *Jonathan Fisher*, 228.

[69] February 18–21, 1799. Carter, "Mind and Ministry of Jonathan Fisher," 125.

[70] 1.) Biblicism: a high regard for Scripture, 2.) Crucicentrism: the centrality of Christ's work of redemption on the cross, 3.) Conversionism: all humans must undergo a conversion experience in response to the gospel, 4.) Activism: the gospel will be worked out in everyday life and culture. See, *David Bebbington, Evangelicalism in Modern Britain: A History from the 1730's to the 1980's* (New York: Routledge, 1989). Thomas S. Kidd would amend "Bebbington's quadrilateral" with an additional feature of evangelicalism: dependence upon the work of the Holy Spirit. Kidd writes, "from the outset of the movement, belief in the active, immediate ministry of the Holy Spirit was precisely what made evangelical Christianity as novel and controversial as it was. It was not just that the new evangelicals tested the limits of what one might expect from the Spirit on a daily basis, in terms of assurance, comfort, understanding, and guidance. The new evangelicals also had fundamental points of disagreement with

Understandably, some pursuits were more controversial than others. Fisher's embrace of temperance was consonant within the growing moral consensus across the nation.[71] The *volte face* is noteworthy considering that Fisher was not given to drunkenness and in fact, had distilled his own liquor for many years. Wine was served at his ordination in 1796. On balance, Fisher did witness firsthand, the harm inflicted by alcohol on clergy and laity alike.[72] The widespread distillation and consumption of whiskey, precipitated by an embargo on sugar, hurt the region's poorest classes. Warning and admonition against conventional societal ills — whether real or perceived — were a consistent theme in Fisher writings. Gambling and dancing were targets of the pastor's social critique.[73]

Two areas that incited greater opposition were the pastor's Federalism, and his incremental approach to freeing slaves. Fisher's political sympathies coincided with his self-understanding as a member of New England's elite — a cadre of men tasked with preservation of order in class and religion. The changing composition of Maine's electorate to a Democratic-Republican majority by the first decade of the nineteenth century would bode ill for Fisher.[74] The same period coincided with the end of the

---

their adversaries — especially Anglican opponents — about the doctrine of the Holy Spirit." Kidd, Thomas S., "The Bebbington Quadrilateral and the Work of the Holy Spirit," *Evangelicals: Who They Have Been, Are Now, and Could Be*, ed. Mark Noll (Grand Rapids: William B. Eerdmans Publishing Company, 2019), Chapter 17.

[71] See William Rorabaugh, *The Alcoholic Republic* (New York: Oxford University Press, 1981). The American temperance Society was founded in 1826.

[72] James Boyd, installed as pastor in the Bangor community was dismissed for "drunken lewdness" in 1801 after only two years into his appointment. See Fisher, "Hancock Association," 13 October 1801.

[73] Jonathan Fisher, "Believer's Column," *Gazette of Maine* (March 1807).

[74] See Ronald F. Banks, *Maine Becomes a State: The Movement to Separate Maine from Massachusetts, 1785-1820* (Middletown, CT: Wesleyan University Press); Murphy, *Jonathan Fisher*, 170; Chase, *Maine Parson*, 256-260. Democratic-Republicans flooded the area, inviting "the common people to reject the politics of paternalism," often resulting in the demolition of the religious establishment. "Federalists wanted to sustain a society where men could clearly identify their superiors, from whom

Hancock revival. Though not one to typically preach on political topics, Fisher gave a message in August of 1812, condemning the United States' war with Britain. This act led two hearers out of the church, and made scores of others hesitant to associate with the church at Bluehill.[75] Insistence that state taxation pay the salaries of Congregationalist ministers, resistance to Maine's independent statehood—advocacy for positions in New England politics that eventually lost—did not help Fisher's reputation. Furthermore, notable Congregationalist pastors sympathetic to Jeffersonian Democracy eventually became Baptists.[76] An unfortunate convergence of associations and alliances, and a broader clash with the spirit of Jacksonian democracy created inevitable barriers to growth.[77]

As for slavery, Fisher believed in the sovereignty of individual state legislatures to decide the matter, a moderate—and from the pastor's perspective—politically-principled position, which he explained in the following:

> By the constitution of the U.S.A the management and concern of slavery within its own limits is left to the legislature of each state itself. Any individual has a right to treat upon the subject of slavery, and to point out its nature and tendency, if it be done in a discreet and becoming manner, but he has not right to interfere directly with the proceedings of the slave-holding states.[78]

---

patronage flowed, and their inferiors, from whom deference was due ... Federalists posed as 'Fathers of the People'—well-meaning superiors ready to assist their lessers ... Thus Republican challengers spoke of themselves as 'Friends of the People"—equals rather than superiors." See Taylor, "From Fathers to Friends of the People," 469–470.

[75] Murphy, *Jonathan Fisher*, 113.

[76] Murphy, *Jonathan Fisher*, 114.

[77] In an early ordination message, Fisher echoed governor John Winthrop's famous 1630 sermon, when he wrote, "The ministers of Christ hold an eminent station; Ye are the light of the world a city on a hill cannot be hid." See *A Sermon, Preached at Machias, September 3, 1800, at the ordination of Rev. Marshfield Steele: to the pastoral care of the church and society in that town* (Boston, MA: E. Lincoln, 1801), 4.

[78] Hall, *Biographical Sketch*, 5.

Fisher neither owned slaves, nor offered any biblical defense of the matter, calling it "a serious evil." If he did not oppose abolitionist motives, Fisher expressed reservations about their methods. While it is tempting to impugn Fisher for prevarication or moral indifference, he was not offering a veiled defense of slaveholding. His "gradualist" approach involved the liberation of African slaves upon the satisfaction of particular criteria such as literacy and trade skills. Additionally, Fisher devoted energy to *Society for the Colonization of Free People of Color of America*, which labored to transport slaves to Liberia. Abolitionists, notably William Lloyd Garrison (1805–1879), were vocal critics of the *Society*.[79] Whatever the faults of Fisher's conservativism, it was certainly not mercenary or naïve. The parson feared that national disunity would lead to a civil war, and expressed concern that freed slaves would be vulnerable to exploitation and degradation. Both predictions proved true.

In contrast to Jeffersonian supporters centered in the south, Fisher advocated the Federalist position that criticized the exploitation of Native tribes.[80] Believing, in his own words, an obligation to "plead the red man's cause," Fisher insisted that mistreatment of America's indigenous peoples was a blight on the gospel of Jesus Christ.

Prompted by concerns about the substance of President Andrew Jackson's "Annual Message" in December, 1831, Fisher took to print. The *Christian Mirror* published "An Alarming Prospect" in early in 1832.[81] In a diary entry from December 1831,

---

[79] William Lloyd Garrison, in his *Thoughts on African Colonization* (1832), called the *Society* "a fraud." Only several thousand of the millions of Africans in America eventually arrived in Liberia.

[80] One particular scandal, known as the "Yazoo Land Deal" involved a fraudulent scheme to take Indian land. In fact, many of these Indians had become Christians through revivals in the south.

[81] Jackson had asserted that, "it is confidently believed that perseverance of a few years in the present policy of the Government will extinguish the Indian title to all lands lying within the States composing our Federal Union, and remove beyond their

Fisher made pointed criticism of abuse of Indians. He wrote, "it holds an implausible main principle, in the operation of which the poor Indians must suffer the greatest cruelties, principle subversive to the faith of treaties, and the principle which, if carried into effect, will probably ruin them."[82] Bluehill's pastor believed self-rule and Indian claims to land were fully legitimate, averring that fair treatment was the proper mode of ethical action and the best path towards conversion to Christianity. The December 1831 entry continues,

> Oh, that God would impose and deliver these oppressed suffers from the arm of oppression. The course pursued by the dominant part of the nation toward the Indians is an awful demonstration that the nation as such, is selfish and that no confidence can be placed for obtaining justice where selfishness reigns any farther than present self interest may seem to prompt.[83]

As would prove true in other areas of his life, Fisher's views cut against the cultural grain. By the time the fiery confidence of Manifest Destiny had died down, the damage done to many tribes was, in large part, irreversible.

---

limits every Indian who is not willing to submit to their laws." See "State of the Union Address" 1831. By 1833, the president's rhetoric struck a more ominous tone, "those tribes can not exist surrounded by our settlements and in continual contact with our citizens is certain. They have neither the intelligence, the industry, the moral habits, nor the desire of improvement which are essential to any favorable change in their condition. Established in the midst of another and a superior race, and without appreciating the causes of their inferiority or seeking to control them, they must necessarily yield to the force of circumstances and ere long disappear." See "State of the Union Address," 1833.

[82] Jonathan Fisher, Diary Entry, 12/19/1831.
[83] Jonathan Fisher, Diary Entry, 12/19/1831.

Conclusion

After a mutual agreement between the congregation and their pastor, Fisher retired after serving at Bluehill for 41 years.[84] Remarkably, he and Dolly had not saved for retirement, and labored on their farm for subsistence into their 70's. The fact that the Reverend Fisher's thrift—the likes of which prompted the creation of a novel shorthand—could not sustain the couple, hint at the economic hardships experienced on the Maine frontier during the era. His decision not to pastor at Ashby and thus forfeit greater financial security, attests to the Fisher's unfeigned commitment to Christ and his church. Letters and diary entries reveal that Jonathan and Dolly were content during their final years, farming, traveling, and usually surrounded by family and friends. He died after a brief illness that began with "pain in the bowels" in 1847. His daughter Betsey, who was present on her father's deathbed, described him as being "calm, and resigned to the will of God." She then offered a theological interpretation of the event with allusion to 2 Corinthians 5:1, "...as his earthly tabernacle was desolving [*sic*], he felt that he had a building above, a house not made with hands, Eternal in the heavens."[85] Dolly would live another six years as a widow before passing in 1853 at the age of 82.

Jonathan Fisher continues to be an object of academic fascination, though the subject(s) of interest possibly reveals as much about the scholar as it does of Fisher himself. Mary Ellen Chase, drawing from a first-person account the legendary sternness and rigor by which an elderly resident of Bluehill remembered Fisher,

---

[84] In a letter dated four years before retirement, Fisher wrote the following to his daughter, "I feel the infirmities of age creeping upon me, sight is growing dim, hearing obtuse, and memory failing; your mother's memory is very much impaired. We must soon both lay down our frail tabernacles in the dust. My mind loses its vitality; I cannot make unseen things appear so real to me as once I could." Letter to Betsy Stevens, 16 November, 1833. Senility notwithstanding, Fisher preached five or six times a year when his successor, Robert Cole, was absent.

[85] Murphy, *Jonathan Fisher*, 229.

recounts the then-boy's attempt to hide in an outhouse upon recognizing the approaching pastor. "Father Fisher, who knew every child in his parish, regenerate or unregenerate, came in person to haul him bodily from his hiding place by the scruff of his neck and back within the catechumenical circle."[86] Chase's account functions as a fitting allegory for the reception by modern New Englanders—a reception that began in the late nineteenth century—of an earlier generation of Yankees in the Puritan mold. Like the portrait of Colonel Pincheon in Nathaniel Hawthorne's *House of Seven Gables* (1850), the old preacher evokes reverential fear juxtaposed with detached avoidance. The Jonathan Fisher of Chase's anecdote is at his core, a stern, rigid, disciplinarian. The actions of a pastor motivated by an unwavering conviction that every hearer inside (and outside) his congregation was on the road to an eternity of heavenly bliss, or unspeakable horror in hell. Fisher's actions and person are obtuse, even incomprehensible to those who do not grasp the magnitude of a life lived where the theological stakes are as high as they were for Bluehill's pastor.

Fisher's self-portrait is significant in that he admired the work, believing it to be an accurate depiction of himself.[87] As others have noted, Fisher's finger is pointed to the Hebrew text of an open Bible. This detail is not insignificant, for Puritan portraits consistently featured a pastor's finger on the Bible, and for Fisher, the association was intentional. Unlike the average clergymen, Fisher was an accomplished painter, yet his art was not divorced from an evangelistic vision. New World settlers, whether Puritan or Separatist, had deep reverence for the Old Testament and believed their spiritual and civic life closely resembled that of ancient Israel. Thus, it seems appropriate that even as a young pastor,

---

[86] Chase, *Maine Parson*, 70.

[87] In his illuminating study on the role of representation in Fisher's cultural productions, Kevin D. Murphy opines that Fisher sought to convey virtue and erudition. See *Jonathan Fisher*, 222.

Fisher interpreted his ministry as resembling that of a biblical patriarch. He was not alone. Ebenezer Price, a friend and pastor, wrote the following in a personal letter to Fisher in 1797:

> We are, also in a sense, tho young, the Fathers of an extensive Country-our Faithfulness, & setting a pious example, will effect [sic] the present, & doubtless generations to come.[88]

Fisher agreed, understanding his influence to extend far beyond his lifetime. Despite his own ability and example however, American Congregationalism was moving in a different direction than Fisher. As is often the case, a pastor's ministerial career does not attain an earlier vision and outcome. Evangelical Christianity, however, did have a vibrant future in America, even if it assumed new forms and emphases. Just as Fisher could not transport himself back to seventeenth-century Massachusetts, contemporaries sympathetic to his ministry can likewise only persevere in their own context within the boundaries of a fixed horizon, and instrumentally, by the same faith.

---

[88] Ebeneezer Price to Jonathan Fisher, 11/18/1797, JFM 1465.201. Cited in Kevin D. Murphy, *Jonathan Fisher*, 110. In January of 1823, Fisher records a missionary journey of 167 miles to communities around present-day Dover-Foxcroft, "154 of it travelled upon foot." He characteristically noted the variety of trees in the region, their growth, and the richness of the soil. He then remarked, "Very desirable it is that as this land shall be sown with the seed of men, it should be sown with the seed of pure religion also. The prosperity of future generations in this state no doubt depends much upon this." Jonathan Fisher, January 6, 1823, *The Diaries of Jonathan Fisher*, 588. Taylor, "From Fathers to Friends of the People."

2
Appointed:
Daniel Merrill, "Gospel Ranger" on the Eastern Frontier

"We do not desire to use offensive words needlessly, but we wish to be understood distinctly." Daniel Merrill

The ministries of both Daniel Merrill and Jonathan Fisher had similar beginnings, and consequently, similar trajectories. Both pursued formal education and theological training in preparation for Congregational ministry at two elite institutions of their time: Merrill at Dartmouth, and Fisher at Harvard. Both desired to go into new territories and communities where the gospel had not been preached, either to support or plant churches in the District of Maine on the Eastern Frontier in the Commonwealth of Massachusetts, "down east" from Boston. Fisher would serve his entire life in the town of Bluehill Maine, while Merrill ministered in the neighboring town of Sedgwick,[1] with an absence serving the Nottingham West Baptist congregation in Hudson, New Hampshire from 1814 to 1820.[2] Both were sons of the Commonwealth,

---

[1] Sedgwick comprised what are now the towns of Sedgwick, Brooklin (Port Watson), and Brooksville, as well as other neighborhoods or villages such as Sargentville.

[2] Academic interest in Daniel Merrill began to blossom at the turn of the 21st century. Readers now have greater access to biographical material assembled in the form of dissertations and academic publications. See Ron Baines, "Daniel Merrill 1765–1833," *A Noble Company: Biographical Essays on Notable Particular-Regular Baptist in America Vol. 6*, ed. Terry Wolever (Springfield, MI: Particular Baptist Press, 2015); Ronald Baines, *Separating God's Two Kingdoms: Regular Baptists in Maine, Nova Scotia, and New Brunswick, 1780 to 1815* (2020) Electronic Theses and Dissertations. 3183. University of Maine; Richard Carter, "Mind and Ministry of Jonathan Fisher." Brittany P. Goetting, "Bound by Print: The Baptist Borderlands of Maine and the Canadian Maritimes, 1770-1840" (2022). Electronic Theses and Dissertations. 3571.

touched intimately by the Revolutionary War. As noted, Fisher was Merrill's junior by three years and lost his father, Lieutenant Jonathan Fisher, who died at the age of 33, leaving his widowed mother, Katharine Avery Fisher, to support their 7 children. Merrill fought in the Revolutionary War as a teenager and would survive the conflict.

Born on March 18, 1765 into a typical New England family in Rowley, Essex County Massachusetts, north of Boston, Daniel Merrill was reared by his parents Thomas and Sarah Merrill in a Congregationalist home. Near the end of his life, he described the residence as his "beloved paternal mansion." The Rev. James Chandler baptized the boy when he was less than a month old on April 7, 1765. By all accounts, Daniel, along with his eight brothers and two sisters, enjoyed a pleasant childhood, free from the extremes of want and wealth.[3]

Daniel's father served as a deacon for over 30 years in a church with New Light sympathies. When Merrill was about five years old, George Whitefield traveled to preach in the neighborhood. The British evangelist would die a month later in nearby Newburyport. Like Fisher, Merrill experienced an evangelical conversion. His change of heart, which happened at age 13, is memorialized in his *Autobiography*. "The Lord gave me to hope in his mercy," he wrote. By the age of 14, he sensed a call "to be a minister and witness" of Christ, but those aspirations were put on hold when Merrill enlisted in the Continental Army at the age of 15.[4] From January 1781 until 1784, Merrill served, venturing "into

---

[3] Ron Baines, "Daniel Merrill 1765-1833," *A Noble Company*, 342.

[4] Daniel Merrill, *Autobiography of Rev. Daniel Merrill* (Philadelphia: Baptist General Tract Society, 1833) From the first page: "The following narration of some portions of the Rev. Daniel Merrill's history, written by himself, was forwarded to the Agent of the Baptist General Tract Society, for publication, a few weeks previous to his decease, which took place in June, 1833. A letter accompanying the manuscript was written by his daughter, at his dictation; disease having rendered him unable to perform the labor."

most of the States then in the Union."[5] Family history claims that "he at one time was an aide-de-camp to Gen. George Washington," though this has yet to be confirmed.[6]

Like many through the ages, Merrill witnessed the worst of human nature while serving as a soldier. On the other hand, he did find "decent morality and hopeful piety" while in the company of Mr. Israel Evans, a military chaplain of upright character.[7] What initially appeared as an interruption to Merrill's plans, and hindrance to his growth as a serious Christian, likely hastened the Holy Spirit's work of sanctification. Upon being discharged, Merrill pursued formal theological training, a period that would span approximately seven years. He entered Dartmouth College at age nineteen and graduated at the top of his class with both a Bachelor's and Master of Arts degrees in the year 1789.[8] The content of Merrill's studies, instruction of mentors, his military experience and travels throughout the young nation, would prove providential. Merrill followed what he believed was the Lord's calling as a Congregational minister to the far-flung settlements and communities on the Eastern Frontier in the District of Maine.

As to his physical appearance, Merrill was described by his son as, "not exceeding ... five and a half feet" and, "rather short of stature ... possessed of a vigorous and solid physique, florid complexion, blue eyes, quick motion and ready speech."[9] In seeking

---

[5] Daniel Merrill, *Autobiography*, 1.

[6] *The Allens from William Allen (1602-1679) of Manchester England, and of Salem and Manchester, Massachusetts, in the direct line of descent through Nathaniel Allen (1744-1789) of Beverly, Massachusetts and Sedgwick, Maine, to Lt. Raymond Frederick Allen, Jr. (1931-) of Rochester, New York, with certain other descendants and collaterals"* (no publisher: The State Historical Society of Wisconsin, original copy at the University of Wisconsin, n.d), 52.

[7] Daniel Merrill, *Autobiography*, 1.

[8] *Daniel Merrill*, The Bible Baptist Tribune, November 25, 2013, www.tribune.org /daniel-merrill.

[9] Samuel Pearce Merrill, "Rev. Daniel Merrill, An Appreciation," *Centennial of the First Baptist Church, Sedgwick, Maine, June 11-18, 1905* (1905), 42; and Baines, "Daniel Merrill 1765-1833," in *A Noble Company*, 350.

to capture the essence of his life, historian Ronald Baines gives the following description of Daniel Merrill:

> Merrill applied himself diligently to his studies at Dartmouth, giving recitations in his senior year in John Locke, *On Human Understanding*, and Jonathan Edwards, *On the Freedom of the Will*, among others. The remainder of his life would evidence his indebtedness to the political principles espoused by Locke and the evangelical Calvinism defended by Edwards. Merrill graduated with high honors in a class of twenty-three students in 1789 ... He was taken under the tutelage of Dr. Samuel Spring (1746-1819) ... an ardent supporter of both domestic and foreign missions, being one of the principal founders and leaders of *the Massachusetts Missionary Society*. He was also involved in ministerial training and in the founding of Andover Theological Seminary. As was the teacher, so was the student; both of these traits would be prominent in Merrill's ministerial life.[10]

Around the time Merrill was preparing for ministry, settlers homesteading Township Number Four along the mid-coast of the District of Maine were petitioning the General Court in Massachusetts to incorporate the area as the Town of Sedgwick.[11] The settlement would be named after Major Robert Sedgwick, Oliver Cromwell's handpicked commander for the expedition that captured the French fort at Castine—located just across the Bagaduce River from the town—a century before, in 1654. The legislature passed a special enabling act that granted the proprietors and

---

[10] Baines, "Daniel Merrill 1765-1833," *A Noble Company*, 345-346.

[11] See, *Life and Times in a Coastal Village, Sedgwick Maine-1789-1989*, 4. This book was "printed to commemorate the two hundredth anniversary of the incorporation of the Town of Sedgwick," by the Bicentennial Committee, with "special thanks" to a number of former and current residents who the author has known personally, most of whom are now deceased. The book is 110 pages in length and undated. The committee drew from original local documents in personal and public collections, many of which have been photomechanically reproduced.

settlers their request upon completion of four conditions in the span of five years, namely:

1. If there were 60 frame dwelling houses;
2. If there were 60 protestant families;
3. If there were built a meeting-house;
4. If there was employed and settled a learned protestant minister.[12]

The first two conditions had already been met by 1788 and the proprietors built the first meetinghouse just across the Benjamin River from the village of Sedgwick in what is the present-day Town of Brooklin. The Act of Incorporation was passed on April 6, 1789, the same month and year the government of the United States first convened. The proprietors began in earnest to settle a minister and establish a Congregational Church. Daniel Merrill was licensed to preach, summoned by the *selectmen* to "fulfil a four months' engagement," and delivered his first sermon in the town's original meetinghouse on the Lord's Day in April of 1791.[13] Of the occasion he wrote, "In the first discourse which I here delivered, the Lord mercifully worked with me and confirmed the word, as the signs which followed abundantly evinced." Merrill was not the settled minister, yet over a period of a few months, his ministry bore abundant fruit. One-hundred residents testified to conversion, claiming to be overwhelmed by an "affecting sense of the exceeding sinfulness of sin ... and the necessity of being

---

[12] Rev. Arthur Warren Smith, *Historical Sketch of the Town of Sedgwick*. "Centennial of the First Baptist Church Sedgwick, Maine: June 11-18, 1905, Two Historical Papers" (no publication date or publisher, bound 64 pages), 15. Laurel Thatcher Ulrich provides an informative and detailed account of how a minister was settled in the District of Maine in 1786 from the diary of Martha Ballard of Hallowell Maine. See Laurel Thatcher Ulrich, *A Midwife's Tale: The Life of Martha Ballard, Based on Her Diary, 1785-1812* (New York, NY: Knopf, 1990), 104-108.

[13] Rev. Arthur Warren Smith, *Historical Sketch of the Town of Sedgwick*, 27.

forgiven."[14] His immediate success led the young Congregational Church in Sedgwick to grow. Outside his own church, Merrill's preaching produced a similar harvest. He records that,

> near one hundred were turned from darkness to light, and from the power of Satan unto God, during the twenty-three weeks in which I was with them [Sedgwick] that season. The same appearances and fruits manifested themselves in every town where I preached more than one Sabbath, during eighteen months in which I was absent from this place.[15]

The spiritual blessings notwithstanding, Merrill was unsure of the Lord's leading. After experiencing similar manifestations of revival throughout northern New England, he believed it imperative that he settle on the eastern frontier. Merrill would later distinguish himself and other evangelists who ranged "to and fro" across the Eastern Frontier as "Gospel Rangers." In a selfsame sermon from Daniel 2:4, "Many shall run to and fro, and knowledge shall be increased," Merrill drew upon military imagery familiar to contemporary audiences, likening this band of itinerant evangelists to army rangers—resolute soldiers, familiar with the terrain, effective in engaging the enemy, and devoted to their Sovereign and the welfare of his people.[16]

---

[14] Daniel Merrill, *Autobiography*, 2

[15] Daniel Merrill, *Autobiography*, 2

[16] Daniel Merrill, *The Gospel Rangers. A Sermon Delivered at the Ordination of Elder Henry Hale*, Second Edition (Springfield: Henry Brewer, 1807). Rangers were formed during the Colonial Period as a kind of light infantry—skilled marksmen, trackers, and frontiersmen who could move quickly and fight effectively in wilderness situations. The *Gospel Ranger*, military motif, was a common feature of Merrill's life and preaching his entire life. In 1825, he cheered on his band of brothers in the ministry: "As warriors you are, like soldiers of the sovereigns of the earth, to be bold, courageous, persevering, and never to halt, till the word is given. You are never to learn the art of retreating, for your backs are never to be turned to the enemy, nor are you to yield to them an inch of ground." Daniel Merrill, *A Sermon Preached at the Ordination of Rev. PHINEAS BOND, PASTOR OF THE FIRST BAPTIST CHURCH IN STEUBEN, May 25, 1825*, (Waterville: Wm. Hastings, 1825), 27.

Daniel Merrill, "Gospel Ranger"

Merrill refused the town's first offer, but when the proprietors agreed to the stipulation that he would be free to "be useful to the adjacent towns, as their servant for Jesus' sake," and furthermore, "be at liberty to go and preach to them ... in the week time," the "Gospel Ranger" became their settled pastor.[17] Merrill was ordained on September 17, 1793. The ordination sermon preached by Dr. Spring from 1 Corinthians 2:2, "For I determined not to know any thing among you save CHRIST and him crucified," charged Merrill to move beyond the abstractions of philosophy and peculiar winds of doctrine blowing through the academy and preach the plain gospel of the cross undergirded by the doctrines of grace. The trajectory of his ministry proved that Merrill heeded Dr. Spring's counsel.[18]

Marriage and Family

The Lord's blessings were not limited to Merrill's preaching alone. During his deliberations with the town of Sedgwick, he found the woman whom be believed would partner with him on the frontier. Joanna Colby of Sandown, New Hampshire seemed the right fit to assist him in planting a church, forming a community, rearing children, and building a Christian home in the wilderness. They married on August 14, 1793. Merrill's motive in accepting the call to Sedgwick and his hopes for their relationship are expressed in this letter to Joanna dated June 17, 1793:

---

[17] Daniel Merrill, *Mr. Merrill's answer to the Christians, and other inhabitants of Sedgwick also the confession and covenant of the Ch. of Christ in that place* (Newburyport, Massachusetts: Edmund M. Blunt, 1801), 5.

[18] Samuel Spring, A.M., *Mr. Spring's Sermon. A Sermon Preached at the Ordination of the Rev. Daniel Merrill in Sedgwick. Sept. 17, 1793* (Newburyport: Edmund M. Blunt, 1794). Over 30 years later, Merrill echoed Dr. Spring in a sermon upon the ordination of Phineas Bond, "have nothing to do with uncertainties. These are for the dreamers. You have to testify what you have seen and what he may show you, as truth, as certain truth. This you are to testify boldly, and unequivocally. *When you have performed this,* YOU ARE TO CEASE. You have delivered your message. The Lord will look to the result. It is presumption for any minister to contend for uncertainties." Daniel Merrill, *A Sermon Preached at the Ordination of Rev. PHINEAS BOND*, 25.

My dear friend,

This has been a solemn day to me. I have given my answer. I have given it, as though the Lord Jesus Christ, in his providence, called me to. I hope that I shall have this consolation, that I have not been influenced from motives of wealth, ease, or honor, but from love to the Church of Christ. I considered that I was not my own, but Christ's in the service of his Church. The town has done on some amount more than I asked. Their union is surprising. It has continued for two years ... I think I shall be able to explain my conduct to [you] when I have opportunity to see my dear Joe [i.e. Joanna]. ... I hope that our presence will make almost any place appear agreeable to each other. Remember... that it is Christ who calls you to come unto this place. I hope, I pray, that you may come in obedience to him, and out of love to his dear children. Pray do not have one backward feeling with regard to coming; for I have full enough. Come as cheerfully as you can.[19]

But alas, their union was tragically brief. The following month, with the leaves barely off the trees in Sedgwick, Merrill's faith would be tested, joy threatened, and his Calvinistic view of God's sovereign purposes, tried. Joanna died suddenly on October 28, 1793, two months after their wedding.

Whether by conviction or necessity, Merrill stolidly channeled his grief into preaching the gospel on brief missionary tours, away from Sedgwick through that first winter. The church had agreed that as their settled minister he would preach abroad on occasion and assist struggling congregations. Merrill's preaching sparked revival in New Hampshire, and introduced him to the woman who would become his "yokefellow" in ministry to Sedgwick. One year after the death of Joanna, Daniel married Susanna Gale of

---

[19] Daniel Merrill, Letter to Joanna Colby, dated Sedgwick, June 19, 1793. Moses Merrill Papers. Cited in Ron Baines, "Daniel Merrill 1765–1833," in *A Noble Company*, 347.

Salisbury, New Hampshire on October 14, 1794. She proved to be "a woman of strong constitution, excellent economy, rare industry and a true helpmeet," essential virtues for any woman raising thirteen children.[20] Six sons and seven daughters all lived to adulthood. Susanna and Daniel named their first child Joanna, in tribute to his first wife.[21] Remarkably, twelve of the thirteen children experienced an evangelical conversion.[22]

Daniel and Susanna's first son, John Gale Merrill, graduated from Colby College and became a medical doctor. He died at the age of 29 in Sedgwick. Susan Gale Merrill married Colonel Rowland Carlton at Sedgwick, where they were members of the Baptist Church. Susan bore ten children. Daniel Merrill Jr. married Mary D. Greeley. They made their home in Worcester MA, where he served as a deacon. They had five children. Joseph Merrill, another son who became a deacon, lived in Sedgwick, Nottingham West NH, and Michigan. He was married to Nancy Baldwin, whom he praised as, "one of the most useful and faithful of women." Sarah Merrill married Rev. Charles Webster Bradbury, a teacher and Baptist Minister in Maine. They had six children together.[23] Samuel Merrill became a wealthy ship captain and later, owner, in Sedgwick and Surry, Maine. Samuel's wife would produce twelve children. Like her sister Sarah, Hannah Weeks Merrill married a Baptist pastor, the Rev. Dura D. Pratt, D.D. In 1832 Pratt, "was invited to take the pastorate of the Baptist church in Nashua, N.H., where he had a most successful ministry for twenty-three years, baptizing during that period not far from 600 individuals." Hannah died at age 36 with two children,

---

[20] Samuel Pearce Merrill, "Rev. Daniel Merrill, An Appreciation," 41.

[21] Joanna married Reuben Greely, a Deacon of the Baptist Church at Nottingham West. They had twelve children. Joanna lived to 95 years of age.

[22] See Samuel Pearce Merrill, 59 and, *The Allens from William Allen (1602-1679) of Manchester England, and of Salem and Manchester, Massachusetts*, 54-57.

[23] Sarah survived Rev. Bradbury by more than a decade and "was quite a generous donor toward the education of the colored people by the Home Mission Society."

predeceasing her husband seventeen years. One son, Thomas Merrill, after serving as a pastor in Maine and New Hampshire, became a missionary to Native Americans in Michigan. Moses Merrill moved west as a missionary to the Otoe tribe in present-day Nebraska. Mary Barnard Merrill married Deacon Isaac Allen of the North Sedgwick Baptist Church. They had six children.

Like Jonathan and Dolly Fisher, Daniel and Susanna Merrill lost children in their twenties. Harriet Rebekah Merrill died of tuberculosis just before her twentieth year. She is buried beside her father and mother in the Rural Cemetery, behind the meeting-house and across the road to Bluehill from the family home in Sedgwick. Eliza Wheelock Merrill married a wealthy merchant from Boston, Charles H. Nichols, and died without children at the age of 29.[24] Reflecting on the family legacy early in the twentieth century, Samuel Pearce Merrill proudly noted that, "Five members of the family have been ministers of the Gospel. One a judge. Six deacons of Baptist churches. Six have been practicing physicians."[25]

Such spiritual fecundity lay, however, in the distant future. In the meantime, Daniel and Susanna would need to clothe and feed their prodigious family. Like virtually every minister in the region, they relied on the Maine woods for lumber and heat, as well as an adequate patch of farmland to provide food, miscellanies, and supplementary income for his family. His annual salary was more generous than Jonathan Fisher's, which plausibly explains why Merrill had greater freedom to travel and engage in the numerous initiatives throughout his tenure. Like Fisher, Daniel Merrill

---

[24] Samuel Pearce Merrill wrote of his aunt, "Eliza was the youngest ... she was a woman of fine culture and a most amiable spirit. Her life was beautiful as one could well be. Her friends were every one who knew her. Some of my earliest and most cherished recollections are associated with this most excellent and cultured Christian woman."

[25] Samuel Pearce Merrill, "Rev. Daniel Merrill, An Appreciation," 63 (Sargentville Library Historical Archive online).

devoted time to raising funds, even canvasing door-to-door. Merrill was an unusually successful fundraiser for various associations and missionary societies. Reflecting a century later, Merrill's grandson offered the following snapshot of the household:

> He was thrifty. On the farm that he occupied, and in the great house which was his home, he had for his family all the comforts and conveniences of that time. On a salary of $400.00 [annually], his family did not want. They were clad well, schooled well, and given every useful advantage which the times and their desires required ... The inventory of his estate ... tells of a house comfortably furnished, and its items reveal the fatherly care and provision for his children in case of need ... His wife was a woman of poise and good sense. She was loyal and affectionate ... of considerable education for that time.[26]

Settling into his role as the ideal New England minister, Merrill was serving not only as the town's pastor, but as a politician and pioneer who brought culture and learning to the "howling wilderness."[27] Records attest, that on January 1, 1794, Nathan Tenn[e]y, Moses Eaton, Israel Robinson, Eben Eaton, and Theo Stephens [Theodore Stevens?] met to form the Hancock Library in the town of Sedgwick, which would serve the entire county. Nathan Tenney was chosen to "get" the initial catalogue of books, "half History & half Divinity," and "the Rev. Mr Merrill should have the privilidge of makeing out one Quarter of The Catalogue of Books." A list of books purchased in Boston was accounted for and the Hancock Library was born at Sedgwick. The holdings of

---

[26] Samuel Pearce Merrill, "Rev. Daniel Merrill, An Appreciation," 58. *Daniel Merrill Estate Inventory*, photographic copy of the original and transcript, Sedgwick-Brooklin Historical Society, Sedgwick, Maine.

[27] James Gilpatrick, "Biographical Sketch of the Rev. Daniel Merrill," from the funeral sermon he preached upon the death of Merrill, *The Baptist Memorial and Monthly Record* (New York: John R. Bigelow, 1845), 4:313.

the library were later divided between Sedgwick and Bluehill in the Autumn of 1796. Daniel Merrill was chosen President of the Hancock Library for the year 1795.[28] The books "bought at the Boston Store" suggest a broad, urbane readership that included, not only history and divinity, but popular novels, comedy, satire, and moral tales or guides, reflecting a religious or Biblical worldview.[29]

Throughout his life, Merrill served in various civic roles. His name appears in the minutes and records of sundry associations and committees. Sources consistently portray him taking the lead in enterprises of all kinds, and histories of Baptist publications throughout the nineteenth century place him in the constellation of luminaries from 1804 onward.

A number of other evangelical pastors joined Merrill in answering the call to serve in the Massachusetts Missionary Society and settle in the harsh, isolated, District of Maine.[30] Jonathan Fisher traveled to the area, preaching during the same period and was later called as pastor in neighboring Bluehill. Merrill and Ebenezer Eaton, a licensed minister from Sedgwick who was serving the Church at Mount Desert, examined young Fisher in July

---

[28] The Records and Constitution of *The Hancock Library*. This bound leather ledger records the founding of *The Hancock Library* and resides in archival care at the Sargentville Library, Sedgwick ME. The unlined, handwritten ledger details the creation of the library and contains an ongoing record of its acquisitions, spanning decades. The library was originally maintained at Sedgwick. Officers were chosen on January 1, 1794 and in the Autumn of that year "The Rev. Mr. Merril[l]" was chosen to serve as President for the year 1795.

[29] The Records and Constitution of *The Hancock Library* list over fifty volumes including multiple standard works by Doddridge, Jonathan Edwards, Baxter, and Bunyan. Books for and by women include Hannah More's *Strictures on the Modern System of Female Education*, Charlotte Palmer's *Female Stability*, Ann Yearsley's *The Royal Captives: a Fragment of Secret History, Copied from an Old Manuscript* and Hannah Adams's *View of Religions*. The novel, poetry, comedy, and satire are represented by such works as Thomas Brown's *The Remains of Mr. Thomas Brown,* Henry MacKenzie's *Julia de Roubigne*, Frances Burney's *Cecilia*, and Oliver Goldsmith's *Vicar of Wakefield*.

[30] See https://www.swhcc.com/history-of-swhcc (accessed on March 2, 2022).

of 1796. The sober proceedings were led by Alden Bradford of Wiscasset, the venerable Peter Powers of Deer Isle, Jonathan Powers of Penobscot, and delegates from the Sedgwick, Penobscot, and Deer Isle Congregational Churches.[31] Merrill and Fisher initiated a close friendship which they would maintain until separated by death. Their fraternity was, however, nearly wrecked at the beginning of Fisher's examination. According to Mary Ellen Chase, Fisher had, "certain involved and obscure disagreements and prejudices, centering about the Reverend Daniel Merrill of Sedgwick."[32] Chase does not disclose their nature, nor did Fisher reference them in his diary. Whatever the disagreements were, she claims,

> Fisher was so unnerved that he was able to get little sleep that night. He also lost his appetite … there were some in the Bluehill congregation that were not entirely satisfied with Fisher and opposed his ordination and settlement rather roughly; the council closed the evening with Fisher's ordination clouded in uncertainty. They reconvened the following morning, July 13, 1796, and re-examined the disaffected folks and found them more moderate in their sentiments. The majority of the council voted to proceed with the ordination, while only Jonathan Powers and the delegates from his Penobscot congregation withdrew and left for home.[33]

---

[31] Ron Baines, "Daniel Merrill 1765-1833," *A Noble Company*, 354.

[32] For a detailed discussion of Fisher's ordination and Merrill's involvement in the controversy, see Richard Carter, "Mind and Ministry of Jonathan Fisher," 98–102.

[33] Ron Baines, "Daniel Merrill 1765-1833," *A Noble* Company, 354; Chase, *Maine Parson*, 59-61. "Necessary matters being duly considered, the Council, on the 13th of July 1796 voted to proceed to ordain Mr. Jon. Fisher to the pastoral care of the Chh of Ct. at Blue hill. Not far from two on the clock P.M. Mr. Fisher was ordained accordingly. Attest. Daniel Merrill Scribe to said council. True copy on file." *Photocopy of original town records*, Town of Blue Hill Maine.

Fisher's ordination did take place, outdoors in the field of Daniel Osgood, a leading citizen and merchant in Bluehill on July 13, 1796.

Merrill and Fisher's lives would remain interwoven during the joyous times of revival as well as the doctrinally-driven sectarian struggles. While these disagreements would invariably place them in opposing camps, they esteemed one another as co-laborers, even friends.[34] Fisher appears to have regarded Merrill as a respected elder, mentor, and trailblazer. As noted in chapter one, Fisher's legacy would grow to near legendary proportions in regional Maine culture and academia, albeit, posthumously. Merrill's influence as a pioneering Baptist would extend far beyond his own congregation during his lifetime yet fade over time to the role of a supporting character in the life of Jonathan Fisher.[35]

With Merrill and his wife settled, and the pastorate of the Church of Christ in Sedgwick solidified, the couple's godly reputation and penchant for civic involvement helped the town grow and flourish. The following vignette from the Thurston family genealogy captures the sentiments of many who would become leading citizens of this Eastern Frontier "city on a hill," beyond the Penobscot River:

> David Thurston was a farmer in New Rowley [MA] till 1795, when he made a prospecting journey to Maine on horseback, stopping at many places to see what advantages they offered, but with the resolution that he would not locate where there was no orthodox minister. In conversation with a gentleman in Bangor he said, 'I have money in my pocket to buy this land,' which included all that is now Bangor city, 'but I will not settle where my family cannot have the gospel.' So he went on forty miles to Sedgwick, where

---

[34] Mary Ellen Chase, *Maine Parson*, 98.

[35] Cf., David Benedict, *A General History of the Baptist Denomination in America, and other Parts of the World*, Vol. 1 (Boston: Lincoln and Edmands, 1813).

Daniel Merrill, "Gospel Ranger"

Rev. Daniel Merrill, a pupil of Dr. Spring, senior, was pastor of a Congregational church. Having purchased a farm he returned to Rowley, and in April, 1796, he took his son Richard and went to Sedgwick to sow and plant for the season, and then returned for his family, who took passage in a sloop from Newburyport to Bluehill Falls[36]

The Church of Christ in Sedgwick was established with twenty-two members in 1793, and under Merrill's preaching and leadership, grew to 189 members within a decade, becoming the largest church of any denomination or tradition in the District of Maine.[37] The renowned Baptist preacher and church planter, Elder Isaac Case, traced the beginnings of the revival in that part of Maine to a travelling Congregationalist preacher, Jotham Sewall, during the latter part of 1802. Case gave the following account of the revival:

others were awakened under my feeble labors when here last April. But the work hath been mainly carried on under the preaching of Brother Pilsbury, and the prayers, exhortations, singing and private conversation of three pious young men, who have been studying with Mr. Merrill, with a view to the ministry. One of these young men is a member of a Baptist church.[38]

In his memoir, reverend Sewall describes the church in Sedgwick under the influence of spiritual renewal:

---

[36] *Thurston Genealogies Compiled by Brown Thurston, Portland, Maine* (Portland: Brown Thurston, 1892), 39.

[37] Daniel Merrill, *Autobiography*, 10; A.W. Smith, "Historical Sketch of the Town of Sedgwick," 20; Henry S. Burrage, *History of the Baptists In Maine* (Portland, ME: Marks Printing House, 1904), 142; Joshua Millet, *A History of the Baptists in Maine; Together with Brief Notices of Societies and Institutions* (Portland: Charles Day & Co., 1845), 263. Richard Carter, "Mind and Ministry of Jonathan Fisher," 228.

[38] Henry S. Burrage, *History of the Baptists In Maine*, 113.

I think I never enjoyed more solemnity and freedom in prayer and preaching. The Lord seemed to be present and to fill my soul and my mouth. Many tears were shed in the assembly. I was told that two-thirds of the congregation were Christians. All the adult persons in the family where I spent the night, eight in number, are professors [believers]... Last winter and spring witnessed the fourth revival since Mr. Merrill's settlement. The Church now consists of nearly two hundred members. Could scarcely find a person who was not a professor."[39]

Sewall would later become one of the first trustees of Bangor Theological Seminary and his son, Jotham Sewall, Jr., would succeed the pulpit of the First Congregational Church of Bluehill in 1843, after Jonathan Fisher's retirement. [40] The reverend Peter Powers of Deer Isle, one of the few men living at the time who experienced the first Great Awakening, described the revival at Sedgwick from his vantage point across the Eggemoggin Reach:

I now come a little nearer home. In the beginning of winter, this glorious work began in Sedgwick, under the pastoral care of the Rev. Daniel Merrill. Perhaps there hath not been a work so powerful, and so much like the work fifty eight years ago [The Great Awakening]. In a time of such extraordinaries, it could not reasonably be expected but some things would be a little wild and incoherent, considering the various tempers, infirmities, and dispositions of mankind: But I believe my young and dear brother Merrill, together with experienced Christians were very careful to distinguish the precious from the vile to correct errors, 'to set the people in the way of his steps,' so that there appears to be no prevalence of enthusiasm among them, according to the best information. How great the number is of those who

---

[39] Jotham Sewall, *A Memoir of Rev. Jotham Sewall, of Chesterville, Maine* (Bangor: E.F. Duren, 1853), 102–103.

[40] Jotham Sewall, *A Memoir of Rev. Jotham Sewall*, 358.

have been brought to hope, I am not able to give any tolerable good account: Some say there are about an hundred, others double that number ... And now, dear Sir, let your imagination paint to your view the striking scene of an hundred souls, men, women, and children, at the same time under the work of the law. The tears, sobs, groans and cries issuing from scores at a time ... Hear them freely confessing their old abominations, their former enmity to the great doctrines of original sin, election, the sovereignty of the divine, free grace, the power of God displayed ... above all, the justice of God in their damnation. How often are souls brought out into the peace and comfort of the love of God, and the sweet consolations of the Holy Spirit. The dead hear the voice of the Son of God, and live.[41]

This work of God's Spirit was also taking place under Jonathan Fisher's ministry in Bluehill, in which he likewise noted, "there were pretty evident indications of a commencing revival. Light beamed upon many minds, and they attained to a joyful hope of salvation. ... By June, 1799, the healing streams of Divine Mercy and Grace were in full flood," resulting in 57 received into fellowship in the Bluehill Church of Christ.[42] In his own locale, Powers saw a harvest of "about forty, men, women, and children, who have obtained a hope; and great numbers are under pressing conviction," though the results at Deer-Isle did not attain that of Sedgwick.[43] Merrill rejoiced in that "great reformation" which took place toward the close of the eighteenth century, as well as in 1802. In Sedgwick, "the divine influences were remarkable in both the church and society." It was at this time that Baptist

---

[41] *A Brief Account of the Late Revivals of Religion in a Number of Towns in the New-England States, and Also in Nova-Scotia. Extracted Chiefly from Letters Written by Several Gentlemen of Unquestionable Veracity. To Which is added, A Very Interesting Letter, From a Minister in London to His Friend in Massachusetts* (Boston: Manning & Loring, 1799), 11-12.

[42] Mary Ellen Chase, *Maine Parson*, 108.

[43] *A Brief Account of the Late Revivals*, 13.

ministers "hearing of the good hand of our God upon us, visited us and preached many lectures" in private homes and the meetinghouse. Although his fellow Congregationalist ministers may have thought the young pastor naïve or even foolish, Merrill and the congregation "received them kindly, for they proved to be men of God."[44]

Merrill's cooperation with Baptist pastors and evangelists began years before his installation at Sedgwick. While still a student, he travelled with itinerant missionaries and preachers from Massachusetts in the Eastern Frontier. Merrill's willingness to cooperate with Baptists is indicative of warm evangelical convictions. At the time, however, he nevertheless possessed a negative, albeit unfounded, opinion of the sect, claiming to have never, "seen more than one Baptist minister, nor heard anyone commend the peculiar tenets of the Baptists."[45] Merrill's change of heart toward the Baptists was partly the result of his calling to take the gospel message to the frontier. Missionary work brought him into close contact with like-minded, evangelical Baptist laymen and preachers. He noted in his *Autobiography* that,

> From time to time my acquaintance with the Baptists increased, and my affection for them, as partakers of the divine nature, and possessing like precious faith, also increased; so did also my desire for a union with them—not by turning to them, but by their conviction of what I believed to be their error, and by turning from it, as least so far that we might appear one people, and have nothing to mar our union, or hinder our work.[46]

Like many Congregationalist clergymen of that time, Merrill was compelled to consider Baptist arguments and determine, to

---

[44] Daniel Merrill, *Autobiography*, 2.
[45] Daniel Merrill, *Autobiography*, 2.
[46] Daniel Merrill, *Autobiography*, 2-3.

his own satisfaction, whether infant baptism was a Scriptural practice, or simply a longstanding human tradition without New Testament support. Convinced of the efficacy of infant baptism at the time of his ordination and settlement, Merrill chose to accommodate those with Baptist convictions. His view on the matter is reflected in later changes to the original covenant of the Church of Christ at Sedgwick. The initial covenant was composed and ratified on July 8, 1793 when the church was formed with 22 members, designating Daniel Merrill as the first member in the list.[47] Concerning baptism, the church followed their minister in affirming the original standard from the Westminster Larger Catechism, rejecting the Halfway Covenant,[48] and baptizing only those

---

[47] *A Record book belonging to the Church of Christ in Sedgwick. 1794*, 17. The authors began working from a photocopy of what appeared to be a bound book of 51 8 " X 14 " pages. The records in the photocopied version begin on July 8, 1793 and conclude with entries regarding the events of May 15, 1805, when the church united with the Baptists. The text of a confession occupies pages 9-17, is dated 1792 and was presumably drawn up during the Congregational period when Merrill considered the Proprietor's offer to settle in Sedgwick. Pages 22-26 are blank, separating the statement of faith, covenant, and record of new members from pages recording church business. It appears that pages 22-26 were left intentionally blank for addition of new members. Page 27 begins with the ordination of Daniel Merrill, followed by chronological entries regarding discipline and other matters up until deliberations on February 14, 1805, when the Church of Christ in Sedgwick was seeking affiliation with the Baptists. The May 15, 1805 entry records formal affiliation with the Baptists, along with the names of those baptized that day, followed by others added to the Church up to the final entry in the photocopy on June 2, 1805. Some text from this Record book appears in Daniel Merrill's published work *Mr. Merrill's answer to the Christians*. Merrill's published work presents us with a "snapshot in time" — the original Record book continued beyond 1801 to 1878. The original text of the Sedgwick covenant is identical to Merrill's published version with the exception of some punctuation. In July 2022, the authors received a digital copy of the entire original Record Book from the Selectman's Assistant of the Town of Sedgwick Maine. The original Record Book is held by the Eggemoggin Baptist Church of Sedgwick in a safe deposit box and was not available for physical examination. The first 51 pages are identical to the photocopied version in the authors' possession. In addition, the authors were given digital copies of the records of the North Sedgwick Baptist Church from the Selectman's Assistant who is currently a member of the North Sedgwick Baptist Church. These records, which were previously reported to have been destroyed by fire, begin at the organization of the church on March 8, 1843 and fill an entire volume.

[48] See Williston Walker, *The Creeds and Platforms of Congregationalism* (New York: Charles Scribners, Sons, 1893), 238-339. The Halfway Covenant is summarized on

children with one or both parents professing Christ, in communion with the visible church.[49] There were a number of members, however, who were not satisfied with the practice of infant baptism, and people holding Baptist convictions continued to seek membership. "In the year 1798 and '99, a great reformation took place among the people" and a meeting was called to examine eight people for membership.[50] The following amendment was added to the covenant:

> 1799. Feb. 8. This day at a Church meeting and conference the church conferred upon and voted ~~as~~ the following. It has long been our opinion, and is still, that it becomes the disciples of Cr to condescend to each other, in all things, which are not dishonorary to Christ, or prejudicial to his kingdom amongst men. We therefore agree, that the article respecting baptism, which is inserted in our confession of faith, and

---

page 261: "there was doubtless substantial agreement in the conclusions at which the assembly arrived. The membership of the children of church members was affirmed. That membership was declared to be personal and permanent, and sufficient to entitle the member by birth, even though not personally regenerate, to transmit membership and a right to baptism to his children, on condition of an express acknowledgement on his part of at least an intellectual faith and a desire to submit to all the covenant obligations implied in membership. Yet though this membership is complete, as far as it goes, it is not sufficient to admit to full communion or to a vote in church affairs. For these further privileges a profession of personal regeneration is necessary." Walker goes on to discuss the controversy over the status of infant baptismal candidates, whose parents had not made a public profession of faith: "The 'Great Awakening' under the preaching of Whitefield in 1740-41, led to a sharp division between the holders of the two positions, nicknamed at that time the 'Old Lights' and the 'New Lights.' The principles of the school of theology which came out of the revivals were thus of necessity opposed to the Half-Way Covenant, and to that school its destruction was due. Of that school the founder and pioneer was Jonathan Edwards." See, also pp. 284-285.

[49] "Q. 166. Unto whom is baptism to be administered? A. Baptism is not to be administered to any that are out of the visible church, and so strangers from the covenant of promise, till they profess their faith in Christ, and obedience to him, but infants descending from parents, either both, or but one of them, professing faith in Christ, and obedience to him, are in that respect within the covenant, and to be baptized." James Benjamin Green, *A Harmony of the Westminster Presbyterian Standards with Explanatory* Notes, (Richmond: John Knox Press, 1951), 206. See *A Record book belonging to the Church of Christ in Sedgwick*, 12.

[50] Daniel Merrill, *Autobiography*, 2

in our covenant, is not considered by us, to be so essentially binding upon any who do not see it duty to practice infant baptism as to render it as a term of communion. At the same meeting examined the following persons, who manifested a desire to come out from amongst the world and separated from them, that Christ might receive them.[51]

Baptist preacher Isaac Case, who was traveling through Sedgwick in the autumn of the same year, met with the Hancock Association of Congregational Churches. He recalled that "about thirty of the number could not be satisfied with infant baptism and Mr. Merrill hath led them to the water and there hath, what he calls, baptized them."[52] Despite theological controversy, Baptists began to surpass Congregationalist and Methodist missionaries in terms of sheer numbers sent to the frontier regions. For a number of doctrinal, political, and cultural reasons, the fields of Maine were ripe for harvest. By the close of the eighteenth century, there were forty Baptist congregations in the District of Maine with a total of 2,186 members in fellowship within the newly-formed Bowdoinham Association. Isaac Case and James Potter were

---

[51] *A Record book belonging to the Church of Christ in Sedgwick*, 33. This amendment is treated as a footnote to Article 14 in *Mr. Merrill's answer to the Christians*. In the original document, it comes as the result of a Church conference held on February 8, 1799 admitting 8 new members and Article 14 directs the reader to the accommodation quoted above on page 33. The meeting adjourned until evening when 13 additional persons were examined for membership. We are not told who, if any, of the prospective and new members held views contrary to Article 14 of the original confession. On May 14, 1805 the original Article 14 is struck through and an arrow points to a note directing the reader to page 50 for its replacement on that date affirming credo baptism, exclusively. "We believe that baptism is an ordinance instituted by the Great Head of the Church, to be a distinguishing badge of his followers, and that it is to be administered only on a profession faith by an immersion of the whole body, in water, in the name of the Father and of the Son and of the Holy Ghost. We also believe it to be by divine appointment, a prerequisite to communion at the Lord's table."

[52] Cited in Ron Baines, "Daniel Merrill 1765-1833," in *A Noble Company*, 358.

striking out north and east to become legends in American Baptist lore.[53] Henry Burrage describes the following:

> At the eastward the Baptist movement made a more rapid advance. Here settlers from Massachusetts, and some emigrants from the old world, were making homes for themselves in the wilderness, and preparing the way for prosperous communities yet to be. With eagerness they were ready to welcome any servant of God who might visit them, and Case and Potter, full of evangelistic zeal, were not slow to take advantage of the opportunities thus afforded for preaching the glad tidings.[54]

In the meantime, Daniel Merrill's influence as a pastor, teacher, evangelist, apologist, educator, denominational organizer, community leader, and statesman in the early Republic continued to grow. The Hancock Association of Congregational ministers existed to strengthen the seven churches bordering Penobscot Bay and the Bluehill Peninsula with the intention of planting churches further down east, beyond the Penobscot River, Bluehill Bay, and Mount Desert Island. As the leading member of the Association, he was the catalyst for the formation of the "Society for Promoting the Education of Religious Young Men for the Ministry, and Also for the Sending the Gospel to the Destitute," a charitable organization.[55] The Society was tasked to educate young, serious, evangelical ministerial candidates who would become missionaries to "the Frontiers of America," with particular emphasis on "the destitute situation of our *Eastern Country*."[56]

---

[53] Henry S. Burrage, *History of the Baptists in Maine*, 86–107. Jonathan Fisher, *The Diaries of Jonathan Fisher*, 31. See also, Taylor, *Liberty Men and Great Proprietors*, 140.

[54] Henry S. Burrage, *History of the Baptists in Maine*, 86.

[55] Daniel Merrill, *The Constitution of a Society for Promoting the Education of Religious Young Men for the Ministry, and Also for Sending the Gospel to the Destitute.* (Salem: Joshua Cushing, 1803).

[56] Daniel Merrill, *Society for Promoting the Education of Religious Young Men*, 8.

The society, constituted in 1803, elected Daniel Merrill president. By November of that year, 219 donors had raised just over $1,000 with Merrill giving $50, the largest single contribution of all members and more than twice as much as the second largest member subscription.[57]

Throughout his travels and interactions, Daniel Merrill continued to encounter godly, biblical, and even educated Baptists, who would challenge his prejudices and caricatures. In his *Autobiography*, Merrill wrote,

> I occasionally became partially acquainted with some of their leaders, and with a few of their private brethren. Their apparent piety, and the manifest honesty with which they adhered to their sentiments, mellowed somewhat my asperity, and produced a certain kind of pity, connected with a commencing desire that they might see and renounce their hurtful errors, and give us the pleasure of receiving them into the community of the orthodox Congregationalists.[58]

In neighboring Bluehill, Jonathan Fisher was himself parrying off the incursion of Baptist preachers. New England Congregationalists seemed to have greater success in keeping the Methodists missionaries from "poaching" members of their flocks. The Baptists, however, proved particularly formidable. What they lacked in formal education they compensated with their familiarity with the Bible. In doctrinal controversies, appeals to commonsense and a literal sense of Scripture proved persuasive to many. One pedobaptist, frustrated with the progress of the Baptists during the so-called "Watery War," quipped sarcastically

---

[57] The other ministers involved were Jonathan Fisher, Jonathan Powers [Deer Isle], and Mighill Blood [Buckstown, later Bucksport]. The Society boasted 180 members and some 219 donors total. Daniel Merrill, *Society for Promoting the Education of Religious Young Men*, 10–12. See also, Ron Baines, "Daniel Merrill 1765–1833," in *A Noble Company*, 356.

[58] Daniel Merrill, *Autobiography*, 2.

that, "even the Baptist women talk Greek, in disputing with me on the subject of baptism."[59] Within this spirited climate that featured both revival and controversy, three young men were assigned to Merrill for ministerial training in 1803. Though Merrill initially hoped to turn them from their errors, all three came under Baptist influence.

The respective candidates were Henry Hale and Thomas Perkins, who had been preaching in the area with some success, and Phineas Pillsbury, a member of the Church in Sedgwick, who was living in Bluehill sometime after July 1793.[60] Pillsbury was eventually convinced by the arguments for credobaptism by immersion in 1804. He was baptized at Isleborough by Isaac Case.[61] Pillsbury requested release from his membership at Sedgwick so as to join the Baptist Church on Fox Island (present-day North Haven). Merrill attempted to dissuade Pillsbury from his decision but eventually acquiesced, putting the request before the church. The separation was amicable as Pillsbury continued with the educational society under Merrill's mentorship and instruction.[62]

Later in 1804, both Hale and Perkins made the change to credobaptism and were re-baptized by immersion on Fox Island. Isaac Case recorded how this came about and provided this perspective on Merrill's mind on the matter, drawn from a personal visit made during the autumn of that year:

---

[59] David Benedict, *Fifty Years Among the Baptists* (Boston: Gould & Lincoln, 1860), 82. Cf., John of Enon (David Benedict), *The Watery War: or, A Poetical Description of the Existing Controversy Between the Pedobaptists and Baptists, on the Subjects and Mode of Baptism* (Boston: Manning & Loring, 1808).

[60] *A Record book belonging to the Church of Christ in Sedgwick*, 18.

[61] Ronald Baines *Separating God's Two Kingdoms*, 46.

[62] *Records of the Hancock Association formed at SEDGWICK, Septem. 1, 1797. Bluehill Mar. 29. 1830*, Transcript in a Word doc., Jonathan Fisher Memorial Society, Blue Hill ME. Phineas Pillsbury is alternately spelled Pillsbury and Pilsbury, and referred to as a "candidate" and "Deac." [Deacon?].

I have administered the ordinance of baptism to twenty-five. Two of them are young men by the names of Henry Hale and Thomas Perkins. They are at present studying with the Rev. Mr. Merrill of Sedgwick, with a view to ministry. It will be natural for you to inquire, what effect it has on Mr. Merrill, his Students becoming Baptist. I will just say, I have made him a short visit, and find him fully convinced of believers' baptism by immersion.[63]

How did Merrill arrive at this conclusion late in 1804? Apart from the changing convictions of his ministerial students and other Christians in Sedgwick, major changes were taking place in Merrill's heart and mind concerning baptism. At the outset, Merrill approached the issue with a view to church planting, building up existing churches, and expanding the Kingdom of God—even to preaching the gospel alongside the Baptists. Central to this desire was turning his "wayward brothers" from their error, encouraging them join in the revival taking place in Congregational churches. Reflecting decades later, Merrill wrote,

> I gave myself with a degree of decision, to a careful and critical review of the oracles of God, that I might write a book and show the Baptists, from the unerring word of God, the certain scripture evidence of their errors, and of the hurtful nature of those errors, and of their obligation to renounce them, and come up to the help of the Lord, to the help of the Lord against the common foe, by uniting their strength with ours.[64]

---

[63] Isaac Case, "Further Account of Rev. Mr. Case's Mission in the District of Maine, extracted from a Letter of his to the Secretary of the Society, dated at Reedfield, January 8th, 1805," in Baldwin, ed., *The Massachusetts Baptist Missionary Magazine*, 1 (Sept. 1803–Jan. 1808), No. 4 (May 1805): 107-108 cited in Ron Baines, "Daniel Merrill 1765-1833," in *A Noble Company*, 359.

[64] Daniel Merrill, *Autobiography*, 3.

To address the controversy with his students and possibly assist others encountering the same controversy across the region, Merrill planned to publish a book defending pedobaptism from the Scriptures. But upon pursuing such study, he discovered that "in some of the links of my chain there was not that full strength of evidence which I could wish." This "anxious search" continued for several years, after which Merrill concluded that "the sacred scriptures did not afford clear and direct evidence to support my own practice."[65] Merrill's distress reached a crisis when eight children from the town were presented for baptism. As his conscience prevented him from enacting the rite, he refused to baptize them. As will be discussed in the following chapter, few were privy to Merrill's inner conflict. His delay lasted several months. However, he eventually communicated his confusion and troubled thoughts to the church, expressing the desire that they likewise take the matter to God in fasting and prayer. The majority acquiesced, and "the day was observed with much solemnity," though the church did not reach a resolution.[66]

The modern reader may sympathize with Merrill's disquieting realization that on the doctrine of baptism, his biblical and theological footing was shifting. For the ecclesial implications of becoming a Baptist were far-reaching. Daniel Merrill was an ordained Congregationalist pastor, supported by the Standing Order, New England's centuries-old partnership of church and state. Staunch advocates of Federalism, the Standing Order assured that the salary of Congregationalist pastors was financed by compulsory taxation. By embracing credobaptism, Merrill would not only be breaking with his Puritan heritage and educational pedigree, but risked the forfeiture of his income, home, and position as the respected minister of the Church of Christ in

---

[65] Daniel Merrill, *Autobiography*, 3–4.
[66] Daniel Merrill, *Autobiography*, 4.

Sedgwick. The prospect of splitting what was the largest church in the District of Maine at the time also weighed heavily on his heart.[67] For a duration of three months, Merrill experienced an acute anxiety concerning baptism—an anguished period he would later call "Egyptian darkness." The shadows would however, flee when, by his own account, Merrill submitted his heart and will completely to God. He describes the event:

> I said, Lord make me what seemeth thee good. At this moment, I surrendered myself and the whole concern unto the Lord, without so much as a known mental reservation. Thus, by an unconditional submission to the will of God, I was enabled to roll my burden upon him, and found peace.[68]

With the matter of baptism settled in his own mind, Merrill began the task of "showing these interesting particulars to my people," in a series of seven sermons which were published in December of 1804.[69] The content of these messages created a rift in the town of Sedgwick that extended to Bluehill and Congregational assemblies throughout the District of Maine. Over time,

---

[67] Daniel Merrill, *Autobiography*, 5

[68] "I have frequently heard persons speaking as though it were a small thing to become a Baptist, as though they would as readily become a Baptist as continue what they were, provided the Baptist sentiments were correct. Such persons possess a very superficial knowledge of what it takes to remove the strong and deep-rooted educational prejudices which those possess who have always believed, and have undertaken to teach and defend the long established traditions of their fathers." Daniel Merrill, *Autobiography*, 5.

[69] Daniel Merrill, *Autobiography* 7–8; Daniel Merrill, *The Mode and Subjects of Baptism Examined, in Seven Sermons; to Which Is Added, a Brief History of the Baptists* (Salem, MA: Joshua Cushing, 1804) The book begins with a note to the reader dated December 27, 1804. We are working from both a first edition, as well as the tenth edition published by Manning & Loring in 1812 and bound by William Willis with Merrill's *Letters Occasioned by Rev. Samuel Worcester's Two Discourses* published in 1807 and *The Second Exposition of Some of the false Arguments, Mistakes, and Errors of the Rev. Samuel Austin, Published for the Benefit of the Public*, (Boston: Manning & Loring, 1807). These bound pamphlets reside in the *The Willis Collection* at the Portland Public Library, Portland ME.

with the exception of a few families, the entire church in Sedgwick was persuaded by Merrill's preaching on credobaptism. There did come a reckoning with Massachusetts state law, for Merrill received his salary as Sedgwick's Congregationalist minister. Seven individuals called for a town meeting—held on January 28, 1805—for the following purposes:

> 1. To choose a Moderator. 2. To see if the town will receive the Rev. Daniel Merrill as a town minister upon the Baptist platform. 3. To see if the town will reject the Rev. Daniel Merrill from his salary, since he has become a Baptist. 4. To see if the town will reject Rev. Daniel Merrill from the pulpit since he has become a Baptist.[70]

"It was a day of storm and tempest, and the wind and sleet such as usually keep people at their firesides. Yet the meeting was full and the majority for sustaining their minister, decisive."[71] Surprisingly, the town representatives cast their votes in favor of Merrill. His income was secured, his family remained in their home, and he continued as the minister of the Church in Sedgwick under the original conditions of his settlement in 1793. The following month, on February 15, the Church in Sedgwick met to resolve a matter of discipline concerning a certain Thomas Cousins, and then held a vote to convene a meeting in order that two articles be, "proposed to the Chh [Church] for their particular consideration," followed by a vote. These included a request for Baptist ministers and delegates to place the church on the

---

[70] Daniel Merrill, *Autobiography*, 9.

[71] *Minutes of the Fifteenth Anniversary of Hancock Baptist Association Held with the North Church in Sedgwick, Tuesday, Wednesday, and Thursday, Sept. 4ᵗʰ, 5ᵗʰ, and 6ᵗʰ, 1849* (Portland: A. Shirley and Son, Printers, 1849), 14.

"Platform," and settling Daniel Merrill as the congregation/s minister.[72]

The meeting was held on Friday, February 28, 1805. The Church in Sedgwick voted to convene this "Ecclesiastical Council" to include pastors Samuel Stil(l)man of the First Baptist Church of Boston, Thomas Baldwin from the Second Baptist Church of Boston, Elisha Williams of the Baptist Church of Beverly, "Mr. Bowles" (Rev. Lucius Bolles) from the Baptist Church of Salem, Abraham Cummings of Vinalhaven, Isaac Case from Readfield Maine, Elisha Snow of Thomaston, Maine, and Joseph Bailey of Balltown, Maine (now Whitefield).[73] John Pitman of Providence, Rhode Island and pastor of the Baptist Church at neighboring Seekonk, Massachusetts was not on the invitation list, but "being present, voted that he take a seat in the Council."[74] Thomas Baldwin preached the ordination sermon and Elisha Snow prayed. Abraham Cummings gave the pastoral charge. Elisha Williams welcomed the Church into Baptist fellowship, openly acknowledging the Church of Christ at Sedgwick as, "the most numerous of any church of any naming in the District."[75]A ceremony was followed by the baptism in which dozens of the Sedgwick congregants were baptized by immersion in the Benjamin River. Merrill described the day as follows:

On the 10th of May, 1805, the principal part of the ministers and delegates were landed upon our shore. On the 13th, if I mistake not, they buried sixty-three of us with Christ in baptism, upon a personal profession of our faith in him, and the

---

[72] *A Record book belonging to the Church of Christ in Sedgwick*, 46. Daniel Merrill, *Autobiography*, 10.

[73] Ron Baines supplies a partial list in "Daniel Merrill 1765–1833," in *A Noble Company*, 363. The list is corroborated and expanded in *A Record book belonging to the Church of Christ in Sedgwick*, 47.

[74] *A Record book belonging to the Church of Christ in Sedgwick*, 49.

[75] Daniel Merrill, *Autobiography*, 10.

next day twenty-three, and thus prepared us to be constituted into a church of God, and pronounced us to be so, and ordained the former minister to be the under shepherd of this little flock. In about six weeks' time, I baptized fifty-eight more. From one time to another, I have baptized some of the remnants of the Congregational church who were not before ready to submit to the baptism which was from heaven. And some, very few of them, are yet apparently believing that the baptism which is of men will answer for them and thus reject the counsel of God against themselves.[76]

Reflecting on the centenary of the occasion, Samuel Pearce Merrill mused on the significance of that day:

That must have been a stirring time! The brethren from far and near; the experiences; the baptisms; and a pathetic scene it was when being troubled for his master, the faithful old New Foundland dog went down into the water, calling for the devoted response from Mr. Merrill, "I hope I shall always follow my Master as faithfully as my dog follows me." How glorious a Jordan became the Benjamin's river that day![77]

Despite a new denominational identity, Merrill remained a member of the Hancock Association of Congregational Churches. The Association, formed in 1797, initially welcomed Baptist pastors to fellowship and appeared intent on maintaining this policy even after 1804.[78] Baptist students and preachers—including

---

[76] Daniel Merrill, *Autobiography*, 10.

[77] Samuel Pearce Merrill, "Rev. Daniel Merrill, An Appreciation," 43.

[78] See *Records of the Hancock Association Full Transcription,* Jonathan Fisher House (Word document) This document appears to be Fisher's transcription. Merrill and Fisher are identified as "scribe" at various meetings. Fisher is "scribe" but Merrill is *scribe pro tempore*. The position of Moderator seemed to rotate.

Isaac Case—attended the Association during these early years.[79] Baptist and Congregational Churches even cooperated in cases of discipline and disputes between parishioners. Daniel Merrill's rising stardom in the Baptist movement and his uncompromising views on ecclesiology and closed communion, however, necessitated a parting of ways, which was, by all accounts, amicable. According to the Association's minutes, Merrill consistently functioned as a leader among the clergy. During the meetings, he would preach sermons as well as give lectures and reports. Moreover, Merrill was the sole instructor and mentor for educating young ministers. Yet the first indication that a breach was forming comes from the Association's minutes in late autumn, 1804:

> Meeting at Sedgwick failed. Bluehill Nov. 13. 1804 … Conversation principally upon the mode of Baptism, on account of the late change in Mr. Merrill's views, who has declared for plunging as the only scriptural mode … Jon. Fisher, Scribe.[80]

The Association met again on January 9, 1805 in Buckstown, where Jonathan Fisher spent the afternoon at the home of Mighill Blood. Jonathan Powers of Penobscot and Daniel Merrill were present. Prior to the evening lecture, they "conversed the rest of the time principally upon the subject of Baptism, and Mr. Merrill's embracing the sentiments of the Baptists."[81] On March 13, 1805 the Association discussed, "whether the Pedobaptists can have ministerial communion with the close-communion Baptists, and they with them. Mr. Merrill preached." [82] The subject was

---

[79] *Records of the Hancock Association Full Transcription*, Jonathan Fisher House (Word document) 4 & 5. Jonathan Fisher, *The Diaries of Jonathan Fisher*, 67.

[80] *Records of the Hancock Association*, 13 ("*on* account of the late change in Mr. Merrill's views" is the correct transcription of the original document. The transcription reads "an account").

[81] *Records of the Hancock Association*, 13.

[82] *Records of the Hancock Association*, 14.

discussed and debated for three subsequent months, and though, "our views divided," the conclusion stood that "the ministerial communion is consistent with the gospel principles in the above case."[83] It appears that a crisis had been averted. Congregationalist and Baptist ministers would, for the time being, cooperate within the Hancock Association. The issue, at least for Daniel Merrill, remained unsettled.

Merrill evidently had a change of heart following the March meeting. On August 14, 1805, Jonathan Fisher recorded in the Association's minutes that, "on account of a change of sentiments in Rev. Dan. Merrill, Voted; That the Rev. Jon. Powers be Moderator of this Association. To whom Mr. Merrill resigned the Chair."[84] The next entry from the Association's minutes contains Jonathan Fisher's sobering observation that, "this day Mr. Case and Mr. Merrill with his delegates, came to this town to form a Baptist church," at Bluehill which—with the exception of one person—consisted of former members of Fisher's Church.[85] On February 13, 1806, Fisher wrote in his diary, "This day … 12 males and 6 females, were formed into a Baptist church. A mournful event! But the Lord reigneth."[86] Concerning the following day, Mary Ellen Chase writes:

---

[83] *Records of the Hancock Association*, 14.

[84] *Records of the Hancock Association*, 14.

[85] *Records of the Hancock Association*, 15. This entry in the *Records of the Hancock Association* is a portion of the larger entry recorded in: Jonathan Fisher, *The Diaries of Jonathan Fisher* 197. The "Baptist Society of Bluehill" was established in 1806 and would become "The First Baptist Church of Blue Hill" in 1959. *A Condensed History of First Baptist Church of Blue Hill*, https://firstbaptistchurchbluehill.org/a-condensed-history-of-first-baptist-church-of-blue-hill (accessed March 10, 2022).

[86] Jonathan Fisher, *The Diaries of Jonathan Fisher*, 198. Chase records the same events without citation on page 98, "This day 18 persons, 12 males, 6 females, all but one members of my church, were gathered into a Baptist church by Mr. Case and Mr. Merrill. To me a mournful event. But the Lord reigneth!" This quotation appears to be an embellishment of what appears in the transcribed diaries and there are two differences in punctuation. On page 97, Chase attributes the following quote to Fisher which goes on for three more paragraphs: "The Rev. Daniel Merrill of Sedgwick, having been led with a number of his church to renounce the mode of Baptism by any other

Rev. Daniel Merrill, before returning to Sedgwick ... called very early and took breakfast with [Fisher]. One would give a great deal to know what was said at that breakfast table by the two close friends of many years! But that Mr. Merrill both felt assured of his welcome and desired to come speaks eloquently and well both for Parson Fisher and for himself.[87]

After this doleful parting of ways, Fisher records that on July 21, 1806 he left Deer Isle and, "set across the reach at Carter's Point. Came on and dined at Mr. Merrill's," home, about three miles up the hill from the shore and across the road from the meetinghouse.[88] Two years later, in 1808, Fisher, "took breakfast at Mr. Merrill's" after a meeting of the Hancock Association of Congregational ministers on Deer Isle. [89]

During this period, a variety of factors strained, if not splayed the chasm between Daniel Merrill and Jonathan Fisher. These include: an abundance of published polemics, public disputations, invective, divisions within families and communities over baptism.[90] Yet evidence drawn from their writings and biographies indicate they continued to share a warm friendship, collegial respect, and even brotherly affection. Both preached, wrote, and published on the subject of baptism and closed communion, yet refrained from ad hominem attacks and abusive language. Merrill and Fisher did not debate the matter publicly, though such a

---

way than immersion as a nullity, and having withdrawn from the fellowship of the churches and received Baptism and ordination anew, and a number of his church also being withdrawn from the fellowship of the rest, and about 30 of the church under my care having followed their example, it has been a time of serious inquiry with me whether immersion be essential to the ordinance of Baptism..." This material does not appear in the transcription of Fisher's diaries and is not sourced by Chase beyond this statement in her Preface on page vii: "This book has been made by many hands and many minds. I am but its scribe... It is based almost entirely upon the 'Common Journals,' or Diaries, of Jonathan Fisher..."

[87] Mary Ellen Chase, *Jonathan Fisher, Maine Parson*, 98.
[88] Jonathan Fisher, *The Diaries of Jonathan Fisher*, 208.
[89] *Records of the Hancock Association*, 18.
[90] Samuel Pearce Merrill, "Rev. Daniel Merrill, An Appreciation," 47.

course would have appeared warranted given the seriousness of the community divide on this single doctrine. One is reminded of Richard Baxter (1615–1691), who was no stranger to controversy, and the interpersonal loss that comes with doctrinal division. Baxter's maxim on the importance of preserving "bosom friends," is applicable to Fisher and Merrill: "An old friend, *caeteris paribus*, is to be preferred before a new one and is not to be cast off without desert and necessity."[91]

When Jonathan Fisher published his thoughts on the meaning and mode of baptism, Merrill had already left Sedgwick for Nottingham West, New Hampshire.[92] There is no indication he planned to return. When Merrill did return to Sedgwick in 1820 after a six-year absence, he did not respond to Fisher's *Short Essay on Baptism* in print. It is reasonable to believe that Fisher, who esteemed Merrill as an elder counselor and friend, intentionally published his treatise on Baptism after Merrill's departure from Sedgwick.[93] It is possible that, upon returning to the area, Merrill believed the matter to be sufficiently settled and thus did not wish to sow discord. Considering the conduct of these men both before and after Merrill's embrace of credobaptism, and additionally, their cooperation in matters of mission and discipline, the textual silence is understandable. As uneasy as the peace between these congregations stood, it nevertheless remained a priority to

---

[91] Richard Baxter, *A Christian Directory* (Ligonier: Soli Deo Gloria Publications, 1990), 880. We know that Fisher read Baxter's "Saints Rest" from entries in his *Diaries* on pages 313 & 377. Baxter's *"The Saint's Everlasting Rest"* and *"A Call to the Unconverted to Turn and Live"* appear in the holdings of *The Hancock Library,* Sargentville, Sedgwick ME.

[92] Jonathan Fisher, *A Short Essay on Baptism, Designed for the Benefit of Common Readers* (Boston: Samuel T. Armstrong, 1817). Jonathan Fisher's "short essay" runs to 105 pages and never mentions Merrill.

[93] Richard Carter describes Jonathan Fisher's reasonable and measured writings on controversial topics, including one critique of Merrill in the *Gazette of Maine*: "During this when a 'certain force' was powerfully with and upon the Baptists, Fisher refrained from being drawn into an arena of personal public debate with skilled combatant Daniel Merrill…" See "Mind and Ministry of Jonathan Fisher," 303.

maintain to these ministries. For his part, Fisher urged the remaining members of the Bluehill Congregational Church to maintain Christian charity toward their friends, who he regarded as erring brothers and sisters:

> It is not without grief, my dear hearers, that I find the state of things in this place now proves an occasion to bring forth this subject. It has not been without secret grief that I have contem[plated]... a wide separation of some from us, who were for a time happily united in the bonds of a solemn cov[enantal] relationship. I believe, my dear Christian friends, that the greater part of those who have withdrawn from us have done that conscientiously... and that they are indeed the children of God.[94]

In a sermon dated March 2, 1806, about a month after the Baptist Society of Bluehill was established, Fisher appeared to hold out hope that a future resolution and reunion was possible:

> So far as it may spring from error, it is desirable to remove the error; so far from ... feelings of heart, it is desirable to rectify the effects ... I have not assumed the subject by us with a desire to widen the breach but to heal it; and if I succeed not, I hope God will enable me to resign humbly to his will, and that I may have the testimony of my conscience that I have sincerely endeavored.[95]

The largest church of any kind in the District of Maine in 1805 was now a Baptist church. With an energetic and gifted administrator and church planter for a pastor, and supported by a

---

[94] Jonathan Fisher, Sermon 914, February 29, 1806 (Archives, Jonathan Fisher Memorial, Blue Hill, ME; transcription from Fisher's shorthand by Michael McVaugh, July 2023), 1.

[95] Jonathan Fisher, Sermon 916, March 2, 1806 (Archives, Jonathan Fisher Memorial, Blue Hill, ME; transcription from Fisher's shorthand by Michael McVaugh, July 2023), 1.

congregation with missionary zeal for the expanding of God's kingdom, Merrill leapt into the "Watery War" with the publication of *The Mode and Subjects of Baptism Examined in Seven Sermons*.[96] The essay, whose contents will be discussed in the subsequent chapter, had a sustained impact spanning several decades beyond the District of Maine and the Canadian Maritimes.[97] Moreover, the ecclesiastical implications of Merrill's credobaptism landed him in further controversy. Merrill came to understand the visible church and God's Kingdom as practically indistinguishable. For the remainder of his life, he would engage in polemics with Congregationalist pastors on this particular theological position.

Merrill embraced the role as promoter and spokesman for the Baptist cause, as is clear from the 18-page autobiographical sketch, composed near the end of his life in 1832, and published shortly thereafter. The *Autobiography of Daniel Merrill* contains only a few opening pages of what would be considered, in a traditional sense, "biography." The remaining details document his coming to embrace the Baptist message, and his later work of turning others from the pedobaptist, "confused church," to the "primitive Platform," a congregation composed of visible saints, baptized by immersion upon profession of faith. In published remarks from the centennial celebration of the Sedgwick Baptist Church in 1905, Merrill's grandson Samuel declared under the heading of *His Publications*:

---

[96] Daniel Merrill, *The Mode and Subjects of Baptism Examined*.

[97] See Brittany P. Goetting, "Bound by Print: The Baptist Borderlands of Maine and the Canadian Maritimes, 1770-1840," 76. Goetting argues "*Seven Sermons* had an immense impact on the New England and Canadian Maritime Protestant community. MBMS missionary Ezra Willmarth announced that the work had deeply influenced readers in central New Hampshire, even leading to the conversion of former Congregational minister Pelatiah Chapin. ... Merrill's work had a similar effect in western New York. Missionary Rev. David Irish wrote that a former Presbyterian had turned to Merrill's *Seven Sermons* when he had questions about the nature of baptism. There is also evidence that *Seven Sermons* was popular in the Maritimes."

As an apologist for Baptist Church Constitution and Ordinances, I do not know of any one who at that period in America had been the author and publisher of so many ... They awakened a general and far reaching interest, and one that was not ephemeral. They were spread over a space of fifteen years.[98]

Both at home and abroad, Merrill was a force to be reckoned with. Though small in stature, he loomed large in his influence upon major changes taking place in New England during the period of the early Republic. He was immediately thrust to the forefront of Baptist dissent and nonconformity, yet in many ways remained true to his roots in the Standing Order. Like Jonathan Fisher, he believed in the ideal of a New England minister who functioned as the principal influencer in regional politics, education, and culture. For Merrill, immersion into these notionally "secular" matters remained subordinate to the greater enterprise of gospel proclamation and the expansion of God's Kingdom on earth. The truly serious Christian minister would not, however, allow civic duties to supplant spiritual ones. Reflecting at the end of his life on his role in these momentous changes, Merrill acknowledged that his involvement in state matters were justified as contributing to the expansion of God's Kingdom:

And to his mere mercy are we indebted for the civil and religious liberty which is now enjoyed by this favored nation; and to this am I specially indebted for preservation from violent death, and for liberty to relate to you these first principles of the kingdom of God. For this kingdom should be our first petition, its prosperity the prime motive in every action, and for its advancement should we readily sacrifice present reputation, pleasure and profit. In full assurance

---

[98] Merrill, "Rev. Daniel Merrill, An Appreciation," 47.

that this kingdom is commenced, and will fill the whole earth.[99]

Sedgwick became embroiled in the growing regional grievance among Baptists that their taxes supported Congregationalist ministers whose churches they did not attend. As Baptists, Methodists, Unitarians, and others increased across New England, growing numbers refused to pay, at times appealing to a key issue that sparked the Revolution, namely, the practice of "taxation without representation." Merrill's case was unique in one respect: the town voted to support him after becoming a Baptist in 1805. Thus, it was, peculiarly enough, *Congregationalists* in Sedgwick who raised their voices against this practice and indicates that perhaps Merrill's grasp of the "Baptist platform" was not fully formed regarding disestablishment.[100] Or, he was willing to make an exception in his own case. This situation did not continue for long as the members of the Sedgwick Church moved to support Merrill almost immediately, voting in 1806 to raise "350 dollars ... for Mr. Daniel Merrill, for the present year" and later to raise another 100 dollars to "make up the [illegible] of his salary for the present year."[101]

This volatile period featured contentious town meetings, strained friendships, and even forcible seizure of property by the authorities. The Standing Order was increasingly pressured from the growth of religious populism, the rise of Democratic-Republicanism, and the waning of Federalism across New England.[102] Merrill's adoption of Baptist theology and practice brought him

---

[99] Merrill, *Autobiography*, 12.

[100] Clark, *History of the Congregational Churches in* Maine, 2:321: "In 1820 the [Sedgwick Congregational] church is reported as consisting of about thirty members," including the community of Brooksville.

[101] *A Record book belonging to the Church of Christ in Sedgwick. 1794*, 60-61.

[102] Stephen A. Marini, "Religious Revolution in the District of Maine 1780–1820," 128-145.

in line with the notion of Two Kingdoms, or spheres of authority, which had precedent in Baptist thought from the late seventeenth century.[103] As the disestablishment movement, grew, fewer citizens supported taxation as a means to pay the salaries of Congregationalist ministers.[104] When Daniel Merrill arrived in New Hampshire in 1814, he found himself strategically placed to lobby for its abolition in the state.

Merrill's formal involvement with politics began in Sedgwick when he was elected to represent the town in the Massachusetts Legislature, serving, respectively, in 1809, 1811, and 1812. In early nineteenth-century America, it was possible to be a politician at the state level while serving as a pastor, full-time. The Baptist's Two Kingdoms doctrine allowed them to view the secular government as distinct from the Church and a positive vehicle for participation within their communities that could sidestep direct clashes with the Congregational religious establishment. Understandably, Merrill indicated that the appointment proved to be a distraction from the work of ministry, his true passion, though he fulfilled his legislative terms with characteristic energy and assiduity.[105] In a striking break with the Federalist tradition, Merrill sided with the Jeffersonian Democratic-Republicans by supporting the War of 1812. On the other hand, he expressed concern that

---

[103] For example, article 24 of the *London Baptist Confession* 1677/1689.

[104] Stephen A. Marini portrays events in New Gloucester, Maine as typical of disestablishment in towns across New England, observing that "dissenters were ... better organized and continued to press their claim to exemption from ministerial taxes ... the sectarians [including Baptists] swiftly gained political control of town meeting and then used their new majority to dismantle the religious establishment." Stephen A. Marini, "Religious Revolution in the District of Maine 1780–1820," 132.

[105] Legislators during this period generally did not campaign, in the modern sense, but were appointed or nominated and affirmed by vote. There is no indication that Merrill sought or ran for office. Yet, said Merrill, "When I have been a legislator, it was my fixed principle that fair claims upon common justice should be heard. I never knowingly suffered a petition, manifestly founded upon principles of equity to fail, without interposing my firm and best exertion for its support." Merrill, "Rev. Daniel Merrill, An Appreciation," 56–57.

the war would damage relations with Baptists in Britain and elsewhere, even hindering cooperation in missions. Writing to Edward Manning in Nova Scotia leading up to the conflict, Merrill lamented, "I wish the differences between your government and ours may be so accommodated as to promote the good of both, and subserve Zion's best good. But I fear a contest is before us ... However the differences may be between the governments among men, be it our concern to be in obedience to the government of God."[106]

In addition to Baptist Associations formed earlier—the Bowdoinham Association in 1787, and Lincoln Association in 1804—the Cumberland Association was established in 1810, while Merrill was serving in the Legislature.[107] A primary reason for such cooperation was to found institutions to educate ministers. The number of Baptist churches planted throughout the District outstripped the number of educated, qualified pastors. From his firsthand experience in the Hancock Association, Merrill knew the need for theological education on the Eastern Frontier was dire. In this he agreed with Jonathan Fisher. An unlearned pastor could not do what Merrill himself had done—participate in politics and establish institutions of higher learning. Uneducated men could not be expected to exert lasting impact on their communities. It is noteworthy that only three-quarters of a century after his death, Merrill's name, according to his grandson, Samuel, was best-known for a school he helped found.

> Perhaps in no one thing is his name so usefully associated as with the origin of what is now known as Colby College. At the time of the early agitation of the establishment of an institution of learning by Baptists, the predominating idea was that of a school for the education of the young men for the

---

[106] Cited in Baines, "Daniel Merrill 1765–1833," in *A Noble Company*, 381.
[107] Merrill, "Rev. Daniel Merrill, An Appreciation," 53.

ministry ... Mr. Merrill was from the first an advocate for the formation of a school in Maine."[108]

Along with a committee representing the Lincoln and Bowdoinham Associations, Daniel Merrill drew up a petition to the General Court in Boston, seeking the establishment of a Baptist college or seminary in the District of Maine. The initiative failed in 1812 as it was perceived by the Congregationalist establishment to be in direct competition with the newly-formed Bowdoin College in Brunswick, Maine. Though he lacked financial and political support, Merrill would not be deterred by this setback. His years in the Massachusetts legislature would soon prove advantageous for Maine Baptists. In a letter to his wife from Boston, dated February 21, 1813, he reported:

> My Dear Partner ... My ways please my Lord for he causes my enemies to be at peace with me. And, astonishing to say, in the very town where my brethren in the seventeenth century were whipped by order of the government for preaching the gospel, I have obtained by order and an Act of the General Court a corporation for the Maine Literary and Theological Institute, together with the grant for one township of land. This is the Lord's doing, and it is marvelous in our eyes.[109]

Although the charter for a Baptist college could not be obtained, the Maine Literary and Theological Institution was established by an act of the legislature on February 27, 1813. Endowed with land outside Bangor—which later proved unsuitable for a school—the location was moved south to a plot donated by the citizens of Waterville in 1816. Instruction began at the Wood House in 1818. After Maine separated from Massachusetts in

---

[108] Merrill, "Rev. Daniel Merrill, An Appreciation," 53.
[109] Merrill, "Rev. Daniel Merrill, An Appreciation," 54–55.

1820, the new legislature recognized the original charter, and re-named the school *Waterville College* on February 5, 1821. Over time, the theological department diminished and the school developed into an exclusively liberal arts college. Through all these changes, Merrill remained a devoted supporter of the institution until his death.[110] T. Champlin, in commemoration of school's fifty-year anniversary, reminded his audience that,

> The Rev. Daniel Merrill ... as we have seen, was one of the original corporators of the Institution, and he remained a Trustee through all its vicissitudes till the year 1833, the sixty-eighth year of his age. During all this period he was rarely absent from any meeting of the Board, and always active and efficient when present ... he was frequently engaged in raising funds for the general purposes of the Institution, and generally with good success. On the whole, perhaps there was no more useful Trustee on the Board.[111]

The creation of a school for the education of Baptist clergy remained a priority for Merrill. One year before his death, he served on a committee reporting to the Maine Baptist Convention in 1832, that discussed the dire shortage of suitable ministers to serve the increasing numbers of Baptist congregations in the state.

---

[110] Merrill evidently viewed the non-denominational literary or liberal arts college as a necessary institution for the development of young Baptist ministers to serve the churches proliferating throughout the District, and later, the State of Maine. Merrill, the Dartmouth man of letters, maintained the conviction throughout his life that a thoroughly educated and literate pastor would best serve the church, though Christ often called the unschooled to minister to great effect. Merrill said, "Education is of inestimable value to a gospel minister; yet, it is not one of the ingredients which come into the composition of a minister of Jesus Christ. The possessor of it is no more a minister of Christ, than the one that possesses it not. He is however, better qualified for some special parts of the service." *A Sermon Preached at the Ordination of Rev. PHINEAS BOND*, 16. Merrill would serve as the President of the Maine Baptist Education Society in 1826, followed by his student Phineas Pillsbury in 1827, as well as various committees related to the education of ministers.

[111] T. Champlin, *Historical Discourse Delivered at the Fiftieth Anniversary of Colby University, August 2ⁿᵈ, 1870* (Lewiston: Journal Stream Press, 1870), 22.

Even at close of his life, he sought to educate aspiring pastors by founding an additional school. Merrill would not live see the results of this last pursuit. By 1836, however, Thomaston Theological Institute was established.

Immediately following the creation of the Maine Literary and Theological Institution, Merrill received the call in 1814 from the Nottingham West Baptist Church of Christ in New Hampshire. The church was formed by a number of converts from his labors as a Congregationalist missionary a decade earlier. Many had become Baptists in the years following, and consequently formed a society in the town. The Nottingham West Baptist Church was notable for being one of the first churches in New England to ordain a black minister.[112] Brother Thomas Paul, educated at a Baptist school as a child and baptized by Reverend S.F. Locke, was ordained by the Reverend Thomas Baldwin in 1804. Paul regularly preached at the Church at Nottingham West before becoming the minister of the First African Baptist Church of Boston in 1805 (also known as the Joy Street Baptist Church). He played the primary role in the establishment of the influential Abyssinian Baptist Church in New York City, the first black Baptist Church in the State of New York.[113]

Unfortunately, we have few details regarding Merrill's decision to resign his fruitful ministry at Sedgwick[114] but perhaps, as

---

[112] Benedict, *A General History of the Baptist Denomination in America*, 331.

[113] Owen D. Pelt and Ralph Lee Smith, *The Story of the National Baptists* (New York: Vantage Press, 1960), 48–51. Dietrich Bonhoeffer attended the Abyssinian Baptist Church and taught in its Sunday School while studying at Union Theological Seminary, 1930–1933. https://abyssinian.org/timeline/1930-3 (accessed March 7, 2022).

[114] "October 17, 1813 ... Elder Daniel Merrill, our beloved Pastor, who has been with us, in joys and sorrows for more than twenty years ... having manifested to us, that in his judgment, God in his providence, is about to remove him to another part of the Lord's vineyard ... and his Wife, our beloved sister Susanna Merrill to the Chh of Christ in Nottingham-West." *A Record book belonging to the Church of Christ in Sedgwick. 1794*, 79. On page 81 we find recorded on the date May 15, 1814, "This Day and Date Elder Daniel Merrill and his wife & family left Sedgwick bound to Boston and from there to Nottingham West."

both a Revolutionary War veteran and vocal critic of Britain, he was motivated out of concern for the safety of the community, his family, and himself. The Merrills left in the spring of 1814 and by September of that year, the British had occupied the coast of Maine and captured Castine. The British garrison could be clearly seen and heard just across the Bagaduce River from the western shore of Sedgwick or present-day Brooksville. In hindsight, the move was providential for it was at Nottingham West that secular and ecclesial politics would compete with the pulpit for his attention, redounding to greater religious freedom for Baptists and other dissenters across New England. Merrill continued to maintain focus on pastoral ministry and the formation of Baptist institutions. This included serving as a delegate to the Boston Baptist Association and pursuing his lifelong passion—preparing young men for the ministry.

In the Early Republic, the battle for religious freedom was particularly acute in Connecticut, Massachusetts, and New Hampshire, where the Standing Order remained entrenched. By the second decade of the century, however, Federalist strength was waning. Dramatic victory over Great Britain at New Orleans in 1815, and the disastrous results of the Hartford Convention with its rejection of proposals by the Democratic-Republican Congress, sealed the fate not only of Federalism, but Congregationalism in New England as a whole. In commemoration of a restored peace via the Treaty of Ghent, and the United States' recent military success, president Madison issued a proclamation to set aside the second Thursday, April 13, 1815 as a National Day of Thanksgiving. On that day, Merrill preached a sermon titled *Balaam Disappointed*, which drew parallels between God's deliverance of Israel from oppressive rulers, to the United States seemingly-miraculous victory over the most powerful nation on earth.[115] The trenchant, albeit controversial sermon, urged hearers to consider what "God hath wrought for our nation" and to thank the Lord for the precious liberties its citizens enjoy:

> We cried to the Lord in our distress, and put in operation the means with which he had furnished us; and after a long and arduous struggle, we obtained our independence, and an acknowledged right of self-government. Since which time we have enjoyed those civil rights and immunities which, but seldom, are enjoyed long; and which many, Absalom like, would now gladly wrest from us with a kiss.[116]

Merrill moved quickly to what he viewed as the most important civil right—religious liberty—of which he shrewdly noted, had never been fully extended to Baptists in New England. Though Congregationalists are not explicitly named, Merrill offered thanksgiving for God's triumph over a cluster of contemporary adversaries: "the ruling Clergy," the Federalists, with their "*Hartford Convention*," and lastly, Britain, "the scourge of the world." With the remaining twelve pages, devoted to "Application," Merrill returned to the struggle for religious liberty, New England Baptists' most immediate concern. Final deliverance, which he claimed was dawning on New England, would entail the following:

> Where these two powers, the civil and the ecclesiastic, are separated, religious liberty will prevail; where they are blended in the hands of superstition, religious tyranny is the natural and sure consequence ... By the good providence of God these two powers are separate ... Hence we have

---

[115] Daniel Merrill, *Balaam Disappointed a Thanksgiving Sermon, Delivered at Nottingham-West, April 13, 1815 a Day Recommended by the National Government* (Concord, New Hampshire: Isaac & W.R. Hill, 1815).

[116] Merrill, *Balaam Disappointed*, 7.

opportunity, every one to sit under his own vine, and his own fig tree, and none to make afraid.[117]

Daniel Merrill the Baptist pastor never discarded his identity as war veteran and patriot. "He would have men carry their religion into all departments of life," wrote Adam Wilson. "He would have Christian rulers, Christian merchants, Christian farmers, Christian men everywhere."[118] Like the original Puritans, early evangelicals such as George Whitefield, and scores after him, Merrill believed that patriotic sermons were theologically justified and civically salutary.[119]

Along with other Baptists, Merrill contributed to the victory for religious liberty that came five years later. As early as 1791, state legislation provided exemptions for religious minorities, though the process was cumbersome and arbitrary, varying from town to town. In 1816, the assessor at Nottingham West demanded that Merrill pay the local ministerial tax. After filing a

---

[117] Merrill, *Balaam Disappointed*, 20. "Among the arguments deployed by pro-war clergymen, the separation of Church and State figures more or less prominently depending on church affiliation, but also on regional location. The most thundering example comes indeed from the New England Baptist Daniel Merrill, who... as it could be expected, exults in identifying the Unites [*sic*] States with Israel, and heaps scorn and insult on the defeated enemy and its allies, the New England Federalists." Lucia Bergamasco, "Religion, patriotism, and political factionalism during the war of 1812," *Revue française d'études américaines*, No. 139, Wars of 1812 / Guerres de 1812 (Paris: Editions Belin, 2014): 46–47.

[118] Adam Wilson, "Daniel Merrill," in *The Annals of the American Pulpit; or Commemorative Notices of Distinguished American Clergymen of Various Denominations, from the Early Settlement of the Country to the Close of the Year Eightenn Hundred and Sixty. With Historical Introductions*, William B. Sprague, D.D., Vol. VI (New York: Robert Carter & Brothers, 1860), 510.

[119] See Thomas Kidd, *George Whitefield: America's Spiritual Founding Father* (New Haven, CT: Yale University Press, 2017), 254–255. Lucia Bergamasco describes the patriotic sermons of the day: "Ministers composed their sermons within a long honored structure: biblical text, explanation, doctrine, reasons, uses (or application) ... especially on the occasion of Fast days called by the State or national governments, we also find sermons in the traditional form of the *Jeremiad*, calling to repentance, pointing at war as a divine scourge for the nation's long list of sins." "Religion, patriotism, and political factionalism during the war of 1812," 45–46.

grievance before the selectmen, none of which were Baptists, he lost the case. Merrill then petitioned the New Hampshire legislature, appealing to the State Constitution, with the claim that, "the Baptists have the right of Citizens, and are entitled with the rest of their fellow citizens to the enjoyment of common privileges and immunities. The constitution requires no more."[120] After the legislative session of 1817, Merrill's petition was granted. He was henceforth exempted from paying the ministerial tax. There are indications that Merrill continued to push for change as part of the Disestablishment Movement. Two years later, on June 24, 1819, New Hampshire passed "The Toleration Act," which essentially dismantled the parish-town model throughout the state.[121]

The Toleration Party was formed in 1816, they won a narrow majority in Connecticut by 1817, and their Tolerationist Platform was adopted at the Connecticut Constitutional convention in 1818, ending formal Congregational dominance in civil affairs. Maine ended local taxation for the support of clergy with statehood and all states entering the Union from that time forward prohibited establishment and included protections for religious liberties. Massachusetts took over a decade for courts to untangle

---

[120] Cited in Baines, "Daniel Merrill 1765-1833," in *A Noble Company*, 389–390. Smith observed, "In so far as Merrill forced the issue in his petition, he instigated the larger issue. For this was the entering wedge" [leading to the Act of Toleration] ... Thru the New Hampshire career of Daniel Merrill one can see the evident, the marvelous, the splendid triumph of Baptist principles ... turning the tide of New Hampshire history into the current of our national destiny." Arthur Warren Smith. *A Baptist Factor In A Critical Decade Of New Hampshire History: a paper setting forth the contribution of Daniel Merrill, as pastor of Nottingham-West Baptist church, to New Hampshire history; read before the annual meeting of the New Hampshire Baptist Historical Society at Dover, October 7, 1908.* Typed manuscript, New Hampshire Historical Society archives, 9–10.

[121] That is the arrangement by which a single Congregationalist church in each town drew funds from local taxes. "Daniel Merrill was a valiant, brave investigator of the agitation which continued until the Toleration Act was passed, whereby no church or person must pay taxes for a church against his choice. His activity for soul liberty covered nearly the entire period of his New Hampshire pastorate." Smith, *A Baptist Factor*, 6.

claims to title and properties between Congregationalists and Unitarians, finally amending their constitution in 1833 effecting a clear separation between church and state.

The year 1820 brought two important events in the life of Daniel Merrill. First, he was called to return as pastor of the Baptist Church of Christ in Sedgwick. Second, the District of Maine succeeded in obtaining its independence from the Commonwealth of Massachusetts. Maine entered the Union as part of the Missouri Compromise whereby Missouri was admitted as a slave state, while Maine would remain free. Merrill returned to the largest church within the newly formed Eastern Maine Association of Baptists. Shortly thereafter, he was elected as its moderator. Ebenezer Pinkham would serve as his ministerial assistant and later as pastor of the Second Baptist Church in Sedgwick. Though in his fifty-fifth year, still in possession of physical and mental energy, Merrill was entering the twilight of his ministry. From 1821 forward associates shared the ministry load in and around Sedgwick. "Elders Amos Allen and Benjamin Lord and Mr. Jedidiah Darling, have been helping in the reformation, and are, as is hoped, ministers for God." he wrote in a letter. Esther Wood described Amos Allen as "a miller, farmer and ship owner ... turned revivalist and with telling effect used the slogan, 'join the New Lights or be damned.'"[122]

At the close of 1821, the Eastern Maine Association joined with the venerable Bowdoinham Association in designating the fourth Wednesday in October as a day of "fasting, Humiliation, and Prayer to God, that he would be pleased to return unto us and revive his work in this region" and that the churches would pray

---

[122] Daniel Merrill, "Revival in Sedgwick, Extract of A Letter From Rev. D. Merrill to One of the Editors," *American Baptist Magazine and Missionary Intelligencer*, Vol. III (Boston: James Loring, and Lincoln & Edmands, 1822), 472. Esther E. Wood, *SKETCH OF THE BLUE HILL BAPTIST CHURCH Given in June of 1956*, 1-2. Typescript copy of the manuscript for a presentation at the 150th anniversary of the First Baptist Church. First Baptist Church of Blue Hill in Maine, archives.

for revival the first Monday of every month. Merrill, who served as an itinerant minister early in his career, was appointed to a board at that same conference, tasked with sending preachers to the "most northerly inhabited parts of Maine, New Hampshire, Vermont, New York, Pennsylvania, Ohio, the Michigan territory generally and in Indiana and Illinois."[123] The vision of this board would find its fulfillment, at least partially, in two of Merrill's sons, Thomas and Moses, as well as his grandson Daniel David Merrill.

With his eye always on the horizon to new territories, revival came again to his own neighborhood and those surrounding Sedgwick. In a letter to an editor of *The American Baptist Magazine and Missionary Intelligencer*, he reported:

> the wind of the Spirit was not publicly visible, nor did the healing waters begin to flow, till past the middle of March … we had four or five lectures, and the religious excitement spread with unusual rapidity. Before the week closed, several were hopefully delivered from the power of darkness, and rejoicing in hope of the glory of God. At this time, and for several succeeding weeks, the operations of the word and Spirit of God upon the people, appear to be, by nothing in nature more fitly represented, than by a strong and dense wind passing over, successively, the several parts of a large forest … The work has been quick and powerful without noise, and free from any organized opposition. For the people of this town, with few exceptions, admit the doctrine of *Free Grace*, and hold to the Baptism of Repentance … Whilst the power of God has been overshadowing us, and his grace been distilling as the dew, or coming down like the gentle rain, a solemnity almost universal, has rested upon the people. Those whom God has set apart for himself, have manifested little or no distressing apprehension of the wrath of God, but a painful sense of their deserving it… the

---

[123] Burrage, *History of the Baptists in Maine*, 156-157. See also, Baines, "Daniel Merrill 1765-1833," in *A Noble Company*, 394-395.

doctrine of salvation by grace is, apparently, deeply fixed in their minds ... Beholding the water issuing from the mouth of Benjamin's river, in which thirty-two persons had just been baptized, confessing their sins, was the means by which one or two, or more of them, were awakened to a sense of their guilt and danger ... It came upon us somewhat like a sudden, mighty rushing wind. Before the saints of the Most High were well prepared to look on, and see what God was doing, the reformation was on every side of them ... The number who have come forward is one hundred and four. Sixty-eight have been baptized ... Of the sixty-eight ... fifty-three are from ten to twenty-one or two years of age ... We are still hoping that more vessels will be filled, before the oil shall be stayed.[124]

In addition to the 1821 revival described above, Sedgwick experienced at least one more noteworthy outpouring of the Spirit before the end of Merrill's life. Ron Baines cites a letter Merrill wrote to his son, Thomas, a student at Waterville College, in which he noted that, "Many are disposed to attend lectures. We have for more than a week past, had meetings daily. The present week we have had meetings multiplied. I appointed on the Sabbath four lectures to be holden in the week time, in different parts of the town, on each of the four first days of the week."[125]

Merrill's Personality: Real and Perceived
Though an unashamed Baptist apologist, Merrill apparently made efforts to remain cordial, friendly, and even warm with his Congregational friends and neighbors on the Bluehill peninsula. As mentioned earlier, he dined with Jonathan Fisher and was involved in controversial local affairs without incident. His settled

---

[124] Merrill, "Revival in Sedgwick," 472–473.

[125] Baines, "Daniel Merrill 1765–1833," in *A Noble Company*, 396. Jonathan Fisher also mentions a localized revival that, though smaller than the Hancock Awakening, was significant enough to record in his diaries.

thoughts at the end of his life reveal much about the man. While his forthright, at times, abrasive public writings conveyed a contentious and partisan spirit, this was not Merrill's intention. Conscious of this reputation, Merrill wrote—interestingly enough in the first-personal plural—in his *Autobiography* that, "We do not desire to use offensive words needlessly, but we wish to be understood distinctly."[126] Some otherwise congenial figures thought Merrill went too far, Jonathan Fisher among them. Though Fisher believed there were excesses among Congregationalists as well as Baptists. Perhaps, like Richard Baxter, Merrill's heart was in the right place but his "wish to be understood correctly" proved counter-productive at times.

Adam Wilson, editor of the Maine Baptist newspaper, *Zion's Advocate*, provided this thoughtful, sympathetic, yet frank assessment of Merrill in *The Annals of the American Pulpit* published in 1860:

> My personal acquaintance with Mr. Merrill commenced about 1822. He was then on the down hill side of life. Yet he was active both in body and mind ... Courage in the cause of the Master was, with him, a cardinal virtue. Good Christians were "veterans"—right living was showing ourselves as men for Christ. Some have thought he dwelt too much on the *manly* part of religion ... His idea of Christian union was union in truth and love. He despised compromise, and did not perhaps always make sufficient allowance for human infirmity ... The religion of Daniel Merrill, like that of Martin Luther, had its rough places. Timid friends might counsel to greater moderation; but such a change might have diminished, rather than increased, his usefulness ... he was in spirit, a reformer; and like all efficient reformers he sometimes used rough words. But his friends believe that even these came forth

---

[126] Merrill, *Autobiography*, 12.

from a heart deeply imbued with the love of Christ.[127]

How does one reconcile the apparent contradiction between Merrill, the bucolic village minister, and the outspoken, foremost Baptist controversialist and pastor of one of the largest congregations in Maine? Was it rank hypocrisy, pragmatism, or simply an inflated ego? To the contemporary reader, Merrill's writings and sermons can appear harsh and hyperbolic. It is helpful to remember that Merrill's delivery and content reflect his generation's experiences. As a religious Dissenter, Merrill witnessed, first-hand, extreme violence, persecution, civil and societal disruption, seizure of property, and denial of civil (and in some cases, human) rights. Baptists were among the most bullied sects in New England at the end of the eighteenth century. Thus, the sobriety and urgency of the closing words of his *Autobiography* are anything but platitudinous when we read:

> And to his mere mercy are we indebted for the civil and religious liberty which is now enjoyed by this favored nation; and to this am I specially indebted for preservation from violent death, and for liberty to relate to you these first principles of the kingdom of God.[128]

There are glimpses of collaboration with those outside of the "Baptist platform" who, nevertheless, shared his Evangelical faith and wider social goals. These include his cooperation with Congregationalists in the formation and maintenance of Bible Societies. Merrill served as president of the *Eastern Maine Association's Bible and Religious Tract Society* in 1821, and the Eastern Maine Association's auxiliary to the American Bible Society at its

---

[127] Wilson, "Daniel Merrill," *The Annals of the American Pulpit*, 509–510.
[128] Merrill, *Autobiography*, 12.

founding in 1824.[129]

In 1825,[130] Merrill wrote to Edward Manning, the pioneering Baptist evangelist and pastor in the Canadian Maritimes, confessing that he was under pressure to hearken to the "Syren song of Union, Union, amongst all Christians ... for missionary and Bible societies."[131] He laments that, among his fellow Baptists, "It is a remarkable time for union. Union Lectures, union prayer-meetings, Sabbath-School unions and I know not how many other hypocritical unions ... Brethren have so fallen in love with these unions." This was not only a concern about ecumenical enterprises in other parts of Maine or Canada. Fisher recorded a meeting in 1827 with Ebenezer Pinkham, Merrill's assistant, to discuss

---

[129] The Society agreed with distributing the Scriptures "without Note or Comments," however "even in this Merrill was at some times "in doubt." See *Eighth Report of the American Bible Society, Presented May 13, 1824. With An Appendix, Containing Extracts of Correspondence, &c. &c.* (New York: Abraham Paul, 1824), 176. Baines, "Daniel Merrill 1765-1833," in *A Noble Company*, 397. Records indicate that Merrill's sons, Rev. Moses Merrill and Rev. Thomas W. Merrill, served as Corresponding Secretaries in their respective auxiliaries of the ABS in the Michigan Territory with Moses recognized in 1830 and Thomas in 1831. See *Annual Reports of the American Bible Society: With An Account of its Organization: Lists of Officers and Managers, of Life Directors and Life Members. Extracts of Correspondence &c. &c.* (New York: Daniel Fanshaw, 1838), 554.

[130] Daniel Merrill, *Letter to Edward Manning dated April 18, 1825.* Acadia Archives, Acadia University. Photographic copy of original letter at https://archives.acadiau.ca/islandora/object/research%3A4547?search=Merrill (accessed May 4, 2022).

[131] For example, "the Eden Baptist Church ... was instrumental in the establishment of the Eastern Maine Baptist Association ... and even hosted the association's annual meeting in 1829. The records noted, 'Many things of important interest to Zion engaged the attention and received the support of the Association among which were Bible and Tract Societies, Missions, the cause of Temperance, etc.'" *Records of the Eden Baptist Church*, 123, cited in Brittany Goetting, "'He Has Abundantly Poured out His Holy Spirit in Eden and Mount Desert': The Baptist Connection on Mount Desert Island, 1790-1840," *Chebacco: The Magazine of the Mount Desert Island Historical Society*, ed. Tim Garrity, vol. XX (Newcastle: Lincoln County Publishing, Co., 2019), 59. The ordination of Enoch Hunting as pastor of the Eden Baptist Church in 1818 was "attended by Elder Amos Allen of Brooksville [a neighborhood of Sedgwick one year earlier] and Elder Ebenezer Pinkham of Sedgwick." Goetting, "He Has Abundantly Poured out His Holy Spirit in Eden and Mount Desert," 57. Amos Allen and Ebenezer Pinkham were both close Merrill confidants and fellow ministers at Sedgwick, as well as his partners in other Baptist endeavors. Pinkham would become the pastor at the Second Baptist Church in Sedgwick, now Brooklin.

establishing Sabbath Schools and, later that year, Fisher visited the Pinkham's school in Sedgwick, dined with them, and "preached to the children from Eph. 6:1 on obedience to parents."[132]

On one hand, Merrill expressed "zeal for missionary and for Bible Societies." He immediately countered that desire; "but my motto is Obedience is better, than sacrifice." Merrill's deliberations on the matter cover two pages in the letter and conclude with this genuine appeal, before moving on to other subjects:

> There is one thing in which I have thought we might have a union with the Paedobaptists, that is in spreading the Bible without Note or Comment. I seem almost to begin to doubt the propriety of even this union. Please, in your next, to give me your thoughts upon this subject. For a long time it has been somewhat settled in my judgment, and I hope in my heart, too, that the better and safer way is to agree with men, so far as they agree with God, and there stop. I say to my Brethren, as Azariah said to Asa, and to all Judah and Benjamin. 2 Chron. 15.2[133]

---

[132] Fisher, *The Diaries of Jonathan Fisher*, 775–776.

[133] 2 Chronicles 15:2 (KJV) reads: "And he went out to meet Asa, and said unto him, Hear ye me, Asa, and all Judah and Benjamin; The LORD is with you, while ye be with him; and if ye seek him, he will be found of you; but if ye forsake him, he will forsake you." Merrill, *Letter to Edward Manning*. Merrill's appeal to Manning is significant, given Manning's development on closed communion: "On 19 Oct. 1795 Manning was ordained as pastor of the Cornwallis New Light Congregational Church, an uneasy alliance of 'awakened' Congregationalists and Baptists. For the next few years Manning baptized adults and infants, by sprinkling or immersion, according to the wishes of those concerned. The excesses of the 'new dispensation' movement... and the continuing instability of the evangelical churches in the Maritimes led Payzant and Manning in 1797 to urge the New Light clergy of Nova Scotia to form an association … The late 1790s also saw an important movement toward the Baptist position of believer's baptism by immersion. Manning was convinced of the correctness of this stand and was himself baptized by immersion in 1798, although he continued to minister to his mixed congregation. In 1800, at a meeting at Lower Granville, the association was transformed into the Nova Scotia Baptist Association, organized on the 'mixed communion' plan." "Manning, Edward," in *Dictionary of Canadian Biography*. http://www.biographi.ca/en/bio/manning_edward_8E.html (accessed May 4, 2022).

Merrill's remaining years consisted of ministry and civil service, albeit it closer to home. He was chosen to sit on the Governor's Council from 1823 to 1826, Maine's first decade of statehood.[134] Ron Baines observes that in the last decade of his life, Merrill, "continued to take a keen interest ... in the ordination of young ministerial candidates," preaching at ordination services, respectively, in May of 1825, 1826, and 1829.[135] Ebenezer Mirick, a member of the Sedgwick Baptist Church of Christ, was ordained as an evangelist and served alongside Merrill as co-pastor from 1829 until his death. The year 1828 marked an important milestone with the birth of the Second Baptist Church in Sedgwick, and installation of its first pastor—former ministerial assistant to Merrill—Ebenezer Pinkham. With the incorporation of the town of Brooklin in 1849, it became the First Baptist Church of Brooklin.[136]

---

[134] Merrill, "Rev. Daniel Merrill, An Appreciation," 54–55.

[135] Baines, "Daniel Merrill 1765-1833," in *A Noble Company*, 400. Merrill installed Phinehas Bond of the Baptist Church in Steuben, Maine (1825), preached the ordination sermon for John Billings, who was installed as pastor of the Baptist Church in Addison, Maine. He installed James Gilpatrick as pastor of the Baptist Church in Bluehill and also preached the ordination sermon for Jedediah Darling of the First Baptist Church in Brooksville.

[136] Some sources spell the name Merrick. Mirick was an alumnus of Colby College. See *CATALOGUS COLLEGII WATERVILLENSIS M DCCC LXIII.* (Boston: Johannes-Milton Hewes et soc., 1863), 12. Mirick appears to have graduated the year following Daniel's son, Thomas Ward Merrill, and came to Sedgwick as a teacher. See also, Rev. Arthur Warren Smith, "Historical Sketch of the Town of Sedgwick," 36 and *The Allens from William Allen (1602-1679)*, 37: "Rev. Ebenezer Merrick" married Lois Allen of Sedgwick on April 22, 1834—this is an apparent misspelling of "Mirick." *The American Baptist Magazine, published by the Board of Managers of the Baptist General Convention*, Vol. IX (Boston: Lincoln & Edmands, 1829), 359. There is no indication that Merrill ever resigned as minister — local histories list Merrill as pastor until 1827, but others speak of co-pastors serving along with Merrill. Chapman, in *Sketches of the Alumni of Dartmouth College*, relates that Merrill returned from New Hampshire in 1820 and "resumed the pastorate at Sedgwick, retaining it until death." George T. Chapman, *Sketches of the Alumni of Dartmouth College from the First Graduation in 1771 to the Present Time, with a Brief History of the Institution*, (Cambridge: Riverside Press, 1867), 51. "He was pastor till his death ... " "Merrill, Daniel," in *Appletons' Cyclopaedia of American Biography*, ed. James Grant Wilson and John Fiske (New York: D.

Merrill's wife of 37 years, Susanna, passed away early in the Spring of 1832. Merrill followed her just over a year later on June 3, 1833. He was 68. Husband and wife lie buried at the Rural Cemetery in Sedgwick, alongside daughters Harriet and Eliza. The cemetery is located behind the meetinghouse where Merrill preached for years, to full capacity, and situated across the road from the "beloved paternal mansion" which Daniel and Susanna, along their thirteen children, called home.

Conclusion

Outside the Eggemoggin Baptist Church on Reach Road in Sedgwick, stands a stone memorial to Daniel Merrill. The epitaph contains three respective titles: PASTOR EDUCATOR LEGISLATOR. Merrill came as a "Gospel Ranger" and pioneer of the faith to the District of Maine in the Commonwealth of Massachusetts, at the time, quite literally, "almost a waste, howling wilderness, and morally almost a barren desert."[137] First and foremost, he was an evangelical pastor and preacher. Embracing the role as a Congregationalist parish minister and Dartmouth graduate, he fit snugly within the paradigm of the Standing Order, fulfilling the civic and religious duties expected of a New England

---

Appleton and Company, 1888), 306. Merrill's descendants dedicated a plaque to Merrill in the village church built in 1837, indicating Merrill served as pastor for "twenty-one-years," citing the founding of the Baptist church in 1805. Were they dating his service from 1805 or the period between 1793 and his removal to Nottingham West in 1814? Perhaps Merrill was seen as *Pastor Emeritus* in the final years of his life and records continued to refer to him as "Elder Merrill" after Mirick's appointment, indicating some form of leadership in the Sedgwick congregation. The revival of 1828 is memorialized by Rebekah P. Pinkham in *Narrative of the Life of Miss Lucy Cole, of Sedgwick, Maine. In Which is Exhibited the Controlling Power of Piety in Early Life* (Boston: James Loring, 1830), 6.

[137] Gilpatrick, "Biographical Sketch of the Rev. Daniel Merrill," 313. In this endeavor, Jonathan Fisher shared the same passion: "He loved unfamiliar country and odd places of sojourn. He liked to speculate upon the future of any wilderness wherein he might find himself, to look forward to the years 'when, under God, it should blossom as the rose and contain, in place of forests, the habitations of piety and peace.'" See Chase, *Maine Parson*, 172.

clergyman.[138] He would come to reject infant baptism, consequently adopting the "primitive" or "Baptist platform." Furthermore, he led a movement that would ultimately dismantle the very system that brought him to prominence in Sedgwick, Bluehill, and beyond.

Notwithstanding these shifts, he did not forsake Reformed theology, evangelical praxis, and passion for God's glory. In this respect, he was in accord with New Light Congregationalist ministers Jonathan Fisher, Jonathan Powers, and fellow revivalist and church planter, Jotham Sewall. Though Merrill rejected the parish system, he remained true to his New England upbringing and Puritan impulse, laboring to educate the young, defend civil liberties, and improve the morals among all within his sphere of influence on the Eastern Frontier. Samuel Pearce Merrill composed the following poem as a tribute to his grandfather in 1909. The poem is significant in that it was written from upstate New York — the very fields the Eastern Maine Association of Baptists commissioned missionaries to evangelize nearly a century prior — evidence that Sedgwick's pastor did not labor in vain.

The Rev. Daniel Merrill, A.M.[139]
An Appreciation.

He was a man!
Whatever path of life his feet have trod.
He honored it;
And well he served his fellow men and God.

---

[138] Mary Ellen Chase referred to Merrill as "the intelligent and indefatigable pastor of the Congregational Church. This Daniel Merrill had already written his name large in the District of Maine by his energetic labors in the cause of God." *Maine Parson*, 95.

[139] Samuel Pearce Merrill, *My Loves and My Lovers* (Jamaica, N.Y: Marion Press, 1909), 114–116.

His scroll of life
Emblazoned is with many-mannered praise;
A soldier he
Thru Revolution to its crowning days.

A college youth.
He took the honors that fair Dartmouth,
gives.

And followed on
To fit him for the life the pastor lives.

Settled at length.
He leads his people into "pastures new,"
And builds the church
That follows Christ in what He bids them do.

In missions, too.
He sees the world has need of saving grace;
And so is formed
The aid soci'ty, first to take its place.

To churches weak,
As Paul, he goes about to plant and build;
To error bold
His pen with Gospel argument is filled.

Where'er you see,
This pioneer in Christian-conquest won;
In spirit brave
The modest hero's glorious work is done.

It lives today!
And from the far, yet unforgotten, past
It comes to life
As justly owned and blest of God at last.
So sleeps his dust

Daniel Merrill, "Gospel Ranger"

At Sedgwick, Maine, where his great work was done
Among his church'
Who with him shall be "shining as the sun."

3

Divergence:
Fisher, Merrill and the Meaning(s) of Baptism

Blessed covenant, what extension,
grace abounding over sin!
O the glorious condescension
to take our infants in!
– Jonathan Fisher, "Infant dedication"

Daniel Merrill's leading the Church of Christ at Sedgwick to become a Baptist congregation in 1804 was not a singularly unique event in American history. As noted in the introduction, scores of Congregationalist churches became Baptist during the pre-Revolutionary period. In terms of sheer numbers, Baptists remained a minority in New England, but in the early decades of the nineteenth century, Baptist growth reached unprecedented rates. In the District of Maine, friction between denominations increased as Congregationalist churches lost more of their members with each passing year. In a context where the Standing Order's two centuries-long hegemony was in question, Jonathan Fisher and Daniel Merrill defended their respective understandings of baptism in writings of a polemical nature with the intention of convincing the opposing party.

Jonathan Fisher on Baptism
In 1816, Jonathan Fisher published *A Short Essay on Baptism: Designed for the Benefit of Common Readers*. Though his views on baptism are found in numerous sermons and general correspondence, this brief document provides a succinct summary of a subject

which he claims has "often revolved in [his] mind." Bluehill's pastor concedes that "much has been written upon it by abler hands than mine, yet still there may be room for something more."[1] This "something more" was a treatise accessible to "the poorer classes of people." With characteristic deference, Fisher commented that, "in the present, fallen state, we are liable to be influenced by prejudice; the sad principle of unhallowed self-love lurks more or less in the bosoms of us all, of whatever name of denomination." These remarks are significant in the wider context of baptismal polemics, and Fisher's hope for Baptist readership is implied in the following quote:

> This has sometimes such an effect, that we may read several pages of a book, and think it all well, till we discover that it was written by one of an opposite party, and then it shall appear abundantly defective.[2]

If the *Short Essay* was penned for a working-class audience, it was likely to find itself in the hands of a Baptist, or at least persons familiar with, and sympathetic to, credobaptist arguments. In catechetical form, Fisher asks what is the meaning of baptism, offers a brief answer, and follows with a brief "meditation," devotional in nature. The *Short Essay* provides five descriptions of baptism which include:

> 1. A sacramental washing. 2. The inward communication of grace by the Spirit of God. 3. The shedding forth of the

---

[1] Jonathan Fisher, *A Short Essay on Baptism* (Boston: Samuel T. Armstrong, 1817), 3. See also Jonathan Fisher, Sermons 914-916, (Archives, Jonathan Fisher Memorial, Blue Hill, ME; transcription from Fisher's shorthand by Michael McVaugh, July 2023). Fisher's main concern in these sermons, delivered less than a month after his congregation was split over baptism, was the practice of closed communion. He sought to demonstrate that communion at the Lord's Table should not be denied to those baptized by various modes, nor those unbaptized due to unusual circumstances.

[2] Fisher, *A Short Essay on Baptism*, 3.

miraculous gifts of the Holy Ghost. 4. A system of doctrine, which sacramental washing is a leading feature. 5. Martyrdom, or suffering death in the cause of religion.[3]

Dealing with the literal sense, Fisher describes "sacramental washing" as the application of water in a "religious ordinance," intended to "signify purification or cleansing." Moreover, he uses the terms "token" and "lively emblem."[4] Baptism as a token or "pledge" has a rich history going back to Tertullian of Carthage, who drew on the original Latin meaning of *sacramentum* as a military insignia worn by Roman soldiers. In the *Institutes* John Calvin, and the Reformed tradition broadly, used "sacrament" to describe the rite.[5] Even Baptists in the seventeenth century were comfortable with the term, though such confessions of faith made clear that the intended sense was distinct from Roman Catholic or Lutheran positions.[6]

Baptism as "The inward communication of grace by the Spirit of God" comes from Romans 6:4 in which the Apostle Paul employs the metaphors of death and resurrection. Rather than focus on what this text suggests about the appropriate mode of physical baptism, Fisher notes that any Christian who takes the passage in a literalistic sense will have to admit that martyrdom is intended. He concludes thus, "Whatever allusion there may be in this place

---

[3] Fisher, *A Short Essay on Baptism*, 5.

[4] Fisher, *A Short Essay on Baptism*, 6.

[5] John Calvin's definition of a sacrament as "an external sign by which the Lord seals on our consciences his promise of good-will toward us, in order to sustain the weakness of our faith, and we in turn testify our piety towards him, both before himself and before angels as well as men," emphasized its promissory effect on the believer. See *Institutes of the Christian Religion*, Henry Beveridge, ed., trans. (Grand Rapids, MI: Eerdman's 1989), 491–492.

[6] Tertullian, of course, is often cited by Baptists for his claim that "delaying baptism" is preferable, "especially in the case of little children." Fisher includes this exact quotation and discusses briefly on why Tertullian may have suggested a more nuanced view. See *A Short Essay on Baptism*, 72–74.

to outward baptism, it is certainly an inward, spiritual baptism, which is especially intended."[7]

Fisher mentions another Pauline text, 1 Corinthians 12:13—"For by one Spirit we were all baptized into one body"—as evidence that even within the church, baptism is principally, a spiritual reality—one "done in the work of regeneration."[8] Point three argues from example in the Gospels and the Acts of the Apostles—notably, Christ's breathing the Spirit onto the disciples, and speaking in tongues at Pentecost—that baptism signifies the bestowing of the gifts of the Holy Spirit. Fisher's fourth description notes that baptism, in some contexts, namely, Matthew 21:25 and Mark 11:30, signified John the Baptizer's "whole preaching and doctrine," which of course, included application of water.[9] The *Short Essay* concludes with an explanation of baptism as martyrdom, where the word is figurative, "and the figure is contained in the idea of pouring out affliction upon the suffering person, or the idea of his being overwhelmed in distress, or that of his body being sprinkled with his own blood."[10]

Fisher briefly comments on the Apostle Paul's assertion in 1 Corinthians 10:1-2 that the people of Israel were "baptized ... under Moses," which he believes was an instance of "sacramental washing," but that was more properly, "a type of that baptism, which should come after it, in the days of the gospel."[11] In his *meditation*, Fisher makes a familiar covenantal analogy, a warning to contemporary readers who likewise, "have the name, and all the outward privileges attending it, without possessing the true spirit

---

[7] Fisher, *A Short Essay on Baptism*, 8.

[8] Fisher, *A Short Essay on Baptism*, 8.

[9] Fisher, *A Short Essay on Baptism*, 11.

[10] Fisher, *A Short Essay on Baptism*, 15. He cites Matthew 20:22, 23; Mark 10:38, 39, and Luke 12:50.

[11] Fisher, *A Short Essay on Baptism*, 19.

of Christ."[12] The second chapter of the *Short Essay* explains the meaning of baptism performed by John the Baptist as being distinct from Christian baptism. Chapter three explains the significance of Jesus' baptism, and includes two parallel columns which feature the consecration of priests in the Aaronic line from the book of Leviticus, with New Testament parallels, highlighting Christ's "priestly" office.[13]

The *Essay* proceeds chronologically, explaining the meaning of the baptism enacted by Jesus' disciples as distinct from John's, yet constituting a kind of transitional rite occurring as the Old Covenant was succeeded by the New. Chapter five provides a definition of Christian baptism as "a sacramental application of water to a person in the name of the Father, and the Son, and of the Holy Ghost," whose meaning signifies "the taking away of sin by the blood of Christ."[14] Fisher concedes that the washing by water does not remit sins *ex opere*, yet believes that its function is to illustrate, proleptically, the spiritual reality of regeneration. In the vein of Calvin, he explains, "But while we are here in the flesh, we need visible, sensible signs to recall spiritual ideas to our notice, and lead our minds into spiritual views."[15] Though Fisher had introduced the term *sacrament* early in the treatise, he does not provide a precise definition until chapter five. He explains that the sacrament obligates the recipient to respond in a manner befitting the magnitude of God's grace.

> Because, as a Sacrament signifies an oath or solemn engagement for the performance of a thing, so baptism implies an

---

[12] Fisher, *A Short Essay on Baptism*, 20. Cf. Augustine: "we too receive a visible food today; but a sacrament is one thing, quite another is the benefit (*virtus*) of the sacrament." See Homily 26 (John 6:41-59) in *Homilies on the Gospel of John 1-40* ed., Allan D. Fitzgerald, trans., Edmund Hill (New York, NY: New City Press, 2009), 458.

[13] Fisher, *A Short Essay on Baptism*, 28-29. The threefold office of prophet, priest and king—*munus triplex*—has origins in Eusebius of Caesarea (d. 339/340 AD).

[14] Fisher, *A Short Essay on Baptism*, 35.

[15] Fisher, *A Short Essay on Baptism*, 36.

obligation on the part of those who receive it, to be obedient to the instruction of Christ, and to submit to the way of salvation revealed in him.[16]

Chapter seven discusses the mode of baptism. Fisher is exegetically fair-handed, admitting that New Testament pattern leans towards immersion, though he is not confident that effusion in some form was not practiced. He writes, "there is nothing so conclusive in favor of immersion as warrants me to insist upon the exclusion of other modes."[17] After considering sundry texts which employ "sprinkling" and "pouring" in Hebrew and Greek, he avers, albeit with surprising confidence that, "nothing more than probable inference can be brought in favor of immersion."[18] Fisher's subsequent meditation nevertheless displays a searching, intimate anguish in which he asks why the ordinance was administered and received in different modes throughout the history of the church. While he admits of no answer, Fisher prays, "suffer me not to feel hard and uncharitable toward those, who appear to be thy friends, who yet believe that but one particular mode of baptism is lawful."[19]

Chapter eight considers the proper subjects of baptism, namely, "adults who have not been baptized, and those of their households under their immediate care and command."[20] Such adults are only to be admitted to baptism upon a "credible confession of faith." Children likewise, with the consent of their parents, can be baptized if the same criterion is met.[21] The *Essay*'s ninth

---

[16] Fisher, *A Short Essay on Baptism*, 36.

[17] Fisher, *A Short Essay on Baptism*, 46. Fisher cites the account of the Philippian jailer's conversion (Acts 16:33) in which an entire "household" is promptly baptized, as suggestive that Paul and the family likely did not have access to deep water under such circumstances.

[18] Fisher, *A Short Essay on Baptism*, 47.

[19] Fisher, *A Short Essay on Baptism*, 50.

[20] Fisher, *A Short Essay on Baptism*, 51.

[21] Fisher, *A Short Essay on Baptism*, 52. He again affirms baptism "as the token or seal of the covenant of grace," 53.

chapter covers infant baptism. Fisher begins with possible objections to the practice, granting that there is no positive prescription that infants receive Christian baptism in the New Testament. Acts 16:15, 33 speak of entire households being baptized, the inference being that 1.) a father acted as representative for his wife, children and servants, and 2.) the likelihood that a given household included infants.[22] Fisher considers the objection that infant baptism seems too significant a practice for the New Testament authors to subscribe or forbid its performance. He opines that "one reason why so little is said concerning infant baptism, and concerning the keeping of the first day of the week as holy time, may be this, to excite Christians to engage in a more diligent search of the scriptures, than otherwise they would; another reason may be, to give room for mutual forbearance."[23] Readers detect a genial tone, the kind one finds in a disputant who understands, and is in sympathetic conversation with, his opponent.

Fisher considered the fact that, unlike circumcision—which has its New Covenant complement in baptism—the Lord's Supper is not given to infants on the basis of 1 Corinthians 11:29. He admitted that such discontinuity is the "greatest objection" to infant baptism.[24] Being deeply committed to covenant theology, exegetical and historical considerations carried less weight in Fisher's mind than the prospect of theological asymmetry. A notable comment in the *Essay* is that if an action, by virtue of not being expressly commanded in the Bible, is thereby forbidden, then Sunday, the "Lord's Day," should not be commemorated for Christian corporate worship.[25] While this issue is less

---

[22] Fisher, *A Short Essay on Baptism*, 55.
[23] Fisher, *A Short Essay on Baptism*, 58.
[24] Fisher, *A Short Essay on Baptism*, 58
[25] In a letter to his son Willard [In His Diaries?], he judged the reasoning of Booth for credobaptism as sound, yet felt that theologically, the practice would entail the abolition of the Lord's Day as Christian Sabbath, a Puritan tradition whose abrogation he judged to be untenable.

controversial in Protestant circles today, intense debate sur-rounded the subject in the first half of the nineteenth century.[26]

The tenth and final chapter covers arguments in favor of infant baptism via continuity with the covenant of grace, from Israel and extending to the church. Jesus' welcoming and blessing of chil-dren in Luke 18:16 is another text suggestive of baptism on grounds of Christ's pronouncement, "of such is the kingdom of God." Fisher returns to the twin texts on household baptisms of Lydia and the Philippian jailer, and finishes the treatise by com-paring the actions of Ezra the priest in Ezra chapter ten, and the pronouncement by the Apostle Paul in 1 Corinthians 7:14 that, "The unbelieving husband is sanctified by the wife, and the unbe-lieving wife is sanctified by the husband, else were your children unclean." He comments that "under the gospel dispensation, a milder proceeding should take place," namely, that their children, "were now to be considered, in a covenant respect, holy."[27] Here, Fisher's theological exegesis admitted of discontinuity between covenants.

Conclusion

Jonathan Fisher's defense of infant baptism did not rely heavily on what is colloquially called "proof-texting," today. He fre-quently uses the terms "intimation" and "inference" to make a comprehensive case for pedobaptism. For readers that would give greater weight to continuity between the Old and New Covenants, Fisher's treatise is reasonably persuasive. If one relies on biblical exegesis, however, as Baptist apologists generally have, the *Essay* will likely appear deficient. Fisher's inclusion of supporting

---

[26] Fisher, *A Short Essay on Baptism*, 60. In addition to "Seventh-day Baptists," William Miller and other millenarian sects such as the early Jehovah's Witnesses and followers of Ellen G. White—later identified as Seventh Day Adventists—claimed proper Christian worship should be done on the Jewish Sabbath.

[27] Fisher, *A Short Essay on Baptism*, 65.

arguments for infant baptism from ecclesiastical history, spanning close to twenty pages, comes as an appendix to the document.[28] His decision to structure the *Essay* in this order reflects the presumed patterns and habits of Fisher's intended audience. As a whole, American Protestants of early the nineteenth century resonated with commonsense literalism for biblical interpretation. Arguments from historical precedent are perhaps the strongest in favor of infant baptism, but if there was any context more averse to tradition—ecclesiastical or otherwise—it was the New England frontier in the early days of the republic.[29] With receptive and increasingly large audiences, preachers such as Daniel Merrill would seize the opportunity and draw many into the Baptist fold.

Merrill's Development and Mature Thought on Baptism

Like renowned missionary Adoniram Judson, Daniel Merrill began his ministry as an evangelical Congregationalist. With an eye on the horizon as a "Gospel Ranger," Merrill believed he was given the charge to "penetrate the wilds of America, the burning sands of Africa, the vast regions of Asia" with the good news.[30] In his early years, Merrill expressed antipathy toward Baptists, pitying the supposedly simple-minded followers of this persecuted sect. However, his attitude toward Baptist preachers and revivalists warmed as he partnered with them, ranging across the western frontier and the District of Maine by boat, horse, and foot. In New England's "howling wilderness," Merrill and others were bringing the gospel to the newly established towns.

---

[28] Jonathan Fisher also includes references to baptism of infants in several Talmudic texts in *A Short Essay on Baptism*, 71.

[29] Nathan Hatch comments that, "American Christianity reveled in freedom of expression, refused to bow to tradition or hierarchy, jumped at opportunities for innovative communication, and propounded popular theologies tied to modern notions of historical development." Hatch's thesis is that this description is accurate, even to the present day. See *The Democratization of American Christianity* (New Haven, CT: Yale University Press, 1989), 213.

[30] Merrill, *The Gospel Rangers*, 9.

It appears that Merrill initially viewed baptism by immersion as a peculiar, albeit secondary matter, a perspective shared by many Congregational ministers at the close of the eighteenth century. He was compelled to consider the matter more closely when members of the Church of Christ in Sedgwick sought full communion, but expressed doubts about the propriety and efficacy of infant baptism. As noted in chapter two, the founding covenant of the Church of Christ in Sedgwick in 1793 rejected the Halfway Covenant and sought to establish a pure visible church that maintained order and discipline expressed in its fourteenth article of faith on the baptism of covenant children.[31] That same statement of faith by the Sedgwick church was edited only six years later to accommodate those who did not "see it duty to practice infant baptism as to render it as a term of communion."[32] With the requirement that a public testimony of conversion precede full communicant membership in the church persons baptized as children, as well as adult converts, it appears that Merrill and other New Light Congregationalists were moving closer to embracing credobaptism. The initial points of contention between Maine Baptists and Congregationalists appear to have been the proper mode of baptism, as well as the suitable candidate for the rite.

When the Baptist message and influence burst from a trickle to a flood among Standing Order churches at the turn of the century, pioneering Congregational missionaries like the Judsons abroad, and Merrill, at home, faced similar doubts and fears as they grappled with the Scriptures. They counted the cost of such a radical change that required a newfound hard stance on a doctrine they once considered a novelty to be tolerated. Merrill

---

[31] In *A Record book belonging to the Church of Christ in Sedgwick*, there are over ten large closely written pages devoted to issues of discipline, warnings, casuistry, setting apart days and seasons of prayer, and other public activities associated with revival between the years 1798 and 1805.

[32] *A Record book belonging to the Church of Christ in Sedgwick*, 33.

wrestled with the mode and subjects of baptism, but that narrow concern would prove to be just the starting point. His journey would completely upend his view of the church and the Kingdom of God, the implications would reverberate to every aspect of his life and those of his parishioners.

As the general contours of Daniel Merrill's change of mind and heart on the issue of baptism have been discussed in the previous chapter, we will examine the process in greater detail. Merrill became a leading Baptist apologist, not only in the District of Maine, but New England and beyond.[33] Thus, the development of his thought has been memorialized in writings as a preacher, teacher, advocate, pamphleteer, churchman, civic leader, and educator. Those extant writings and records do not provide a systematic account, yet they do outline the major themes in his Baptist theology, not only addressing which persons were affected by credobaptism and the nature of these effects, but its wider role in defining and demarcating, respectively, the church and God's Kingdom.

During those times, when the influence of Federalism was waning and Democratic-Republicans were pouring into the region, any dispute between Congregationalists and dissenting Methodists or Baptists was loaded—at least implicitly—with partisan political freight. While some Congregationalists may have been critical of, or hostile to, Federalist policy, dissenters uniformly rejected Federalism and the Standing Order's elite institutions. In Merrill's Two Kingdom view,[34] international, regional, and local politics, along with civil affairs, were carried on under the rubric of the "worldly" or secular kingdom. His primary focus was, however, the Kingdom of God, which he viewed as coterminous with the church.[35] His rejection of infant baptism and

---

[33] Merrill, "Rev. Daniel Merrill, An Appreciation," 47.
[34] Baines, *Separating God's Two Kingdoms.*
[35] Baines, "Daniel Merrill 1765–1833," in *A Noble Company*, 370.

embrace of "the Baptist platform" took place within the context of a declining, yet pervasive Congregationalist, Federalist Standing Order. This necessarily drew him into political conflict. Over time, Merrill penetrated the "Second" Kingdom, as his writing and preaching attest. Both the magistrate and minister he took to task, yet it is a fair judgment that his argumentation developed primarily along Scriptural lines. He worked out his conception of an ideal "primitive" or "New Testament church" paradigm—a band of believers sojourning together through a hostile environment, endangered by the forces of nature and subject to harm by world powers. Added to these obstacles were a generally religiously indifferent population and New England's openly antagonistic politicians.[36]

Merrill on Baptism as a Standing Order Minister

In 1793, Merrill's vocation as a New England Congregational minister in the District of Maine and the Commonwealth of Massachusetts was typical—one could say ideal—both doctrinally and culturally. Within a decade, however, Isaac Case reported that Merrill was a fully-confirmed Baptist in the Autumn of 1804. Case wrote: "It will be natural for you to inquire, what effect it has on Mr. Merrill, his Students becoming Baptist. I will just say, I have made him a short visit, and find him fully convinced of believers' baptism by immersion."[37] In order to trace Merrill's transformation between 1799 and the end of 1804, when he published his *Seven Sermons*, two primary documents come to the fore: *A Record*

---

[36] For a thorough discussion of Merrill's theology of baptism and its development regarding covenant and kingdom theology, see Baines, "Daniel Merrill 1765-1833," in *A Noble Company*, 357-376; *Separating God's Two Kingdoms*, 20-62 and 208-258; Carter, "Mind and Ministry of Jonathan Fisher," 219-239.

[37] Isaac Case, "Further Account of Rev. Mr. Case's Mission in the District of Maine, extracted from a Letter of his to the Secretary of the Society, dated at Reedfield, January 8th, 1805," in Baldwin, ed., *The Massachusetts Baptist Missionary Magazine* 1 (Sept. 1803-Jan. 1808); No. 4 (May 1805): 107-108. Cited in Baines, "Daniel Merrill 1765-1833," in *A Noble Company*, 359.

book belonging to the Church of Christ in Sedgwick. 1794, and the *Autobiography of Rev. Daniel Merrill.*[38]

The *Record book* reflects actions taken by Merrill and the church, leading up to, and including the ceremony in May of 1805, when the Church of Christ in Sedgwick was received into Baptist communion, its leaders rebaptized, and Merrill ordained as a Baptist minister. The *Autobiography* was written months before Merrill's death, and though it is not as detailed as his published sermons and pamphlets, the document should be taken as his final thoughts on baptism and the so-called "Baptist platform." The simple structure of the *Autobiography* presents an *inclusio* of sorts, providing a framework for the story of Merrill's remarkable doctrinal shift. The *Autobiography* begins with an introduction to the author that situates him in the town of Sedgwick. The narrative moves immediately to the body of the work on page two, and Merrill's chief preoccupation: credobaptism as the visible emblem of membership in a pure New Testament church, representing the primary expression of God's Kingdom on earth. The twin foils are the so-called "confused church," and the "kingdom of this world." The chronicle arrives at its resolution on the final page, by bringing the reader back to Sedgwick where the saga began, with the following explanation:

> We do not desire to use offensive words needlessly, but we wish to be understood distinctly. What we wish to say, and what we wish to be understood to say, is that there are but two generic churches in the world. One is that church which avowedly and intentionally receives none into her community but saints, and does receive none but upon a profession of their being so ... The other church does avowedly and practically initiate into its community persons who have no

---

[38] *A Record book belonging to the Church of Christ in Sedgwick. 1794*; Daniel Merrill, *Autobiography of Rev. Daniel Merrill* (Philadelphia, PA: Baptist General Tract Society, 1833).

claim to the style of the saints, and who make no such pretensions. This we style the confused church... These things were distinctly testified unto the people in this region... More than four hundred baptized believers are now upon the ground which the Congregational church in this town covered in the year 1805... DANIEL MERRILL, Sedgwick, Maine, Nov.22, 1832.[39]

Merrill's earliest thoughts on baptism as a Congregational minister are reflected in the covenant he composed for the Church of Christ in Sedgwick and of which the first members affirmed on July 8, 1793. The document reflects the New Light Congregationalist consensus, which rejected the Halfway Covenant, a position explained in the answer to Question 166 from the *Westminster Larger Catechism*:

Q. 166. Unto whom is baptism to be administered? A. Baptism is not to be administered to any that are out of the visible church, and so strangers from the covenant of promise, till they profess their faith in Christ, and obedience to him, but infants descending from parents, either both, or but one of them, professing faith in Christ, and obedience to him, are in that respect within the covenant, and to be baptized.[40]

The Sedgwick statement of faith reads, "Art. 14. Of Baptism ... infants descending from parents, either both, or but one of them professing faith in Cr. and obedience to him, are in that respect, within the covenant, and to be baptized." [41] Here we find the subjects of baptism signified with no reference to mode, which assumes most candidates entering the covenant would be infants, or children of at least one parent already a covenanted member of

---

[39] Merrill, *Autobiography*, 12.

[40] James Benjamin Green, *A Harmony of the Westminster Presbyterian Standards with Explanatory* Notes, (Richmond: John Knox Press, 1951), 206.

[41] *A Record book belonging to the Church of Christ in Sedgwick*, 12.

the community. How the infant would be baptized is not discussed. Merrill and the implied reader likely assumed baptism by dipping, sprinkling, or pouring.

The *Record Book* notes, however that, "in the year 1798 and '99, a great reformation took place among the people." [42] The controversy over infant baptism was thrust upon the church when several candidates desiring membership requested to be baptized by immersion. After a discussion, the covenant was amended by Merrill and affirmed by a vote of the members:

> 1799. Feb. 8 ... It has long been our opinion, and is still, that it becomes the disciples of Cr to condescend to each other, in all things, which are not dishonorary to Christ, or prejudicial to his kingdom amongst men. We therefore agree, that the article respecting baptism, which is inserted in our confession of faith, and in our covenant, is not considered by us, to be so essentially binding upon any who do not see it duty to practice infant baptism as to render it as a term of communion. [43]

Merrill and the church consistently viewed baptism, regardless of mode or the age of the candidate, as essential to the Christian's profession of faith, and acceptance into membership. But the steps of bringing baptismal candidates into full communion— where voting rights were the primary consideration—hearkened to controversy concerning the Halfway Covenant. Full membership in Sedgwick would only be conferred upon profession of evangelical conversion—by adults at their baptism via various modes, or by baptized infants who came of age, and were able to articulate an account of regeneration. The Sedgwick church was in agreement on this point. Over the next five years, however,

---

[42] Merrill, *Autobiography*, 2.

[43] *A Record book belonging to the Church of Christ in Sedgwick*, 33. This amendment is treated as a footnote to Article 14 in *Mr. Merrill's answer to the Christians.*

Merrill and the majority of the congregation would undergo a major transformation in their conviction about the proper mode of baptism. Understandably, this led to the question of when the subjects would make a public declaration of evangelical conversion. That sequence or progression in the life of a disciple of Christ would necessarily affect their understanding of membership and the notion of a pure, visible church, set apart from the world. Merrill would ultimately come to articulate his "Two Kingdom" system, which distinguished a visible, pure church on the one hand from the "confused," "Jewish church" on the other. Members of a true church, he reasoned, could not be in communion with false ones.[44]

Merrill Affirms the Baptist Platform

As a convinced Congregationalist, his journey to the Baptist fold began with the Bible, so that in his own words he "might write a book and show the Baptists, from the unerring word of God, the certain scripture evidence of their errors, and of the hurtful nature of those errors, and of their obligation to renounce them."[45] In this conviction, he was in the mainstream of Congregational thought. Merrill became an effective Baptist apologist precisely because he once shared the views of those who became his opponents after 1804. He "contemplated day and night, and perused the sacred volume, and re-perused it," and when he was ready to write his apologetic, he judged some of his arguments for pedobaptism to be weak for their lack of clear Biblical evidence. He wrote,

---

[44] When Merrill labels the Congregational and other pedobaptist churches the "Jewish church," he is speaking figuratively and not literally, of churches that appeal to the Old Covenant and circumcision signified in baptism, as the sign of membership in the covenant of both regenerate and unregenerate, as was the case in Israel before Christ.

[45] Merrill, *Autobiography*, 3.

I therefore sat myself to a renewed research, that I might strengthen any part which seemed not sufficiently strong to move a world. For truth was my object as well as victory, and my eye was principally upon the one, that I might win the other. I did not, in this momentous concern, covet principally the praise of men nor the show of victory, but the prevalence of all-conquering truth.[46]

This project, his "anxious search" as he called it, continued over a span of two years. During this period Merrill concluded that though he was not a Baptist, and still considered baptism a "gospel ordinance," he could find no support for his previous practice in the New Testament, and therefore no longer felt confident in his authority to baptize. He explained:

The sacred scriptures did not afford clear and direct evidence to support my own practice. Yes, I was compelled to believe that there was no certain precept nor plain example in the Bible to authorize the administering of any gospel ordinance to an unconscious babe. I still fully believed that there were gospel ordinances, and that the Bible did define with certainty what these ordinances were, and to whom they should be administered; but I very sensibly felt that I knew not either. For as yet I was not merely no Baptist, but possessed a very strong and powerful opposition against being one. At the same time all satisfactory evidence of the truth of my own practice failed me. This was a painful condition.[47]

Up until this point, Merrill's inner struggle had been largely unknown outside of his family and fellow itinerant missionaries, such as Isaac Case. Matters came to a head when eight children were put forward for baptism by members of the Church at

---

[46] Merrill, *Autobiography*, 3.
[47] Merrill, *Autobiography*, 4.

Sedgwick. Merrill refused to grant the request, claiming that he "was under no obligation to go ... where the Lord would not go with me." He did not, however, explicitly embrace a Baptist identity at this point. In the meantime, he noted, "My pain and anxiety increased upon me."[48]

Merrill's inner struggle became obvious to the congregation and he requested that the church observe a day of fasting and prayer for direction—to discern whether he, and the church with him, should renounce their former practice and tradition, and cease rejecting "the sentiments of the Baptists, if those sentiments were in accordance with his revealed will." All but three of the members observed the day.[49] The day came and went without a clear resolution. Lacking inner tranquility, Merrill continued on in what he described as "Egyptian Darkness."

> In this state of distressing uncertainty and profound ignorance, I continued for nearly three months, growing nothing better, but rather worse. I read, I meditated, I fasted, I prayed, but all apparently to no purpose. The subject was revolving in my mind day and night, sleeping and waking ... At times I thought myself ready, or nearly so, to be any thing the Lord would have me be. However, I had as yet an unconquered antipathy against being a Baptist. At times my carnal nature so lifted up itself that I could not bear the idea of being called one. I was not willing as yet to become as a little child in this case. Therefore the Lord kept me, from month to month, in Egyptian darkness."[50]

Merrill's autobiography does not offer a precise timetable, but the search he described as lasting "not for weeks and months, but for more than two years," began around 1802 and his *Seven*

---

[48] Merrill, *Autobiography*, 4.
[49] Merrill, *Autobiography*, 4.
[50] Merrill, *Autobiography*, 5.

Sermons, representing his settled thoughts during that period, were published in December of 1804.[51] Ron Baines notes that the time of his refusal to baptize the eight children, through his six months of despairing *Egyptian Darkness*, approximately nine months passed.[52]

One entry in the *Record book belonging to the Church of Christ in Sedgwick 1794* may narrow his day of decision to sometime in the late spring or early summer, 1804. On June 21, the Church met to consider motions to "make up the deficiency of Mr. Merrill's salary" and "consult together, whether anything could be done, with respect to the support of the Pastor of the Chh, and also to consult with him upon the subject."[53] They were anticipating the possibility that Merrill would lose his financial support from the town taxes if he and the church sought fellowship with the Baptists. Months later, on September 9, the records show the church convened to take up a common complaint—a matter of discipline regarding "hard drinking, and of very unbecoming conduct and conversation."[54] Sandwiched between those two entries, one dated August 27, 1804 reflects the concerns of a congregation that had recently abandoned infant baptism and embraced credobaptism. With the newfound conviction that baptism by immersion ought to follow a profession of faith, full membership in the Church in Sedgwick would require young people and children, most of whom had been baptized as infants, to give an account of the regenerating work of the Spirit and come forward for baptism by immersion. The entire church, with the exception of a few, had evidently adopted credobaptism. Merrill was convinced that he was not qualified to perform baptisms until he was received into

---

[51] Merrill, *Autobiography*, 3.

[52] Merrill, *Autobiography*, 5; Baines, "Daniel Merrill 1765–1833," in *A Noble Company*, 361.

[53] *A Record book belonging to the Church of Christ in Sedgwick. 1794*, 39.

[54] *A Record book belonging to the Church of Christ in Sedgwick. 1794*. 40.

Baptist fellowship and commissioned, an event that would come the following spring. This move placed believing children and recent converts who desired baptism into a kind of limbo. Merrill recorded that the church set aside the fourth Thursday, "as a day of fasting and prayer to God, that he will pour his Spirit upon the Chh, and give them wisdom and [illegible] His ways, and cause a revival of religion among our young men and maidens, and among our children."[55] These deliberations by the church point to late Summer or early Autumn when Merrill and much of the congregation had settled the matter.

By September, Merrill was a confirmed Baptist and had embarked upon his preaching of the Seven Sermons. Isaac Case visited Sedgwick, and noted in his diary on November 6th and 7th of that same year that Merrill had preached "five sermons upon the Mode." He added:

> Deacons are convinst and agreate part of the Church. He hath taken very prudant measures to remove pregiduses and to seerch candedly for them selves to see whether these things be so or no - there is but avery little disputing but Each searching his Bible to know Duty for him selfe.[56]

Merrill perceived the Church at Sedgwick's tenuous position at the end of the summer 1804. Having won the major battle over the question of Baptism, he recognized that the war was not yet over. Both the church and town would continue to struggle—theologically and practically—over the implications of what had, with striking speed, overturned decades of tradition. The concerns of losing his monetary support and homestead weighed heavily on Daniel Merrill's heart and mind, but upon looking

---

[55] *A Record book belonging to the Church of Christ in Sedgwick. 1794*, 40.
[56] Baines, *Separating God's Two Kingdoms*, 220–221.

back, he voiced no regrets in how he chose to shepherd his flock during this journey. He recalled in his *Autobiography*,

> I soon engaged in the important labor of showing these in-teresting particulars to my people. The first Lord's-day af-ter my mind was relieved from the long and distressing per-plexity, which the hurtful traditions of men had occasioned me, I delivered to my congregation the substance of the first two of the seven sermons, which I speedily caused to be published for their perusal. From Sabbath to Sabbath, I ceased not to preach and show the glad tidings of the king-dom of God. I showed my brethren, in the most friendly and undisguised manner, the difference between what we had been, and what the Lord Jesus in his word required us to be ... They therefore gave me a candid, patient, and solicitous hearing; and then searched the scriptures, that they might know the correctness or fallacy of the things they had heard. The above course, I and my people pursued from week to week, and from month to month.[57]

Merrill's First Published Exposition on Baptism

The Mode and Subjects of Baptism Examined in Seven Sermons was published by Daniel Merrill in December of 1804 and distributed to the church, "for their perusal." [58] This work represents the fruit of the author's years of painstaking study and prayer, done mostly out of public view. The *Sermons* were Merrill's first pub-lished work as a Baptist, and apart from the doctrinal statement and covenant in *Mr. Merrill's answer to the Christians, and other*

---

[57] Merrill, *Autobiography*, 7–8. Ron Baines observes, "Merrill did not exercise dic-tatorial authority over his congregation. He appealed to their consciences and called for them to be like the 'noble Bereans' and 'search the scriptures devoutly, and follow me so far as I follow Jesus Christ.' He asked his hearers and readers not to follow him blindly but laid before them his reasons for embracing Baptist principles." Baines, "Daniel Merrill 1765–1833," in *A Noble Company*, 242.

[58] Merrill, *The Mode and Subjects of Baptism Examined*.

inhabitants of Sedgwick, his first purely theological production.[59] A Baptist apologetic booklet written by a Dartmouth graduate and pastor of the largest church of any kind in the District, was bound to excite attention beyond the town of Sedgwick. After the publication of *Seven Sermons,* Jonathan Fisher saw a third of his congregation defect to Merrill's church in 1805. Fisher would also witness the establishment of a Baptist Society in Bluehill in 1806. Congregational ministers and other pedobaptist apologists quickly responded to the treatise. The "Watery War" commenced with the first edition of *Seven Sermons.*[60] The sermons, representative of Merrill's initial thoughts on believer's baptism, would be republished at least ten times by 1812.

Each of the seven sermons begins with Matthew 28:18-19 as an epigraph in the published version, and Merrill develops his thoughts from the phrase, "Go ye therefore, and teach all nations, baptizing them in the name of the Father, and of the Son, and of the Holy Ghost: Teaching them to observe all things whatsoever I have commanded you."[61] As the title makes clear, his primary concern was the "who" and the "how" of baptism. Merrill's intention was for his readers and hearers to consider the nature of biblical covenants, the purity of the visible church, and the Kingdom of Heaven—in contradistinction to the Kingdom of this World.

Merrill viewed baptism as a positive institution, grounded in the law of Christ and the Apostolic teaching, and narrowly defined by New Testament writings. He commented that, "2. Baptism is a positive institution, about which we can know nothing, as to its being a Christian ordinance, but from what Christ, and those

---

[59] Daniel Merrill, *Mr. Merrill's answer to the Christians.* One other published work took the form of a Constitution and *mission statement* for the newly created association to prepare young men for ministry and was occasional in nature regarding doctrine or theology.

[60] John of Enon (David Benedict), *The Watery War.*

[61] Authorized Version.

inspired by his Spirit, have taught us." He argued that later developments or traditions, "by the precepts and commandments of men, added since, is distinct from the ordinance, and makes no part of it." For such reasons, "Whenever, and wherever, this ordinance is so changed, as to lose the intent of the Institutor, then and there the ordinance is lost, and becomes no Christian ordinance at all." By framing baptism in such a way, Merrill was able to develop an argument for the baptism of those seeking the ordinance upon a profession of faith, administered by immersion. Because Christ and the apostles never positively instituted the baptism of infants, pedobaptism, reasoned Merrill, could only be of human origin and should therefore be rejected. It is, in fact, "no Christian ordinance at all."[62]

The first three of the *Seven Sermons* are concerned with lexical meanings of various terms associated with baptism such as washing, and sprinkling. Merrill considers a compendium of verses regarding the baptism by John, Christ's own baptism, and New Testament verses which mention the rite. Following his "positive institution" motif, the only relevant texts are "those ... which mention Christ's baptism," or the baptism Jesus instituted.[63] It is noteworthy that although he covers the same biblical material as Jonathan Fisher's *Short Essay*, Merrill exhibits greater certitude about baptism, and his deep convictions about the ordinance can be sensed in the following:

> It may be easy for you to gather what is the outward and visible part of the ordinance of baptism. It is to immerse proper subjects in water, in the name of the Father, and of the Son, and of the Holy Ghost. This is the outward and visible part of baptism, the scriptures being judge; this literal and plain meaning of the command being judge; the practice of the

---

[62] Merrill, *The Mode and Subjects of Baptism Examined*, 9–10.
[63] Merrill, *The Mode and Subjects of Baptism Examined*, 10–17.

apostles being judge; the practice of the church for more than a thousand years being judge; and even if we appeal to those who refuse to practice thus, they add their testimony, that it is what was commanded. They pretend not to say that any new command hath been given, or that the old one hath ever been changed.[64]

By the close of Merrill's third sermon, the "mode and subjects of Baptism," is a settled matter. His closing remarks address the audience as Congregationalists and pedobaptists by covenant, though by the time of publication, the majority of the congregation were convinced and would formally declare their full acceptance of believer's baptism the following year.

"If immersion be from heaven, and sprinkling from men," Merrill asked, the path going forward for the Church of Christ at Sedgwick was clear. "1. We who call ourselves Paedobaptists, are as a house divided against itself. To say the least, we appear thus."[65] With each sermon, Merrill's declarations expressed urgency, the implications being starker. His conclusion, which captures theological substance in its rhetorical attire, is worth quoting at length:

> According to the light which for the present appears, we cannot but conclude that our definitions of baptism and to baptize are scriptural, accurate and just ... It appears that it is not left with us to choose what mode we will practice in administering or in receiving the ordinance of baptism; for we find but one mode to it: and we must practice this, or none. We may sprinkle a person in the name of the Father, &c. and we may wash the face, or any part of a person, in the same sacred name; but it is not possible to baptize a person in this way; for sprinkling, or any small partial washing never was, is not now, nor ever will be, what the scriptures

---

[64] Merrill, *The Mode and Subjects of Baptism Examined*, 45.
[65] Merrill, *The Mode and Subjects of Baptism Examined*, 46

mean by Christian Baptism. That a person must be greatly unacquainted with the plain, literal, scripture account of baptism or extremely prejudiced, not to say perverse, to affirm that the Bible says nothing about immersion, or burying in water for baptizing. For it speaks of this mode, and of no other, in the application of water as a gospel ordinance ... It appears that for well-informed Pedobaptists to oppose the Baptists, as to their mode of baptizing, is very great wickedness. For the Baptists have the advantage of plain and express scripture on their side, and the learned, critical and candid Pedobaptists know it. ... Dr. Lathrop appears generously to grant the truth, that immersion is scripture baptism, and only contends that sprinkling be also allowed; which every candid mind would readily do, were there one text of scripture to support it ... No true Christian, if he knew what he did, would ever make light of immersion, which the Lord commands, and the Baptists practice, as the mode of baptizing, or, more strictly, as baptism itself."[66]

With the proper mode and subjects of baptism settled in his mind, the notion of a "confused" pedobaptist church was patently evident. A true and distinctly visible church was marked by the sign of baptism, performed by immersion, bestowed on those professing an evangelical conversion. This was the essence of Merrill's *Seven Sermons*. Additionally, they served as the port of entry into his theology of Two Kingdoms—one of this world, and the other of heaven. Merrill refined his theology of baptism in future sermons and writings, though largely as a response to detractors. Ron Baines observes that it became apparent early in the "Watery War," that Merrill and other Congregationalists who embraced the Baptist message were no longer arguing within the bounds of the intramural debates taking place at the turn of the century, but were developing a more robust and wide-ranging

---

[66] Merrill, *The Mode and Subjects of Baptism Examined*, 46–47.

theology of baptism. Baines comments that what "Austin, Fisher, and other Pedobaptists were beginning to realize is that the Baptists rightly understood their doctrinal differences to be much bigger than the mode and subjects of Baptism; it was the entire formulation of the New Covenant community that was in view."[67]

Merrill's Settled Theology of Baptism

A detailed discussion of the repartee and substantive debate between Merrill and his critics lies beyond the scope of this chapter.[68] The most serious and sustained objections to his *Seven Sermons*, followed by his published responses, however, provide a coherent and straightforward sketch of his developed theology of baptism, as well as some points of departure between Merrill, Fisher, and their neighboring churches. Jonathan Fisher spent over a decade formulating his rejoinder to credobaptism, beginning with a series of sermons late in 1804. He published his *Essay on Baptism* in 1817, when the Watery War in Hancock County was essentially over. Fisher did not directly address Merrill, who had removed to Nottingham West, New Hampshire, and Merrill did not respond in print after his return to Sedgwick in 1820. Richard Carter provides a perceptive analysis of the polemics when he writes, "the views of Fisher based on complicated fineries of Covenant Theology were far more obtuse, and increasingly less than convincing" than those of Merrill and other Baptist apologists and pamphleteers.[69]

Rev. Samuel Austin responded quickly to *Seven Sermons* in the form of letters addressed to Merrill, of which Ron Baines quips,

---

[67] Ron Baines, "Daniel Merrill 1765-1833," *A Noble* Company, 367.

[68] For Merrill's theology of baptism and its development regarding covenant and kingdom theology, see Ron Baines, "Daniel Merrill 1765-1833," in *A Noble Company*, 357–376; Ronald Baines, *Separating God's Two Kingdoms*, 20–62 and 208–258; Carter, "Mind and Ministry of Jonathan Fisher," 219–239.

[69] Richard Carter, "Mind and Ministry of Jonathan Fisher," 225–226.

"only took up half the argument."[70] Austin passed over lexical and scriptural arguments for credobaptism and argued the common pedobaptist position that the New Testament offered insufficient evidence for a normative mode of baptism.[71] He targeted Merrill's "offensive" conclusion that those incorrectly baptized were outside the Kingdom of God and that a pedobaptist church was, by definition, "mixed" or "confused." In other words, Merrill's notion that a pedobaptist communion was no true church was the main point that rankled Austin. Samuel Worcester, the Congregationalist pastor from Salem Massachusetts, entered into the Baptist controversy under a similar set of circumstances as Jonathan Fisher. Like Bluehill's pastor, members of Worcester's church left to join the newly-formed First Baptist Church of Salem in 1804.[72] Worcester likewise understood covenant theology as the key to determining the proper subjects of baptism, while expressing some level of ambivalence regarding the mode. Worcester contended that Merrill's view of the Abrahamic Covenant was deficient, and argued that the New Testament church provides a continuation, or "augmentation" of that earlier covenant. Thus, baptism is prescribed for children of believing parents in the same way that circumcision was enjoined upon infants as entry into the covenant community.

---

[70] Samuel Austin, *An Examination of the Representations and Reasonings Contained in Seven Sermons, Lately Published, by the Rev. Daniel Merrill, on the Mode and Subjects of Baptism: In Several Letters Addressed to the Author, in Which It Is Attempted to Shew, That Those Representations and Reasonings Are Not Founded in Truth.* (Worcester: Isaiah Thomas, 1805). Ron Baines, "Daniel Merrill 1765–1833," in *A Noble Company*, 366.

[71] From the *Advertisement* on page 1, "It will be seen by the attentive and intelligent reader of the following letters, that they were merely designed to meet and refute the arguments contained in the Sermons they cursorily review. The writer does not profess to examine the Antipedobaptist hypothesis on the most extended plan; or to collect and establish the evidence which supports the opposite theory [pedobaptist]." Samuel Austin, *An Examination of the Representations and Reasonings Contained in Seven Sermons*, 1.

[72] Samuel Worcester, *Two Discourses, on the Perpetuity and Provision of God's Gracious Covenant with Abraham and His Seed.* (Salem: Haven Pool, 1805).

Congregationalist Rufus Anderson of North Yarmouth began a dispute with Merrill over closed communion when he published a work in the form of seven general letters, reproving the exclusive claims of Baptists. In summary, Anderson's appeal was for unity and cooperation between the two sides.[73] Merrill responded in the form of eight letters, turning the tables on Anderson with his title, *Open Communion With All Who Keep the Ordinances as Christ Delivered Them to the Saints.*[74] Anderson responded once more on the same issue and Merrill let his rejoinder stand.[75] David Lawrence Morril was a minister, lawyer, and physician, who also served as Governor and Senator of New Hampshire.[76] He responded to Merrill's view of Open Communion, but failed to address Merrill's major themes. Merrill did not reply in print. Still, other New England pastors engaged with the tract over a few years. These included Joseph Field, John Reed, and Jabez Chadwick.[77]

---

[73] Rufus Anderson, *The Close Communion of the Baptists: In Principle and Practice, Proved to Be Unscriptural, and of a Bad Tendency in the Church of God* (Salem Massachusetts: Joshua Cushing, 1805). Rufus Anderson was a Dartmouth Graduate and longtime friend of Merrill. Ron Baines notes that Anderson, Worcester, and Austin were associates and may have coordinated their responses. This is plausible given their various, individual lines of criticism published within a short time frame. Baines, "Daniel Merrill 1765-1833," in *A Noble Company*, 243.

[74] Daniel Merrill, *Open Communion with All Who Keep the Ordinances as Christ Delivered Them to the Saints. Eight Letters on Open Communion Addressed to Rufus Anderson, A.M* (Boston: Manning & Loring, 1805).

[75] Rufus Anderson, *An Estimate of Immersion the Main Principle of Close Communion, as Defended by Rev. Daniel Merrill: Concluded with an Address to Him, in Several Discussions* (Salem: Joshua Cushing, 1806).

[76] David Lawrence Morril, *A Concise Letter Written to Rev. Daniel Merrill, A.M., of Sedgwick Containing Strictures and Remarks on Several Letters by Him, Addressed to Rev. R. Anderson, A.M., Entitled, Open Communion with All Who Keep the Ordinances as Christ Delivered Them to the Saints: In Which the Fallacy of His Propositions and Arguments Is Illustrated* (Amherst: Joseph Cushing, 1806).

[77] Joseph Field, *Strictures on Seven Sermons, with an Appendix, by Reverend Daniel Merrill, of Sedgwick Maine. On the Mode and Subjects of Baptism. In Twelve Sections* (Northampton: Thomas M. Pomroy, 1806). John Reed, *An Apology for the Rite of Infant Baptism and for the Usual Modes of Baptizing in Which an Attempt Is Made to State Fairly and Clearly the Arguments in Proof of These Doctrines, and Also to Refute the Objections and Reasonings Alleged against Them by the Rev. Daniel Merrill and by the Baptists in General.* (Providence: Heaton & Williams, 1806). Merrill mentioned a manuscript response to "Doctor Reed's Apology" in a footnote on page 15 of *The Kingdom of*

Chadwick, a presbyterian minister from New York, had been persuaded by Merrill's arguments and identified as a Baptist for
about three months. Each of these authors followed the well-trod
polemical path by answering Baptists in general, without eliciting
further response from Merrill, whose theology of baptism had
reached its mature development by 1811.

With the dust of controversy over the publication of the *Seven
Sermons* settled, Merrill was established as a Baptist apologist,
leader, and scholar. The Kingdom of Heaven, the nature of the
church, and communion—as they relate to baptism and the "Baptist platform"—were frequent subjects of sermons published over
the next two decades. His address, *The Kingdom of Heaven, Distinguished from Babylon, a Sermon Delivered at the Introduction of
the Lincoln Association, Sept. 21-22, 1808*, was not his final published work, but it adequately represents his definitive theological
assessment of these subjects.[78]

The Kingdom of Heaven

Merrill discerned, as Austin and Worcester noted in their critiques, that the debate over baptism hinged on the relationship between the Old Covenant as contained in the Hebrew Bible, and
the New Covenant as proposed in the canonical New Testament.
The nature of the church and the appearance of the Kingdom of
Heaven on earth depended on one's interpretation of the relationship between covenants. He began his address to the Lincoln Association with the declaration, "This kingdom is the mystery,

---

Heaven, Distinguished from Babylon, a Sermon Delivered at the Introduction of the Lincoln
Association, Sept. 21-22, 1808 (Buckstown, Maine: William W. Clapp, 1810). Jabez
Chadwick, *Four Sermons, on the Mode and Subjects of Christian Baptism. By Jabez Chad-
wick, Pastor of the First Presbyterian Congregation in Onondaga* (Utica, PA: Seward and
Williams, 1811).

[78] Daniel Merrill, *The Kingdom of Heaven, Distinguished from Babylon. Introduction
of the Lincoln Association, Sept. 21-22, 1808* (Buckstown, Maine: William W. Clapp,
1810).

which, from the beginning of the world, hath been hid in God; which in former ages was not made known... is now... revealed unto his holy Apostles and Prophets by the Spirit."[79] Merrill argued that the kingdom "hid in God," was inaugurated with the New Covenant. Thus, pedobaptist appeal to circumcision of infants as the model for Christian baptism—signifying entrance into the kingdom—was their principal hermeneutical error. The New Testament provided the primary sources and arguably, the interpretive lens, with which to evaluate Old Testament ceremonies and church tradition alike. In the words of Baines:

> By affirming that the Kingdom of God did not commence with Israel in the Old Testament, Merrill, like Williams and Backus before him, was assigning to New Testament revelation the task of controlling typological interpretations ... If Israel was not the Kingdom of God, though it could point to the Church in a limited and typological way, it was not to be followed to any conclusion that the New Testament did not warrant."[80]

Merrill appealed to Ephesians 2 to establish "two subjects of the first importance, and which will demand your whole attention ... I. The kingdom of Christ on earth. II. The rules and regulations to which this kingdom of Christ was first set up, and is still in building."[81] The Kingdom of Christ was inaugurated and is

---

[79] Merrill, *The Kingdom of Heaven*, 4.

[80] Baines, *Separating God's Two Kingdoms*, 20-62, 208-258; Carter, "Mind and Ministry of Jonathan Fisher," 28-29.

[81] Ephesians 2:15-19 (AV) reads, "Having abolished in his flesh the enmity, *even* the law of commandments *contained* in ordinances; for to make in himself of twain one new man, *so* making peace; And that he might reconcile both unto God in one body by the cross, having slain the enmity thereby: And came and preached peace to you which were afar off, and to them that were nigh. For through him we both have access by one Spirit unto the Father. Now therefore ye are no more strangers and foreigners, but fellow citizens with the saints, and of the household of God."

manifested in the Church.[82] The Kingdom, which was established between the manifestation of John the Baptist and the suffering of Christ, is continuing to be built around the world.[83] Merrill uses the terms "Kingdom of God," "Kingdom of Heaven," "the gospel Kingdom," "the Kingdom of Christ," "Christ's terrestrial Kingdom," and the "Kingdom of Jesus," interchangeably. This Kingdom of Heaven is contrasted with the kingdoms of this world. The former will one day, "consume, and destroy..." the latter.[84] These worldly kingdoms are amalgamated into a singular adversarial kingdom, which Merrill labeled in conventional Puritan form, "Babylon," the "Church of Babylon,"[85] "mystical Babylon," and the "visible Church ... of Antichrist."[86] This "Babylonish kingdom" stands apart from, and in opposition to, the Kingdom of Heaven up to the present. The inauguration and establishment of the Kingdom of Heaven in "Christ's visible church, or kingdom" through the New Covenant in His blood, has resulted in the abrogation of the "Jewish economy [system]" and its "Ceremonial commandments contained in ordinances." [87] Merrill explains,

> At the commencement of this kingdom, or near it, its divine Author abolished in his flesh, (by his suffering,) the enmity, (the occasion of enmity between Jews and Gentiles) even the law of commandments, contained in ordinances; for to *make in himself twain, (of Jews and Gentiles,) one NEW MAN*, or *body of men, one NEW KINGDOM, so making peace*: that he might reconcile both Jews and Gentiles unto

---

[82] Merrill writes, "the kingdom of heaven, Christ's visible church, or kingdom... his people or disciples... " CHRIST's kingdom, on earth, which is called the kingdom of heaven." "The kingdom of heaven, the gospel Church..." See *The Kingdom of Heaven Distinguished from Babylon*, 8.

[83] Merrill, *The Kingdom of Heaven*, 7, 8.

[84] Merrill, *The Kingdom of Heaven*, 4.

[85] Merrill, *The Kingdom of Heaven*, 28.

[86] Merrill, *The Kingdom of Heaven*, 18.

[87] Merrill, *The Kingdom of Heaven*, 8.

GOD in *one body* by the CROSS, having, by his cross, slain the law of Ceremonial commandments contained in ordinances. Thus was the Jewish economy abrogated.[88]

Merrill reasoned that because the ordinances under the Old Covenant were abolished in the death of Christ, an appeal to circumcision from Colossians 2:11–14—except by analogy—could not be employed as support for infant baptism. Since the Kingdom of Heaven is a mystery revealed, the way one enters the Kingdom sheds light on ordinances of the past, but not visa-versa. As for so-called "ceremonial commandments," these were "slain" at the cross and thus have no bearing on the nature of baptism. The New Testament provides historical accounts and explicit instructions concerning the proper mode and subjects of baptism. Merrill would venture to argue that a single passage, Matthew 28:18–20, definitively settles all controversies over infant baptism.[89]

Merrill's theology of the inaugurated Kingdom of Heaven, manifested in the "gospel Church," logically led him to identify the king's subjects and explain how they gained admittance into the Kingdom of Heaven, that is, "Christ's visible church." With his doctrine fully formed, Merrill returned to where he began in 1804 with his exposition of Matthew 28:19–20 in the *Seven Sermons*. In his address to the Lincoln Association, however, he reiterated with greater force a foundational principle he introduced in sermons six and seven that disciples are first made, and then baptized. As a rule, it follows that any arguments for the efficacy or propriety of baptizing insensible infants are invalid. To enter

---

[88] Merrill, *The Kingdom of Heaven*, 4.

[89] Matthew 28:18–20 (AV): "And Jesus came and spake unto them, saying, All power is given unto me in heaven and in earth. Go ye therefore, and teach all nations, baptizing them in the name of the Father, and of the Son, and of the Holy Ghost: Teaching them to observe all things whatsoever I have commanded you: and, lo, I am with you always, *even* unto the end of the world. Amen."

Christ's visible church—the Kingdom of Heaven—Merrill argues that one must first be a disciple:

> We will now turn our attention to the words and acts of Jesus CHRIST, relative to the building of his kingdom. When he first set up the gospel Church, the kingdom of heaven among men, He called to him *his disciples, whom he would, and they came unto him...* Here were *none* but *disciples, professing friends...* This looks like a *practical, foundation principle.* It is given by the Son of man. He called *none* but *visible disciples, to be either teachers, or members of his visible kingdom.*[90]

Jesus commissioned his followers to do the same. Merrill comments that the Apostles were told by Christ, "to baptize none but disciples," and that no instance can be found where a person was baptized "who did not... appear to be a disciple of Jesus." The church, as far as the New Testament is concerned, is "made up of disciples, of baptized disciples, and of such only."[91]

The New Testament Church

Merrill continued with the application of his address to the Lincoln Association in seven points—the seventh comprised nearly half of the thirteen total pages—describing the relationship between the Kingdom of Heaven and the kingdoms of this world (e.g., Babylon). The nature and composition of Christ's visible church is depicted positively, its foil being pedobaptist churches, counterfeit communions who remain outside God's realm. From *The Kingdom of Heaven, Distinguished from Babylon* we read what Merrill considers "obvious and weighty conclusions," namely:

---

[90] Merrill, *The Kingdom of Heaven*, 13.
[91] Merrill, *The Kingdom of Heaven*, 14.

1. "That gospel churches, in our day, should be composed of such persons, as are first made the disciples of Christ, and afterwards baptized into him."[92]
2. "That the Batized [*sic*] Churches, or those who are now called Baptist Churches, are each one of them, of the visible Church of CHRIST ... made up, according to the commandment and pattern given, of persons who were first discipled, and then baptized.[93] We purposely exclude from our consideration all Churches, which admit to their community any of the unbaptized; for all such pollute, if not destroy, the Church of God."[94]
3. "That the Paedobaptist Churches are NOT of the visible Church of CHRIST ...[95] They baptize first, and disciple afterwards, or never ... Personal faith in Christ is not, generally, and never was, considered by them as a necessary, personal, prerequisite for baptism, or Church-membership among them."[96]
4. "It appears, that the Paedobaptist Church is the visible Church of Babylon, or of Antichrist."[97]
5. "That the Paedobaptist ministers are not ministers in the Church of CHRIST..."[98]
6. "Every disciple, every saint, in the Paedobaptist Church ought to come out of her; and be no longer a partaker of her sins, lest he receive of her plagues also."[99]

Merrill was neither the first, nor the last Baptist to make such propositions. But as a former Congregationalist in a region where the Standing Order still held, it was inevitable that a hearer or reader who came to share his convictions would not only leave, but outright reject the Congregationalist church where he or she

---

[92] Merrill, *The Kingdom of Heaven*, 14.
[93] Merrill, *The Kingdom of Heaven*, 15.
[94] Merrill, *The Kingdom of Heaven*, 16.
[95] Merrill, *The Kingdom of Heaven*, 16.
[96] Merrill, *The Kingdom of Heaven*, 16.
[97] Merrill, *The Kingdom of Heaven*, 18.
[98] Merrill, *The Kingdom of Heaven*, 19.
[99] Merrill, *The Kingdom of Heaven*, 21.

was a member—a sobering prospect for pastors such as Jonathan Fisher, whose moderate defense of pedobaptism could not match the zeal of Merrill's opposition to the practice.

Closed Communion

Merrill's final exhortation to the Association included detailed application that he intended his hearers to draw from the theological substance. With the assumption that such conclusions were self-evident to his audience—a position with some warrant—he asserted in point seven that, "It appears to be, not only an impropriety, but a manifest evil also, for the ministers in the kingdom of heaven, in the visible Church, to exchange pulpits with Paedobaptists."[100] The notion that Baptist pastors would continue to minister closely alongside Congregationalist ministers or share pulpits would be an abomination. He continued:

> To exchange pulpits with men, who are sentimentally and zealously active in bewitching the Church of CHRIST is obviously improper. It also hath a manifest evil in it; for by so doing, we practically say their error is small, when it is, in fact, a grievous and ruining one. We also publicly acknowledge them as ministers in CHRIST's Church, when the fact is, they, as Paedobaptists ministers have no commission from Christ... and, as far as their influence extends, they ruin the visible Church of GOD."[101]

---

[100] Merrill, *The Kingdom of Heaven*, 23.

[101] Merrill, *The Kingdom of Heaven*, 23. At the same time, Merrill was apparently willing to find common ground with Baptists at home and in the Canadian Maritimes who did not share his Reformed view on the human will: "There is, however, a shade of difference, and, perhaps, not a small one, between some of the baptized Churches, as to doctrine, or sentiment. Some, it is alledged [*sic*], hold to a free-will in natural men to do good as well as evil. Others hold to a free-will to evil and to that only. It may be, that this difference is larger in appearance, than in reality. But let this difference be as it may, in Church building they agree ... We purposely exclude from consideration all Churches, which admit to their community any of the unbaptized: for all such pollute, if not destroy, the Church of God and are... Churches, or Societies, of spurious origin; or Churches bewitched." Merrill, *The Kingdom of Heaven*, 16.

While Merrill placed all pedobaptists into a single, errant, worldwide communion, his comments to the Lincoln Baptists are best understood as regional, localized polemic against the Federalist ruling elite, the possessors of institutional and cultural dominance. Merrill's position, drawn from conviction about the meaning of biblical texts, would not soften toward the pedobaptists over time. Undoubtedly, political persecution and compulsory taxation gave Merrill a jaundiced view of the Congregationalist establishment, yet for all he risked to lose, only the deepest-held beliefs could lead a man to call a church of which he was once a pastor, "a Synagogue of Satan."[102]

Granted, Merrill did not go so far as to pronounce individual pedobaptists "unbelievers." He consistently affirmed their status as Christians, called them "beloved brethren," enjoyed their fellowship, participated with them in distributing Scriptures, served alongside them in government, and even noted their individual piety.[103] He did insist, however, that common communion between

---

[102] Merrill, *The Kingdom of Heaven*, 25

[103] "Tho' many of the ministers were as holy as Noah, Daniel and Job, yet we have nothing to do with them as ministers in the Church of Christ. Nor have they anything to do with us to build an house unto the Lord our God, till they renounce the Church of Babylon... We certainly will exercise all kindness towards the Paedobaptists." Merrill, *The Kingdom of Heaven*, 25, 26. Nearly a decade later in 1819, Merrill addresses his audience warmly in the form of an open letter dialogue his published response to Nathaniel S. Prime, "BELOVED BRETHREN, You are born of God, and beloved by him. There are seasons in which the honour and truth of God are the joy of your heart." See, Daniel Merrill, *The Gospel Church, Vindicated by the Scriptures. From the Severe Accusations; the Ingenious but Very Mischievous, Sophistry of Nathaniel S. Prime, Pastor of the Presbyterian Church, in Cambridge, N.Y.* (Concord: Hill & Moore, 1819), 62. This was written in response to Nathaniel S. Prime, *A Familiar Illustration of Christian Baptism: In Which the Proper Subjects of that Ordinance and the Mode of Administration are Ascertained from the Word of God and the History of the Church; and Defended from the Objections Usually Urged by the Opposers of Infant Baptism, and the Advocates of Immersion: In the Form of a Dialogue.* (Salem, NY: Dodd & Stevenson, 1818). Prime does not mention Daniel Merrill by name, but critiques the works of Dr. John Gill and, presumably, Isaac Backus though he is not named. Historian Arthur Warren Smith observed, "Strange as it may seem, the pedobaptists thereabouts sent an appeal to Daniel Merrill to write an answer which ... should be a conclusive answer to ... [Prime's] unfair strictures and ... set forth the scripture teaching." Smith, *A Baptist Factor*, 5.

the Baptist Church and the "confused Church" was not possible. In reality, the question of open communion was not a question at all. His address to the Lincoln Association made this clear, as indicted by the juxtaposition of the following text from the published title page:

> Say ye not, a Confederacy. Isa. 8:12
> Let us build with you; for we seek your God as ye do.
> BABYLONIANS
> Ye have nothing to do with us to build and house unto our GOD.
> ISRAELITES
> Ezra, 4:2. 3.

Merrill's theology of baptism was typical of New England Baptists with roots in the English Baptist Confessions, and the writings of theologians such as John Gill. Merrill's theological writings gained attention as he was one of the few Baptists in America with an academic background, conversant with the leading Congregationalist thinkers of his time such as Dr. Spring, his mentor, and Jonathan Edwards, as well as the theology of John Calvin. In appropriating his theology, Merrill displayed an insider's knowledge of the Standing Order, expressed in a trenchant, directed line of argumentation that friends and allies found engaging and opponents virulently opposed. Merrill's sermons and pamphlets usually found their target—often former colleagues—making him a foremost Baptist champion for over three generations. When reading Merrill's works, it is worth noting that among passages where he is most harsh and condemning, it is typically within the wider context of historic grievances concerning persecution of Baptists, particularly by the hands of New England's elite—even in Merrill's own lifetime.

In his preaching and writing, Merrill appealed to the Bible and common sense. Both emphases found wide acceptance among the religious and irreligious hearers alike who flooded into the District of Maine during the Early Republic. The Standing Order was declining, Democratic-Republicanism was on the ascent. Thus, dissenters filled the vacuum, and with a man like Merrill leading the charge, Baptists outstripped all other sects and denominations, becoming the dominant Christian tradition in Maine. Though his opponents, and even some friends, felt he was too sharp and provocative by pen and pulpit, Merrill could be a genial, affable, and engaging person. Maine was ripe for the evangelical harvest, and preachers with a simple message that appealed to the Holy Spirit's power to initiate revival and employed in egalitarian language could accommodate what the old wineskins of the Standing Order could not.

Merrill's last words, of which we have written record, from the year 1832 reiterated the motive behind his spirited, persistent preaching of the Baptist message. Aware of obstinate detractors in his region and in a self-consciously apologetic vein, he insisted that his desire was not "to use offensive words needlessly," but rather be "understood distinctly." For any who would not take his denomination seriously, Merrill cited a form of evidence that could not be easily refuted, much less, ignored: "more than four hundred baptized believers are now upon the ground which the Congregational church in this town covered in the year 1805"[104]

Conclusion

In *Jonathan Fisher: Maine Parson*, biographer Mary Ellen Chase included an extended quote from the Bluehill Congregationalist pastor on what he considered the consensus opinion on baptism. Fisher opined that he had "the advantage of contemplating the subject with a good degree of freedom from ... self-interest," and that after meditation and prayer, he felt "inward and general

---

[104] Merrill, *Autobiography*, 11, 12.

satisfaction that sprinkling with water ... is acceptable to God."[105] Whatever Fisher's intentions, and despite the mild tone, his language belies an awareness of an elevated position. "Advantage," "satisfaction," these words aptly described the Standing Order, a title of inescapable aristocratic undertones. On the ground, however, a meaningful advantage had already been lost. Daniel Merrill emerged as an underdog, and fought in like manner, with urgency and force. Whereas Fisher felt comfortable leaving a reader with a probable judgment in favor of pedobaptism, Merrill could assert that his definitions of baptism were, "scriptural, accurate and just," by virtue of "plain, literal Scripture."[106] Whether Merrill jettisoned nuance, or Fisher simply understated his case—both of which are arguably true—is perhaps less important than the composition of their audiences, whose inclinations would undoubtedly determine whether Fisher or Merrill proved more convincing.

---

[105] Chase, *Maine Parson*, 97.
[106] Merrill, *The Mode and Subjects of Baptism Examined*, 46.

4

Cooperation:
Fisher and Merrill's Evangelical Co-labors

Bluehill at the turn of nineteenth century was a relatively small community, making for regular interaction between Jonathan Fisher and local Baptists. Despite predictable friction, there is strong evidence of denominational cooperation under the wider evangelical umbrella. As the Baptist fold grew, it drew its members from the same New England stock that once filled Congregationalist pews. At the same time, the Bluehill Baptists served alongside and under the leadership of Daniel Merrill in their respective churches, associations, missionary societies, and educational institutions. Merrill honored the independence of the Bluehill congregation and continued to minister alongside them in the establishment of a Baptist identity. The Eastern Maine Association of Baptists, for example, featured George Stevens and Daniel Merrill—both committed Calvinists. Jonathan Fisher, being a "consistent" Calvinist, had more in common with the Baptists like Merrill and Stevens than the average liberal pastor from the Standing Order. As noted previously, Merrill's uncompromising Baptist positions made cooperation difficult, yet fellow Baptists, contemporaries of their pastor, did demonstrate by—among other actions—the appropriation of their assets, a modest degree of solidarity with Maine Congregationalism without diluting theological convictions. The same was true of Congregationalists who assisted Baptists in Maine.

Fisher and Merrill: the earliest days

If for any other reason, Jonathan Fisher and Daniel Merrill understood each other by virtue of a relationship that remained steady for a 38-year duration. Fisher's first recorded interaction with Merrill dates to October, 1795. Though licensed to preach, Fisher was not permitted to administer communion at Bluehill where he served as an itinerant. Merrill inquired with Fisher as to which members of the congregation were disqualified to partake of the sacrament. In a foreshadowing of future conflict, Fisher cited two men, Joseph Osgood and Joshua Horton, whom he believed Merrill should bar from the Lord's table. Their respective offenses were, drunkenness and quarreling with profanity. One deacon, an original signer of the 1773 church covenant, bitterly objected to Fisher and Merrill's assessment and threatened to take legal action. Merrill wisely proposed a meeting in which a person amenable to the accused presided. Eventually, the church upheld the judgment recommended by the two young pastors. Fisher's principled action did not scuttle his chance to pastoral the Bluehill church which would ordain him nine months after the incident.[1]

Local Maine historian Rufus Candage, born in 1826 and raised in Bluehill, reflected upon those tumultuous times in his *Settlement and Progress of the Town of Bluehill, Maine*. Candage expressed gratitude for the moderation and forbearance that characterized the community and its leaders through those years in the following,

> These are said to have been days of great trial to Mr. Fisher, as nearly all of the seceding members had been converted and brought into the church under his preaching. These were days when denominational feeling was unyielding and rancorous; but it is said, to the honor of Mr. Fisher, that he was not known to express an unkind word against, or

---

[1] See Richard Carter, "Mind and Ministry of Jonathan Fisher," 90–91.

reflection upon, any Christian brother for the course he had taken; and he was known to pray fervently and devoutly for the blessing of God on the new church which had sprung from among his own people.[2]

Candage's claims are consistent with those of others who knew him well. Reflecting on Fisher's example, he made the following conclusion about the pastor's conduct,

> Let us all rejoice that at this day, Christians, though differing in forms of church government, yet holding to the essential points of the Gospel, may live together in the same community in Christian charity and love, and respect each other as brethren.[3]

Missionary Endeavors

A rotating missionary circuit was established by Congregationalists at Belfast in July, 1791.[4] Fisher and Daniel Merrill served on the circuit, walking extensive distances, personally evangelizing a rustic and at times, hostile populace. In *A History of Education in Maine*, Henry Chadbourne described the region during the National Period:

> The province had frequently been an asylum for those people who had been excommunicated. Since the early settlers had immigrated here merely for the purposes of gain, they did not value their privileges as highly as the people of Massachusetts. The opinion generally prevailed that Maine was peopled by those who were too immoral and irreligious to be allowed to remain in other colonies and it used to be

---

[2] R.G.F. Candage, *Settlement and Progress of the Town of Bluehill, Maine. An Historical Address* (Boston: T.R. Marvin & Son, 1886), 30.

[3] Candage, *Settlement and Progress of the Town of Bluehill, Maine*, 30.

[4] Fisher, "Records," 10 July 1797.

tauntingly said, "When a man can find no religion to his taste let him remove to Maine."[5]

Fisher records engaging in a conversation with a certain Mr. Godfrey, a young Deist at Gouldsboro Point, who after debating the parson, challenged him to a draw. Fisher wisely deescalated the situation. On balance, from the same area came pleas for a pastor to preach spiritually-hungry audiences. Henry Burrage cites a local pastor, who recollected a scene similar to St. Patrick's vision of the Irish: "My poor heart yearns when I think of them, and think of their language to me: 'Do not forget us; do come to us again, and if you cannot come, you must try and send some minister to preach to us.'"[6]

As noted earlier, the Hancock Association of ministers supported Baptist missionaries prior to Daniel Merrill's becoming a Baptist himself, yet his insistence on Closed Communion created invariable tension, consequently prompting his resignation in August, 1805. Merrill proceeded to found the Lincoln Baptist Association in 1808. In *The Kingdom of Heaven Distinguished From Babylon*, the association's sermonic manifesto, Merrill condemned the exchanging of pulpits with paedobaptists as "a manifest evil" in his seventh point.[7] To his audience he posed the following question,

Now my brethren, when we exchange pulpits, do we not publicly and directly contradict the word of the Lord, transmitted by Moses? Do we not, by such practice form a

---

[5] *A History of Education in Maine* (Orono, ME: University Press, 1936), 13.

[6] Henry S. Burrage, *History of the Baptists in Maine* (Portland: Marks Printing House, 1904), 13, 111–12, 122.

[7] Daniel Merrill, *The Kingdom of Heaven Distinguished From Babylon; A Sermon Delivered At the Introduction Of The Lincoln Association, Sept. 21–22, 1808* (Buckstown: Press of William W. Clapp, 1810). This judgment was Merrill's seventh point in the sermon. See also Carter, "Mind and Ministry of Jonathan Fisher," 236.

confederacy with mystic Babylon, with her, who spiritually, is called Sodom and Egypt, where also our Lord was crucified?

Since the Reformation, mystic Babylon functioned as an ecclesial foil, possessing rhetorical poignancy for Protestant audiences. Whether the mature Merrill failed to live up to his earlier principles or simply moderated his position, his initial hesitancy to cooperate with Congregationalists was not without reason. A denominational minority for over a century, Baptists grew rapidly in the wake of the first Great Awakening. In 1740, for example, there were only twenty-five Baptist churches in all New England. By 1790, there were 266.[8] Congregationalist pastor Noah Worcester, puzzled by the explosive growth among Baptists penned, *Impartial Inquiries concerning the progress of the Baptist Denomination* in 1794. Worcester's jaundiced assessment focused on the pathos of Baptist preachers as compensating for a lack of education.

> To them the want of knowledge in a teacher ... may easily be made up and overbalanced by great zeal, and affecting tone of voice, and a perpetual motion of the tongue. If a speaker can keep his tongue running ... and can quote memoriter a large number of texts from ... the Bible, it matters not to many of his hearers whether he speaks sense or nonsense.[9]

Prejudiced as Worcester's sentiment was, most Congregational ministers during the period shared his views. The ignorant Baptist preacher was a cultural trope that many found irresistible. As the late historian Winthrop Hudson noted, however, Baptists as a whole did in fact, value education. Investment in academic institutions such as Brown, Andover, and Colby demonstrate

---

[8] Ahlstrom, *A Religious History of the American People*, 375.
[9] Cited in Hudson, *Religion in America*, 122.

Baptist concern for a learned ministry.[10] Numeric increase combined with congregational autonomy did make enforcement of academic standards difficult, yet learned Baptists were not unknown.[11] In addition to the Dartmouth-educated Merrill, Abraham Cummings, a Baptist educated at Brown, served as a member of the Hancock Association.

Cooperation and Communion:
Merrill and the Baptists of Bluehill

As discussed in chapter three, Daniel Merrill's developed ecclesiology grounded his conviction that Baptists could not in good conscience join with Congregationalists in receiving the Lord's Supper, nor permit a pedobaptist to preach in a credobaptist church. God's Kingdom, which Merrill viewed as manifested in the true Church of Christ, could have no "confederacy" with the "confused church." Jonathan Fisher by contrast, never deviated from his desire to partner with ministers and associations in preaching, moral improvement, and the formation of schools for general and theological education. Any church that accepted a hand in fellowship for the purpose of furthering the gospel he considered an ally. In this respect, Fisher resembled Richard Baxter who famously wrote:

> My religion is merely Christian... The rule of my faith and doctrine is ye law of God in Nature and Scripture. The Church which I am a member of is the Universality of Christians, in conjunction with all particular Churches of Christians in England or elsewhere in the world, whose Communion according to my capacity I desire..."[12]

---

[10] Granted, in 1805, there were only three Baptist pastors with a college degree. See Burrage, *History of the Baptists in Maine*, 40, 103.

[11] Hudson, *Religion in America*, 122.

[12] Frederick J. Powicke, *The Reverend Richard Baxter Under the Cross (1662-1691)* (London: Jonathan Cape Ltd., 1927), 72. Baxter's sentiment inspired the title for C.S. Lewis' apologetic work *Mere Christianity*

Merrill, however, remained unequivocal in his public pro-
nouncements on the matter. How those convictions developed
and their effects on his public and private life, his ministry, as well
as among those he most directly influenced, requires further research.[13] There are glimpses of Merrill's interactions with his
Congregationalist neighbors and friends in Sedgwick, Bluehill,
and the surrounding communities that provide the particulars of
cooperation. Of noteworthy interest is an early account of Merrill's former student, Rev. David Thurston. Like most Standing
Order ministers at the time, Merrill was not only a pastor, but a
public-school teacher as well. A collection of anecdotes by The
Brooksville Historical Society recounts,

Before enough schoolhouses were built, schools were held
in some homes where there was an extra room. The teacher
might be a learned man, like the preacher, Daniel Merrill
and Rev. Manning Ellis, both of whom taught several
terms."[14]

---

[13] See, for example, Merrill's remarks in 1825 to Phineas Bond and fellow ministers in *A Sermon Preached at the Ordination of Rev. PHINEAS BOND,* 27: "The present
period appears a new era in the Christian history; the opponents of the distinguishing
characteristics of the Church of Christ, or the kingdom of God on earth, are sounding
a truce, proposing a cessation of arms; and most of the Lord's host manifestly inclined
for the ease and quiet of winter quarters ... to such as continue their faithful testimony,
and are valiant for the truth, there is no peace on earth; their peace is in heaven ... The
victory will soon be yours." This sentiment appears at the close of the sermon, which
can be characterized primarily as a thorough presentation of the gospel, emphasizing
God's "free and sovereign grace" in the life and ministry of the apostle Paul, running
to 28 pages. Merrill characteristically affirms the distinctives of his "Baptist platform"
and caricatures the educated elites who oppose the Kingdom of God at points in the
sermon, but with comparably less piquancy than in his earlier works. The "Watery
War" is no longer front and center, but the "doctrine of free grace, or salvation by
Christ crucified." Merrill speaks of "good men" among "the confused church," who
minister "avowedly, from the best of motives, to prevail upon the world to embrace
the gospel."

[14] *Traditions and Records of Brooksville, Maine, collected by The Brooksville Historical
Society 1935-36* (Auburn: Merrill & Webber Company, undated), 66.

Thurston moved to Sedgwick as a boy and took up studies under Merrill, but "Mr. Merrill set him to parsing, and this 'brought him up very short.'" He soon abandoned his Latin in order to work on the farm.[15] Thurston experienced an evangelical conversion at the age of twenty, was admitted to the Church of Christ in Sedgwick, and went on to Dartmouth to train for Congregational ministry. While on a preaching tour through Hancock County years later, he recorded this illuminating interaction with Merrill, now a Baptist:

> Wednesday, Jan. 1, 1806, brother and I went to father's at Sedgwick. I had not visited my father's family before since September, 1803. A great change had taken place in the

---

[15] Rev. David Thurston recorded in *1635–1880 Thurston Genealogies Compiled by Brown Thurston, Portland, Maine* (Portland: Brown Thurston and Hoyt, Fogg and Donham, 1880), 92. As noted earlier, Merrill was regarded as an eloquent, careful, well-read, and convincing preacher. It seems that language and its use was a priority for Merrill, the teacher, and he could be a stickler with his students on the subject—particularly those training for the ministry. References to Ebenezer Eaton, a ministerial candidate, in the minutes of the Hancock Association support this notion. On September 18, 1797, "Voted; that Mr. Eaton be required for the present to spend three days in the week, namely from Tuesday morning till Thursday night, with Mr. Merrill in the study of the English language, Friday and Saturday being allowed him to prepare for preaching." On May 2, 1799, the Association was concerned about Mr. Eaton's lack of progress: "It is the opinion of the brethren that the cause of religion requires that Mr. E. Eaton, a licensed preacher, not having had the privilege of a public education, shoud [*sic*] spend as much time as possible in the study of English grammar, and reading, as well as for his public discourse, and it is recommended, and enjoined by the Association that he spend, aside from his secular concerns, at least four days every week in attention to grammar, reading, and study." One year later, we read: "Urged upon Mr. Eaton the importance of attending to the rudiments of knowledge." *Records of the Hancock Association.* Isaac Case wrote that Eaton was "a man of little lerning but of Greate piety" who nearly had to "forfit his credenchals to preach," because of the lack of progress in his studies. Ronald Baines *Separating God's Two Kingdoms*, 91. Ebenezer Eaton heeded their urging and went on to become the pastor of the Congregational Church in the Town of Mount Desert: "In October 1801 the town of Mount Desert voted to give Brother Ebenezer Eaton from Sedgwick $250 per year to serve as minister... Even though Ebenezer was mostly self-educated in the Bible and thus considered himself ineligible to be ordained, he 'yielded to the wishes of his people and consented to be ordained in 1823.' He served the church for 35 years until 1836." *History of Southwest Harbor Congregational Church*, https://www.swhcc.com/history-of-swhcc (Accessed April 22, 2022).

minister, Rev. Daniel Merrill, and in the church of which I was a member. The pastor had been immersed and re-ordained by a council of close communion Baptists, and a large majority of the church had gone with him. Nor is it owing to any want of earnest, persevering labors on his part that I am not a Baptist. He deemed it inconsistent to ask me to preach, but he came and heard me preach at several lectures ... I preached about a dozen times in different neighborhoods.[16]

Though Merrill sought to convert Thurston to Baptist views, and did not allow him to share the Sedgwick pulpit, he did nevertheless, listen respectfully to the younger man's teaching in meetings throughout the area. The "Gospel Ranger" had wider objectives that required a reasonable degree of latitude and decorum. Merrill fulfilled important roles in public evangelical, educational, and political enterprises that required cooperation.[17] For some endeavors, he depended on the financial support, not only from pedobaptists, but other sectarian and secular individuals, and their respective associations. It is in the lives of Merrill's contemporaries and associates that the uncompromising rhetoric of *The Kingdom of Heaven Distinguished from Babylon* proved not to be the modus operandi for every Maine Baptist. Three figures, James Gilpatrick, George Stevens, and Thomas Lord give a fuller and more comprehensive understanding of denominational relations during the early to mid-nineteenth century in Hancock County.

---

[16] Thurston, *Thurston Genealogies*, 97. David Thurston went on to become an enthusiastic supporter of the *Bangor Theological Seminary*.

[17] "A Father of a rural county had to perform a delicate balancing act in mediating between his common neighbors and the political elite gathered at the state and national capitols. His standing depended upon a mix of local popularity, expressed at polling places, and social acceptance by the state-wide brotherhood of gentlemen, manifested in the private circles of elites." Taylor, "From Fathers to Friends of the People," 480–481.

James Gilpatrick

Annie L. Clough observed that "Rev. Merrill's influence was widespread in this part of Maine. Following his re-ordination, twenty-eight members of the First Congregational Church of Blue Hill withdrew, dissatisfied with the ordinance of baptism..." They proceeded to join themselves to the Baptist Church in Sedgwick.[18] Some returned years later to rejoin their neighbors in the newly established Baptist Society, formed in Bluehill on February 13, 1806.[19] The Society began under the oversight of Elder Amos Allen and Elder John Roundy, son of Bluehill founder John Roundy, and continued with others until the longest serving pastor, James Gilpatrick, assumed leadership.

Reverend James Gilpatrick, a graduate of the Waterville Theological Institute, was installed in 1828 as the church's first settled minister and served the Bluehill Baptist Church until he was released to pastor the Baptist Church in Topsham Maine in 1845, leaving in 1846.[20] Pastor Rinaldo Olds followed Gilpatrick into the pulpit at Bluehill years later in 1889 and described him as "a strong man, both physically and mentally. He could hold a 'breaking-up plow' for a six-ox team or drive his spiritual plow-share through the fallow ground of his people's hearts, or fight border ruffians in Kansas,"[21] where Gilpatrick moved his family to establish a free state in the 1850s. He later returned and lived out his remaining years in Bluehill. "Elder Gilpatrick, as my Father told me," wrote historian Esther Wood, "was more interested in

---

[18] Annie L. Clough, *Head of the Bay: Sketches and Pictures of Blue Hill, Maine, 1762–1952* (Woodstock: Elm Tree Press, 1953), 14–15.

[19] R.G.F. Candage, *Settlement and Progress of the Town of Bluehill, Maine. An Historical Address* (Boston: T.R. Marvin & Son, 1886), 32.

[20] Joshua Millet, *A History of the Baptists in Maine; Together with Brief Notices of Societies and Institutions* (Portland: Charles Day & Co., 1845), 444. His surname was erroneously spelled "Gillpatrick" in some published works.

[21] R.L. Olds, *The History of the First Baptist Church in Bluehill*, 4. Typescript copy of the manuscript for a presentation at the centennial celebration of the First Baptist Church. First Baptist Church of Blue Hill in Maine, archives.

reform than shipping. He was an advocate of temperance, missions, and the anti-slavery movement and he was a man of positive opinions."[22]

Merrill preached Gilpatrick's installation sermon at Bluehill, and Gilpatrick preached Merrill's funeral sermon at Sedgwick in 1833. At the time of Gilpatrick's arrival, the two congregations and the lives of their respective pastors were tightly interwoven. As noted in Chapter 2, Daniel Merrill was assisted in the ministry at Sedgwick by Ebenezer Pinkham and Ebenezer Mirick until his death. A selection from *The American Baptist Magazine* from the year 1829 reads, "May 20, Mr Ebenezer Mirick was ordained as an evangelist, at Sedgwick. Sermon by Rev. James Gilpatrick."[23] In January of 1831, Daniel Merrill and James Gilpatrick traveled to North Yarmouth Maine and were appointed to an Examining Committee representing the Maine Branch of the Northern Baptist Education Society with the purpose of "ministerial education."[24]

Gilpatrick and Merrill served together with Daniel Faulkner, representing the Eastern Maine Association of the American Bible Society, alongside societies from other denominations—

---

[22] Esther E. Wood, *Sketch of the Blue Hill Baptist Church*, 2.

[23] *The American Baptist Magazine*, Vol. IX (Boston: Lincoln & Edmands, 1829), 359.

[24] *The American Baptist Magazine*, Vol. XI (Boston: Lincoln & Edmands, 1831), 18. Merrill served as President of the Maine Baptist Convention that year and the two following years at Bloomfield and Warren, before his death in 1833. In 1832, Merrill was the primary preacher at the Maine Baptist Convention and Gilpatrick preached the sermon the following year. After Merrill's death, Gilpatrick would become a prominent figure in Maine's abolitionist movement. "The Maine Baptist Anti-Slavery Convention was held in Topsham Jan. 19 and 20, 1841. Rev. J. Gilpatrick was elected president... An address to the Baptists of Maine was adopted; also an address to the Baptist churches in the South. Of the two hundred and fourteen Baptist ministers in the State, one hundred and eighty, it was claimed, were decided abolitionists. Resolutions were adopted, and delegates to the Maine Anti- Slavery Society and to the Baptist National Anti-Slavery Convention were appointed. The secretary, in his report of the Convention, said ' 'this was the most important and best anti-slavery meeting ever held by the denomination in the State." Henry S. Burrage, *History of the Baptists In Maine*, 313.

predictably, Merrill was the President.[25] Gilpatrick also served as a Trustee of Colby College between 1834 and 1851, following in Daniel Merrill's footsteps and working alongside his son, Daniel Merrill Jr., a trustee from 1842 to 1855.[26] On July 19, 1832 Elder Gilpatrick presided over the ordination of Moses Merrill, charged and prayed over the aspiring young missionary and, after Merrill's death, remained involved in Baptist endeavors with both Thomas and Moses, corresponding and sending boxes of clothing in support.[27] These records reveal that Merrill, his sons, and Gilpatrick worked closely together, often under the influence and direction of Daniel Merrill. Yet, there is no indication that Merrill exerted pressure on other Baptist leaders to follow his convictions concerning Closed Communion, nor did others exhibit reservations about aligning themselves with Merrill for Baptist causes.[28] In a

---

[25] *Sixteenth Annual Report of the American Bible Society* (New York: Daniel Fanshaw, 1832), 113. Merrill was the society's president and Gilpatrick the secretary. In an ordination sermon preached in 1825, Merrill urged his audience to "let everyone that is willing-hearted be at the work; *strengthening the things that are ready to die;* and as a pioneer be preparing the way of the Lord, by aiding in the translating; printing and circulating of *the scriptures of truth, without note or comment* in all languages, among every nation and people of the earth." The exhortation comes within the context of his criticism of "some unhallowed confederacy" and "union," inferring that the translation and distribution of the Bible, undertaken with members of "the confused church," was an appropriate partnership in heralding the return of Christ. Daniel Merrill, *A Sermon Preached at the Ordination of Rev. PHINEAS BOND, 19.*

[26] Ernest Cummings Marinner, *The History of Colby College* (Waterville: Colby College Press, 1963), 635.

[27] *A Record book belonging to the Church of Christ in Sedgwick,* 230. James Gilpatrick, *Transcript of Letter Sent to Moses Merrill from James Gilpatrick dated January 25, 1825.* Acadia Archives Acadia University. https://archives.acadiau.ca/islandora/object/research%3A4547?search=Merrill (accessed October 16, 2022). Gilpatrick sent a box of clothing, which never arrived at the mission station, and the letter indicates that he had been corresponding regularly since Merrill's departure from Sedgwick. He writes, "Dear Brother Merrill, I know you have felt neglected by me since I have so long neglected to write. But I certainly have intended no such thing. You know it. I have often thought of you ... Mrs. Gill-patrick [*sic*] is about to write to Mrs. [Moses] Merrill I believe. Tender my regards to Mrs. Merrill."

[28] Merrill's maxim was, as referenced earlier, "it has been somewhat settled in my judgment, and I hope in my heart, too, that the better and safer way is to agree with men, so far as they agree with God, and there stop. I say to my Brethren, as Azariah said to Asa, and to all Judah and Benjamin. 2 Chron. 15.2." Daniel Merrill, *Letter to*

letter to Moses Merrill in 1835, Gilpatrick freely reported "we have had a revival in this place this winter, tho' mostly with the Congregationalists. It began in a protracted meeting held by that church. Eight or ten in our society have obtained hope."[29]

Granted, interaction between Baptists and Congregationalists, as well as other sects differed by context. Merrill chose an intimate communion of fellow Baptists in Sedgwick. Gilpatrick by contrast, engaged in a number of cooperative efforts with Fisher and the Congregational community. James Gilpatrick, George Stevens, and other Bluehill Baptists partnered with Congregationalists in church discipline, prayer for revival, pastoral care of the sick and dying, social welfare, temperance, and education.[30] Perhaps Merrill's mature outlook on how Closed Communion should be expressed in a specific context was influenced by the fact that the Baptist Church in Sedgwick was essentially the only church in town during the latter years of his life. Many of the Bluehill Baptists, on the other hand, had once been members of the Congregational Church, which effectively split when the Baptist Society formed there. The religious community in Bluehill, which included more than a few Methodists, was not as homogeneous as that of Sedgwick. Gilpatrick's ministry at Bluehill and Merrill's final years in Sedgwick, the period when their ministries overlapped and the two pastors partnered in important endeavors. Both were free to work out Baptist distinctives in ways they

---

Edward Manning. The passage reads "And he went out to meet Asa, and said unto him, Hear ye me, Asa, and all Judah and Benjamin; The LORD is with you, while ye be with him; and if ye seek him, he will be found of you; but if ye forsake him, he will forsake you" (2 Chronicles 15:2 KJV).

[29] James Gilpatrick, Transcript of Letter Sent to Moses Merrill from James Gilpatrick dated January 25, 1825.

[30] Brittany P. Cathey notes that, in the founding of Sunday schools in Maine, Jonathan Fisher "spent time with his neighbors Faulkner and Gilpatrick on July 11, 1832 to select suitable books." See "Reverend Jonathan Fisher: One Thread in the Web of Early American Education, 1780–1830" (Unpublished MA thesis. University of Maine. Orono, ME, 2015), 53.

determined best suited to the spiritual health and vitality of their respective congregations. We can conclude that Merrill regarded the Baptist principal of local Church independence as a primary, and not a secondary, principle in the "Baptist platform," along with Closed Communion, and he was able to hold both values in tension. In this matter of local autonomy Merrill, like Fisher, did not depart from their shared Congregational tradition and, perhaps, helped them to empathize with one another through the difficult years.

Rev. Gilpatrick remembered Daniel Merrill as a man who was, "honest, affable, and kind" in his personal dealings. He wrote, "As a Christian, he was sincere, devout, consistent and persevering. He was the same at home and abroad; in his family and in the church; yes, we believe in his closet, and in the world."[31] At the same time, Merrill was direct and, "definite in his preaching. He always had some object in view. To instruct, or to convict his hearers was his object, and to accomplish this he was always plain ... perspicuity was always in his sermons ... his language was simple, but *strong.*"[32] His preaching could also be affectionate. Gilpatrick explained, "Although plain, and pointed, and faithful, he was not harsh and unfeeling. Far from it. A tender compassion for souls characterized his preaching ... he often wept freely."[33] When taken together, the portrait is of a plain-dealing public figure, one who, though he could be perceived as controlling or domineering, was described as personally warm, understanding, and empathetic by those who knew him best.

Reflecting upon Merrill in 1859, nearly thirty years after his first *Biographical Sketch* of the man, Gilpatrick provided greater insight into both his public persona and private practice in a

---

[31] Gilpatrick, "Biographical Sketch of the Rev. Daniel Merrill," 312.

[32] Gilpatrick, "Biographical Sketch of the Rev. Daniel Merrill," 312.

[33] Gilpatrick, "Biographical Sketch of the Rev. Daniel Merrill," 313.

memorial published in *The Annals of the American Pulpit.* He writes, "My personal acquaintance with the Rev. Daniel Merrill was for only a few of the last years of his life ... a period of between four and five years, my intercourse with him was quite frequent, and always agreeable." Gilpatrick refers to him affectionately as "Father Merrill" and adds that, in his final years, he was no longer the physically vigorous and energetic Gospel Ranger, but "inclined to be corpulent," indicating he may have been experiencing the late stages of heart failure. Nevertheless, "he stood very firm and erect," was grave in his countenance, "but mild and pleasant." Gilpatrick continued,

> His manners were bland [pleasantly gentle or agreeable], and his whole appearance gentlemanly. Though he had great firmness and courage, he was remarkable for self-control, seldom, if ever, discovering the least irritation or haste of temper. He possessed a naturally vigorous intellect... As a Christian, he was devout, consistent and perseveringly active. He had great uniformity of character—at home and abroad, in the family, the social circle, the Church, and the world, he always evinced the same high regard to the principles and precepts of the Gospel.[34]

Considering James Gilpatrick's characterization of Merrill in his *Biographical Sketch* and the *American Pulpit*, as well as their close interactions up until Merrill's death, it is reasonable to conclude that the two men shared the same strong Calvinistic Baptist convictions,[35] while taking different paths in cooperation with

---

[34] James Gillpatrick [*sic*], "Daniel Merrill," *The Annals of the American Pulpit*, 510

[35] Gilpatrick explains, "Not only was he successful in the conversion of souls, but in confirming them in the faith—in building up the church of Christ. And particularly in clearing away the unscriptural notions of *infant baptism*... and in supporting the doctrine of believers' baptism..." "Biographical Sketch of the Rev. Daniel Merrill," from the funeral sermon he preached upon the death of Merrill, *The Baptist Memorial and Monthly Record* 4 (New York: John R. Bigelow, 1845), 313.

other evangelicals. Although Merrill was assertive and narrow in his expressions against cooperation among his fellow Baptists, he evidently gave priority to congregational independence. His tolerance toward Baptists such as James Gilpatrick, Adam Wilson, and others may explain, in part, why Merrill the churchman accomplished so much, both within and without the Sedgwick church's walls. James Gilpatrick is not an isolated case of a fellow Baptist within Merrill's circle who exhibited denominational latitude.

George Stevens

George Stevens was a contemporary and life-long friend of Jonathan Fisher, even after Stevens' defection from the Congregational Church to join the Baptist Church in Bluehill. Stevens provided Fisher with his horse on occasion for his missionary journeys, as well as carpentry and building tools for the parson's many projects on the farm. In his diary, Jonathan Fisher memorialized Stevens' conversion: "March 14, 1803: Mr. George Stevens spent part of the day with us, professing to have obtained a hope in Christ."[36]

Most of what is known about Stevens has come down through local lore,[37] his will and estate documents,[38] and by way of his lasting educational legacy, the *George Stevens Academy* in Bluehill, Maine, located in the village at the Head of the Bay.[39]

---

[36] Fisher, *The Diaries of Jonathan Fisher*, 149.

[36] Fisher, *The Diaries of Jonathan Fisher*, 149. Fisher's intercourse with the Stevens spanned several decades, from the turn of the century onward. For example, a January 28, 1806 entry records: "Evening Mr. George Stevens and wife made us a visit" (196). An entry 21-years later: November 6, 1827: "Spent the evening at Mr. George Stevens', making arrangements for collecting money from S.S. [Sabbath School] subscribers who have not paid," (802).

[37] Esther Wood, "George Stevens, Village Squire," in *Deep Roots: A Maine Legacy*, (Camden: Yankee Books, 1990).

[38] George Stevens, "George Stevens' Will" (1851). Blue Hill Documents, 32. https://digitalmaine.com/blue_hill_documents/32.

[39] Esther Wood, *A History of George Stevens Academy*, 5. www.georgestevensacademy.org/Page/5 (accessed March 19, 2022).

In 1898, a new Academy building was constructed on the George Stevens property on Union Street. Mr. Stevens, who died May 1, 1852, had served for many years as an Academy trustee. A highly successful businessman and a devout Baptist, his opinions were often at variance with those of the predominantly Congregational Academy board. His will left the major part of his estate, including his homestead and home lot, in care of a self-perpetuating body of five trustees—to be used for the establishment of an academy when such a step seemed advisable.[40]

Stevens was a shipbuilder and mill owner. He owned vast tracts of woodlands and was the town's leading businessmen, engaging others in a variety of ventures. Early in the 19th century he built a cotton mill in Bluehill that ginned Southern cotton, as well as a carding and fulling mill, and an additional sawmill at the mouth of the Mill Stream.[41] In Fisher's painting, "Morning View of Blue Hill," Stevens' shipyard is seen in the distance with two ships under construction, and another approaching under full sail from the east. Stevens also served as an officer of the Social Library of Blue Hill, after the dissolution of the Hancock Library in Sedgwick, where Daniel Merrill served as president.[42] The holdings of the Hancock Library were divided between the two towns. Thus, a new library was created.

In becoming a Baptist, Stevens worked closely with Daniel Merrill and James Gilpatrick.[43] Minutes from the Eastern Maine Association, which met on October 3 and 4, 1821 in Surry, record Merrill proposing that,

---

[40] Clough, *Head of the* Bay, 14–15.

[41] Clough, *Head of the* Bay, 8.

[42] Clough, *Head of the* Bay, 21.

[43] James Gilpatrick's first wife died in Kansas and, after returning to Bluehill, Gilpatrick married the second wife and widow of George Stevens, Mary. A monument stands in the Seaside Cemetery in Bluehill over the graves of Stevens, his first wife Dorcas, Mary (Stevens) Gilpatrick, and James Gilpatrick, with the erroneous spelling Gillpatrick.

a missionary who has a clear apprehension of the gospel of Christ and of the things of his kingdom, together with sound judgment, a warm heart and good education, should be employed for one year to traverse the above route, keeping the most northerly, passable road, tracing the inlets into the wilderness where small settlements are commenced, and where the gospel may seldom or never have been preached; pursuing this route till he shall arrive at the borders of the Michigan territory, then, and afterwards, conform to circumstances, observing, as nearly as the good of the cause will justify, the instructions he may receive.' The association approved the proposed measure, "provided there be a probability of bringing it into operation."

A committee was established which, in addition to Merrill and three others, included George Stevens.[44] Though not a minister himself, Stevens' wealth would be crucial to the long-term stability of Baptist and Congregationalist institutions in Maine.[45]

Stevens had no children but brought up a nephew and one foster son, who later drowned while a student at Colby College. The college in Waterville was also the beneficiary of his philanthropic endeavors.[46] Esther Wood opines that "perhaps the squire [Stevens], a Baptist, resented the Congregational dominance of the board of trustees," yet this did not cause him to withdraw a

---

[44] The other three men were the Rev. Amos Allen, Rev. Enoch Hunting, and Richard Allen. The town of Surry, where the association met in 1821, neighbors Bluehill and was at that time another shipbuilding community. One of Stevens' most innovative and successful protégés, Thomas Lord, hailed from Surry and went on to design and build, not only ships, but the Congregational Church in Bluehill, the Sedgwick Baptist Church, and others in the area. Thomas Lord also performed a major renovation of the Bluehill Baptist Church. Like Stevens, Lord was a member of the Bluehill Baptist Society. Henry S. Burrage, *History of the Baptists in Maine*, 156–157.

[45] Stevens was, most likely, sent as a "messenger" by the Bluehill Baptist Society to the Surry meeting. Associations received "messengers" appointed by member churches, including both clergy and laypersons. *The Second London* Confession, adopted 1689, Chapter XXVI, 15.

[46] Esther Wood, "George Stevens, Village Squire," in *Deep Roots: A Maine Legacy*, (Camden: Yankee Books, 1990), 160.

handsome benefice that included his "mansion house," mills, money and wild lands—all to the institution.[47] Though a committed Baptist to his death, Stevens bequeathed his estate to the Congregationalist-led Bluehill academy. Jonathan Fisher gave the "dedicatory address" and became the President of the Board of Trustees. George Stevens was the first non-Congregationalist trustee to join the board. Wood describes conflict that arose from Stevens' directive that precluded denominational favoritism,

> In 1832 he offered on his decease and that of his wife to give a thousand dollars and a piece of land to the Academy. His offer included this provision, "The institution shall be put on a liberal scale that all denominations shall have equal rights and privileges." The Academy trustees said, "no." ... Squire Stevens was not to be defeated. In his will of 1851 he provided that after his death and that of his wife his homestead, one hundred and fifty acres of land and a large portion of his personal property should be used to establish an academy. The will specified, "said Academy shall be located on the one half acre northwest of my dwelling house." The Squire chose the first board of trustees, a self-perpetuating board.[48]

---

[47] Wood "George Stevens, Village Squire," in *Deep Roots*, 160. Wood comments that only years after Stevens' death did his academy merge with the old Blue Hill Academy.

[48] Wood *A History of George Stevens Academy*, 5. For the earliest records of the Blue Hill Academy-George Stevens Academy, see Bluehill Academy, "GSA Course of Study, 1831" (1831). Blue Hill Documents, 33. https://digitalmaine.com/blue_hill_documents/33. See also Brittany P. Cathey, "Reverend Jonathan Fisher." Some rural Maine private schools and academies continue to be publicly funded through town property taxes and grants. The United States Supreme Court handed down a ruling in the 2022 case of *Carson v. Makin*, which would likely please Baptists George Stevens, Daniel Merrill, and other sectarian leaders of their day. From the Maine Department of Education: "What does the recent Supreme Court decision mean? In Carson v. Makin, the Supreme Court held that Maine could not exclude sectarian schools from approval for the receipt of public funds for tuition purposes because they are sectarian. In other words, a sectarian school that meets all of the other requirements for approval for the receipt of public funds for tuition

George Stevens likewise demonstrated his commitment to Baptist higher education, bequeathing one-thousand dollars to the "said trustees with interest from and after my decease." To the First Baptist Society in Bluehill he gave,

> all the woodland lying on the eastern side of the road leading from Bluehill to Surry, being about seven hundred acres, for the support of preaching in the said Baptist Society, and it is my desire and wish that the said Society shall by their committee sell said land as soon as may be and invest the proceeds in bank or railroad or other stock and appropriate the income and that only annually for the support of a Calvinistic Baptist Minister, and for no other purpose whatever, also two and a half acres of land adjoining the Parsonage to be added to said Parsonage; to have and to hold the same to said Society and their assigns forever."[49]

Stevens' theological specificity, stipulating that the proceeds of his estate pay the salary of "a Calvinistic Baptist Minister," shows that his cooperation with Congregationalists did not entail relinquishing commitments about ecclesiology and soteriology. Stevens' will stipulated, moreover that, "all the rest, residue and remainder of my estate real, personal and mixed of which I shall die seized and possess...to be disposed of in the best manner.... at a proper time applied to the establishment and support of a Theological Seminary under the direction and control of the Baptist Denomination."[50] This item was later revoked and funds

---

purposes must be approved in the same manner as a non-sectarian school." www.maine.gov/doe/carsonvmakin (accessed August 13, 2022).

[49] George Stevens, "George Stevens' Will" (1851). Blue Hill Documents, 32. The parsonage, which still stands, was built years earlier according to Pastor Rinaldo Olds: "a house was begun in 1831... it may not be possible to ascertain its cost, for material and labor were both largely contributed, and Mr. Gilpatrick did much of the work on the place and the house with his own hands. It was a neat little place and a good home for the minister for many years." Olds, *The History of First Baptist Church in Bluehill*, 10.

[50] George Stevens, "George Stevens' Will" (1851), 4.

redirected to the creation and support of what was destined to become the Blue Hill-George Stevens Academy.[51]

Thomas Lord

Thomas Lord of Surry, son of Baptist Rev. Benjamin Lord, came to Bluehill as an apprentice carpenter at the shipyard of George Stevens when he was 15 years old. Though he had little education and his journals show him to be a poor writer with the penmanship of a child, he was a creative and productive builder, "who could turn his hand to anything from a church to a coffin."[52] Esther Wood comments,

> Two months before he died in 1880, he summed up his life thus: "Have worked on 83 vessels, more or less, built 84 dwelling houses, 12 school houses, 14 meeting houses, 15 barns and sheds, and other public buildings, 10 stern mouldings and heads and blinds and other works."[53]

He shared the same native talent for design, aesthetics, and craftsmanship with Father Fisher. And, like the parson, he also kept careful records and papers, which reside now at Colby College. Lord, like his employer George Stevens, was a confirmed, generous Baptist who "went to meeting every Sunday."[54] Lord lived in Bluehill and was a contemporary of both Fisher and Daniel Merrill.[55] Though a committed Baptist, there are indications that

---

[51] George Stevens, "George Stevens' Will" (1851), 6-7.

[52] Samuel L. Green, "Thomas Lord, Joiner and Housewright," *Magazine of Art: A National Magazine Relating the Arts to Contemporary Life* 40.6. ed., John D. Morse (October, 1947): 230.

[53] Esther Wood "George Stevens, Village Squire," *Deep Roots: A Maine Legacy*, (Camden: Yankee Books, 1990), 164.

[54] Samuel L. Green, "Thomas Lord, Joiner and Housewright," 231.

[55] Lord mentions going "to Merrill, Deer Isle shingling, planing desks and blinds." There is a town of Merrill in Maine, 145 miles away, and there were Merrills living in Bluehill, but the natural reading would suggest that he went to see Daniel Merrill on his way to Deer Isle. Fisher's journal records similar anecdotes when he writes about

he joined the Congregational Church in Bluehill toward the end of his life.

Lord built the First Baptist Church of Sedgwick, moving the congregation down the hill toward the shore from the old Meeting House. In September 19, 1836, Moses Dodge deeded a lot to the Baptists located at the center of the village, on a small hill overlooking the harbor. The town chose Col. Benjamin S. Deane of Thomaston to design a building large enough to accommodate the growing congregation and Thomas Lord was selected to build the house of worship. Commenting on a restoration effort in 2010, Emily Burnham wrote in *The Bangor Daily News* that, "The church, built in 1837, is the finest example of Greek Revival architecture in the state, according to Earle Shettleworth, director of the Maine Historic Preservation Commission."[56]

Thomas Lord shared his talents with the community and after the Congregational Meeting House in Bluehill burned in 1842, he built the new church for Rev. Jotham Sewall and the congregation Fisher had shepherded for forty years.[57] Rufus Candage was a boy at the time and remembered the occasion of its dedication when Baptists joined the Congregational Church in opening the doors to the beautiful Greek Revival edifice:

> THE CONGREGATIONAL CHURCH, built in 1842-3, and dedicated Jan. 11, 1843, stands next to the Asa Clough house... The writer was present at its dedication and sat in his father's pew, No. 9. ... The invocation and scripture readings were by Rev. James Gilpatrick, pastor of the

---

his local treks in the form of an itinerary or travel diary. Samuel L. Green, "Thomas Lord, Joiner and Housewright," 232.

[56] Emily Burnham, "Man Leads Effort to Preserve Sedgwick Church," *The Bangor Daily News*, July 19, 2010: https://bangordailynews.com/2010/07/19/living/man-leads-effort-to-preserve-sedgwick-church (Accessed March 29, 2022). "In the Sedgwick Church he [Lord] placed a carving around the painted date '1838.'" Wood, "Thomas Lord, Builder," *Deep Roots*, 167.

[57] Chase, *Maine Parson*, 277.

Baptist church; sermon by Rev. Jotham Sewall, jr., pastor of the church, from Hag. 2, 9th, "The glory of this latter house shall be greater than the former, saith the Lord of Hosts."[58]

The Baptist Church in Bluehill was built in 1850 and remodeled by Lord in 1856. Lord went on to build other Christian meetinghouses,[59] both Baptist and Congregationalist, in Brooklin, Surry, Somesville, South Penobscot, North Sedgwick, Ellsworth (Union River), and, most notably, the West Brooksville Congregational Church, completed in 1855. The Brooksville Church is considered by some to be his most beautiful interpretation and expression of the Greek Revival style. One wonders what assessment Merrill would make of a magnificent neoclassical Congregational house of worship erected by a Baptist architect and builder—was it a visible manifestation of Baptist success in Maine, or an indication that the simplicity of an earlier era had been lost? Perhaps both are true.

Conclusion

Mary Ellen Chase indicates that it took a considerable amount of time for the Baptists to extend the right-hand of fellowship to Father Fisher, their spiritual counselor and friend since the Congregational Church set down roots in Bluehill at its founding. Writing in her characteristic present tense, Chase notes,

---

[58] Candage, *Historical Sketches of Bluehill*, 54.

[59] "[the church] has in each district a chapel well equipped and many loyal and strong supporters of the work. Thus services are maintained in the home church and in four chapels, where the pastor preaches regularly, and Sunday-schools and prayer-meetings are held weekly." "First Baptist Church in Epitome," *One Hundredth Anniversary of the First Baptist Church Sedgwick Maine 1805–1905*, Anniversary Program June 11–18, 1905 (no publication information) https://www.sedgwickmaine.org/sargentville-library-historical-archive/library/REL/REL.4%20%20First%20Baptist%20Church%20of%20Sedgwick%20100th%20Anniversary%201905.pdf (accessed March 29, 2022).

Not until July, 1822, is he asked to preach in the new Baptist meeting house, erected in 1817, and then only upon the occasion of a funeral; but in August, 1817, he writes of uniting with the Baptists at the village schoolhouse in the monthly "concert prayer meeting," apparently the first union service held by the two churches.[60]

Considering Daniel Merrill's steadfast opposition to sharing a pulpit with Congregationalists, such cooperation within two decades of becoming a Baptist, is more significant than Chase seems to suggest. In an 1826 journal entry, Fisher judged a lecture by the Sedgwick Baptist pastor, Elder Pinkham, to be "very good"—an event at which Fisher was asked to give the opening prayer. The same year saw Baptists and Congregationalists in Bluehill "unite in a season of prayer and fasting for the outpouring of the spirit among us all."[61] Prior to retirement in 1837, he had spoken more than once in the pulpit of the Baptist meeting-house.[62] Notwithstanding Merrill's uncompromising position on cooperation, it arguably produced—whether intentionally or not—concrete forms of denominational unity that many evangelical churches within the same communities could not muster today.

---

[60] Chase, *Maine Parson*, 100. Cooperation between Baptists and Congregationalists across the region was neither uniform nor organized. Brittany Goetting (Cathey) observed that only a few miles away, across Blue Hill Bay, "The two denominations were not able to unite under a common cause until the emergence of the benevolence movement in the mid-nineteenth century. The Mount Desert Island Congregationalists and Baptists then began to participate together in organizations like tract, temperance, and Sunday school societies." Brittany Goetting, "'He Has Abundantly Poured out His Holy Spirit in Eden and Mount Desert,'" 56-57.

[61] The Pinkhams are mentioned ten times in Fisher's Diaries and entries suggest a warm friendship begun in 1814, when Pastor Pinkham of Sedgwick visited the Fisher home for the first time along with his wife, Rebekah. Chase makes additional observations, "In 1827 his church is joining with the Baptist 'to form a common Sabbath School Society'; in 1829 he is working for the cause of temperance with the Rev. James Gilpatrick, the newly-ordained Baptist minister." See also, Brittany P. Cathey, "Reverend Jonathan Fisher."

[62] Chase, *Maine Parson*, 101.

As we have seen, Merrill himself did not approve of every collaborative effort by his disciples and fellow Baptists, yet those decisions made *as* Baptists warrants attention. George Stevens' will is a prime example, for its execution benefited Congregationalists and Baptist alike, yet included a proviso that only a Calvinistic Baptist minister would qualify for compensation. Thomas Lord's service in the construction of Baptist and Congregationalist houses of worship is emblematic for the possibilities and limitations of ecumenicism. Lord's architectural expertise assisted in building churches, that if equal in aesthetic quality and beauty, did not cease to be distinct from one another, confessionally.

5

Legacy:
Fisher, Merrill, and Lessons for the Present

Among the most scandalous, if not humiliating episodes in the Fisher household involved, incidentally, an infant and baptism. As mentioned earlier, Jonathan and Dolly lost one son, Samuel, at two weeks-old, in 1812. A lurid rumor began circulating that the Fisher child died after being baptized and taking ill. An alternative version of the story claimed that Dolly and Jonathan baptized their dead baby. The origin of these tales was traced to a servant in the Fisher household who had become a Baptist named Eliza Day. Both parents vehemently denied the claims. Only after several years, did the accuser admit the account(s) were fabricated. Jonathan and Dolly not only served twenty-five more years at Bluehill, but maintained sanguinity, a testimony to their integrity and resilience. Though no subsequent conflict matched Eliza Day's rumor, friction with the fledgling Baptists was simply unavoidable.

Nineteen years later, two years prior to Daniel Merrill's death and six years from Jonathan Fisher's retirement, a long-time member of the Bluehill Congregationalist church, Samuel Parker, died. Parker's first wife was also a member, though his second wife, Mary Mathews, was a Baptist. Two days passed after Parker's death and Jonathan Fisher had not been asked to preside over Samuel's funeral. A diary entry on December 4 records the following:

> Have had no request or invitation to take any part in Mr. Parker's funeral. I find my mind thrown into a state of perplexity and embarrassment, but I desire to repose my trust in God. I feel that the proceedings of some in the other

society in relation to this funeral must have been overbearing and toward me unkind and disrespectful.[1]

Just as Josiah Fisher's decision to attend Bowdoin College elicited a seemingly disproportionate adversarial response by his father, so was Jonathan's being snubbed for a funeral interpreted as indicative of deeper and more consequential shifts.

Baptist growth in Maine had produced unavoidable partisan attitudes towards Fisher's ministry. The fact that declining fortunes happened near the end of his pastorate made the pain particularly acute. Daniel Merrill, by contrast, who broke with an established tradition and embraced an entirely new one, achieved a level of success most church planters and missionaries rarely attain. Risking reputation and livelihood to become a Baptist led to staggering success. Fisher carefully examined Baptist claims, but remained convinced that infant baptism was supported by Scripture. Each pastor read the same Bible, took seriously the witness of church history, prayed, but reached different conclusions concerning this ordinance. Merrill's ascendance in contrast to Fisher's ecclesial stasis hints at the difficulty of assessing the meaning of these men's ministries. Much less does it answer the question of who chose the correct path.

Making Sense of a Legacy

In *Summa Theologica* (1.2. question 3), Thomas Aquinas (1225–1274) posed the question, "does man's happiness consist in fame or glory?" The scholastic doctor answered in the negative, noting that, "human knowledge is often deceived." Moreover, "fame has no stability; indeed, by false rumor it is easily lost. And if for a time it remains stable, this is incidental."[2] In a short span of time,

---

[1] Diary entries of 12/3 and 12/4/1831; Candage, *Historical Sketches of Bluehill*, 2:19.

[2] Thomas Aquinas, *Selected Writings*, Ralph McInerny, ed., trans. (New York: Penguin, 1998), 500.

a person's reception by successive generations is subject to change. A monument that is built by one community—with the ideals it represents—can be toppled, literally and figuratively, by later descendants. Judging by external considerations, Jonathan Fisher and Merrill's lives followed similar patterns, particularly in their 20s and 30s. Both were educated at elite institutions and ordained in Congregational churches. Both were married with large families. Adherents of evangelical Calvinism, Fisher and Merrill were witnesses and participants of revival in first the decade of the 19th century. Activism accurately described their ministries. Jointly, and later, separately, they established local associations, regular prayer meetings, preached itinerantly, published writings, and advocated for social reform. Each man stayed broadly within the Reformed tradition and guided their churches away from Universalism and Unitarianism. Two institutions of higher learning—Colby College and Bangor Theological Seminary—owe their existence to Daniel Merrill and Jonathan Fisher.

It should, therefore, come as a surprise that Jonathan Fisher is studied with great interest by contemporary scholars, whereas Daniel Merrill's life and work remain largely unknown. Merrill was instrumental in planting scores of Baptist churches prior to his death in 1833. Baptists would soon become the largest Protestant denomination in New England, and by the early decades of 20th century, the entire United States. Fisher, by contrast, pastored the Congregational church at Bluehill that contained as few as forty members by the time he retired in 1837. Granted, Fisher provided historians and sociologists with more material from which to work. Daniel Merrill did not leave assiduous records, a fact that could reasonably be attributed to a vigorous pace of preaching, teaching, traveling, organizing, and the raising of thirteen children.

The above considerations hint at the conceptual challenge of determining a legacy. In recent history, Jonathan Fisher has been studied and admired for secular dimensions of his life, a fact that would certainly puzzle him were he alive today. Daniel Merrill, a Baptist missionary and church planter tour de force who shaped the spiritual contours of the entire region and was a direct participant in the disestablishment of state religion, has less renown than the pastor of a neighboring congregation whose membership never exceeded 100 people. Details of the Reverend Fisher's life and ministry are accessible to the public, but they are typically explored as useful descriptive keys for understanding New England in the National Period. To the present, he is not widely admired for his theological and pastoral vision.[3] Reception—or lack thereof—by modern readers, hints at legacy's ambiguous nature when judged from a finite perspective. Christianity has historically taught that glory and fame are by nature, fickle and fleeting in a fallen world. An eschatological dimension must be taken into account in discussions pertaining to meaning. "Each one's work will become manifest, for the Day will disclose it, because it will be revealed by fire, and the fire will test what sort of work each one has done." So wrote the Apostle Paul in his first letter to the Corinthians.[4] Weighty considerations notwithstanding, we can (humbly) identify patterns, acknowledge foundations, and learn lessons from both Jonathan Fisher and Daniel Merrill.

C.S. Lewis (1898–1963), who, in his 1944 essay, "On the reading of old books," argued for the value of learning from the past. He made the following insightful observation,

> People were no cleverer than they are now; they made as many mistakes as we. But not the same mistakes. They will not flatter us in the errors we are already committing; and

---

[3] This work is hopefully a contribution to a recovery of Fisher's and Merrill's spirituality.

[4] 1 Corinthians 3:13 (ESV).

their own errors, being now open and palatable, will not endanger us.[5]

As interpretive guidance, Lewis' insight can provide modern readers the possibility of attaining wisdom. In contrast to exalting the lives of Fisher and Merrill by virtue of selective evidence (hagiography), or employing them as historical foil for our supposedly superior present age ("chronological snobbery"), we can avoid the twin errors of despair and triumphalism and learn in a disposition of gratitude.

Perseverance

Unitarian Joseph Priestley's prognostications about scientific advancements making modern life unprecedentedly comfortable have, on the whole, proven true. The arduous nature of a typical day's work in the lives of Jonathan Fisher and Daniel Merrill is distant, even incomprehensible for westerners in the twenty first century. What Priestly and scores after him have overlooked, however, is the extent to which ease has not contributed to the development of character, much less an increase in moral goodness. Particularly in the present, technology may be contributing to its very erosion. Granted, no rational person would want to lose multiple children as the Fishers and Merrills did for the reasons they did, nor meet in a church building bereft of heat or electricity during a New England winter, nor preach on a circuit on foot or via horseback for miles on end. As Kevin Murphy notes, Jonathan Fisher, "never doubted the heroic nature of his enterprise," a reminder that Fisher intended to blaze a trail, not model a normative pastorate.[6] Whatever dimension of life we admire in the era is offset by the harshness of frontier existence. Added to this, is the

---

[5] C.S. Lewis, "On the Reading of Old Books," in *God in the Dock: Essays on Theology and Ethics*, ed., Walter Hooper (Grand Rapids, MI: Eerdmans), 202.

[6] Murphy, *Jonathan Fisher*, 2.

biblical claim that human nature has not changed. It would there-fore, be a mistake to idealize Fisher and Merrill's age. As for the differences, we stand to benefit from their example, for as C.S. Lewis observed, figures of the past will not "flatter us in the errors we are already committing."

Jonathan Fisher and Daniel Merrill's decades-long ministry have not been the norm for a majority of pastors in the evangelical tradition. In some cases, explosive growth—as in frontier Meth-odism—required that a minister rotate to a new parish every few years. For most periods, including the present, numerical growth in North America is modest. Under such conditions, a lengthy tenure presents the opportunity for multigenerational investment in a single community—a path which requires a pastor to exhibit the integrity that earns and maintains trust among those inside and outside the church.[7] Understandably, a pastor who leaves a congregation every two to five years will jettison the conse-quences of a reputation that is compromised by accusations—be they true or false. But time is a reliable, if provisional, test of a pastor's character. For a variety of reasons, a minister who is con-sistently on the move arguably does more harm to local congrega-tions. Knowing one's pastor will be gone after a short tenure cre-ates inevitable detachment. Like a lengthy marriage, Fisher and Merrill rejoiced with the highs and endured the lows, thereby maximizing the benefits for themselves, their churches, and the respective towns where they preached week after week and year after year.

---

[7] Kevin D. Murphy observes the following, "On the frontier, three opportunities arise that are not available in established settlements, or at least not to the same degree: the ability to place one's personal imprint on a new community, the potential to ob-serve change clearly, and the chance to profit from the transition from unsettled to settled. Jonathan Fisher was keenly aware of all three of these possibilities and at-tempted to capitalize on all of them over the course of his life in Blue Hill." Cited in Murphy, *Jonathan Fisher*, 3.

The Place of Confessional Standards

As noted, confessions of faith were vital to the ecclesial identity of Congregational and Baptist churches. Without recourse to episcopal authority a doctrinal consensus to which members of a gathered body could assent was the only guard against theological anarchy. Fisher and Merrill did not waver in their conviction that any and all members should in good faith, confess to their churches' statement of beliefs. Of course, such an uncompromising stance was not incompatible with evangelical piety. In addition to assenting to the church's confession of faith, persons who sought full communicant membership were required to provide testimony of personal conversion in Sedgwick and Bluehill. The policy, if it excluded many who would otherwise join the church, assisted in maintaining strength and stability.

Even by the first third of the nineteenth century, Congregational churches, notably in eastern Massachusetts, had loosened confessional standards to accommodate non-Trinitarians. Baptists would also have defections from orthodoxy, but from revivalist origins rather than Harvard's professorial elite. In both instances, philosophical trends would overwhelm congregations that diluted, or chose not to enforce their confessions. Strangely enough, cosmopolitan Unitarians and chiliastic biblical literalists would agree that classic Trinitarianism was untenable for members of their churches—the objection being that this doctrine failed some supposed standard of rationality. The consequences of embracing theological liberalism in the eighteenth and nineteenth centuries are evident in contemporary American Congregationalism, where church attendance has steadily declined for the last half-century. Sectarian offshoots such as early Seventh-Day Adventists and the Jehovah's Witnesses, even as they rejected orthodoxy as articulated in the first four ecumenical creeds, embraced novel dogmas in their claim as the true heirs to supposedly pure churches described in the book of Acts.

Crucial as assent to correct doctrine was for Daniel Merrill and Jonathan Fisher, it constituted only one of two essential components to church membership, the second being a testimony before one's local church providing evidence of personal conversion. This was, and is, a tall order. Even a cursory reading of the New Testament, much more, the doctrine of predestination, suggests that the road leading to eternal life is narrow. In a community that is—at least formally—religiously homogenous, the potential for embarrassment remained high for those who lacked an experiential testimony of God's grace. The compromise that was the Half-Way Covenant loomed large over the descendants of New England's Puritan forbearers. Fisher and Merrill had intimate experience of evangelical conversion and were New Lights by conviction, not expedience. While the outcomes for insisting that candidates provide evidence of regeneration were mixed at different junctures in their careers, relaxing this requisite article would have proven harmful to their churches in the long-run, as recent history has shown.

Merrill's journey to become a Baptist on account of the Bible's witness came at great personal cost. Added to this risky endeavor, the near immediate success in persuading substantial numbers of people, it comes as little surprise that Merrill was particularly zealous in his newfound persuasion. Converts typically make the best evangelists, and Sedgwick's pastor boldly, even shockingly, denounced his former denomination as a false church. Naturally, this made for an awkward relationship to neighboring Congregationalists such as Jonathan Fisher, and Merrill's decision to reject open communion made his departure from the Hancock Association a *fait accompli*. Theologically, the boundary between New Light Congregationalists and Calvinistic Baptists was actually quite narrow. It makes sense, then, that Baptists in Bluehill would invite Fisher to preach from their pulpit in later years, and the two congregations would develop a comparatively genial relationship.

Presently, the divide in evangelical circles over baptism requires that distinct institutional identities remain intact. As in the nineteenth century, disagreements on the nature and extent of denominational cooperation extend to the present. For Baptists in particular, Fisher and Merrill's story compels us to wrestle with the subject of ecclesial unity. With some exceptions, the majority of evangelical churches in the U.S. practice open communion, a phenomenon of which Daniel Merrill would soundly disapprove. As for membership, Baptist churches—particularly in communities with a smaller evangelical presence—the question of whether persons baptized as infants should be admitted as members if they show evidence of conversion but do not desire rebaptism, is vigorously debated.[8] Daniel Merrill and Jonathan Fisher's partisan struggles, accompanied by timely diplomacy, kept their churches from the kind of sectarianism that would hinder health and growth. Their example proves that unity is not attained without struggle, and the fruitful cooperation requires time and a healthy dose of realism.

Processing Patterns in Revival

Evangelicalism, by its origins and historic emphases, is a revival-oriented movement within the Protestant tradition. Fisher and Merrill's connection to Peter Powers, a pastor who was himself converted under Jonathan Edwards' preaching, makes for a familiar story with a kind of apostolic-succession imbedded in the broader narrative. Revivals, by their very definition, have a conventional life cycle that includes an ending. Pastors often move through a process of deliberation and analysis, the kind only possible when the fires of revival have died down. Jonathan Edwards' writings on revival, notably *The Religious Affections*, typify this

---

[8] Some Baptist churches in Britain for example, have allowed paedobaptists to become members with full rights with the exception of casting a congregational vote for a new pastor.

pattern. There is, understandably, a certain degree of disappointment, even grief, that emerges when the fervor of many is unmatched by perseverance on the part of those impacted. For Jonathan Fisher in particular, the Hancock Revival, which had run its course by 1804, was unsurpassed by subsequent experiences. Being 35 years-old at the time, Fisher would serve at Bluehill's Congregational church for 33 more years and live for another 43. Spiritually-fruitful periods did come, but not like the years 1800–1804, a time of abundant harvests in the United States, considered by historians as the Second Great Awakening.[9] This very categorization is possible because of records kept by men like Fisher and Merrill. Their experiences contributed to a general timeline. But unlike us, they had no knowledge of when revival would end, much less, when another awakening would begin.

In the meantime, Fisher and Merrill were active, preaching, evangelizing, and pursuing social reform. Mentoring young candidates for the pastorate formed a crucial component to their ministerial duties. Both pastors trained young men for the ministry in their homes. Several of Daniel Merrill's sons became ministers. Jonathan Fisher mentored his son, Josiah, and son-in-law, Joshua Wood. Josiah went on to become the first pastor of the Congregational Church in Orono Maine, Clyde and Greenbush New York, and Heath Massachusetts. He served his longest tenure at the Succasunna New Jersey Presbyterian Church for thirteen years and provided pulpit supply to the Presbyterian Church at Oliphant Pennsylvania from 1871 until his death in 1875. Josiah and his wife, Elizabeth Davenport Fisher, had only one child who passed beyond infancy, James Boorman Fisher. J.B. Fisher, like his father, became a Presbyterian clergyman.

---

[9] Recent historians have noted the continuous nature of the First Great Awakening makes the category of a Second Awakening misleading. It is true, however, that in New England, there was acute spiritual decline in the latter half of the eighteenth century and that revival came at the turn of the nineteenth century.

An annual pattern of evangelistic preaching in the rustic, and at times, perilous frontier, reveals a deep commitment to the spiritual destinies of Mainers. Fisher and Merrill were atypical of clergymen—but not unlike early evangelicals such as Philip Doddridge (1702-1751)—in using their allotted vacation for evangelistic preaching. Critical as these individual efforts were for preserving and transmitting the faith, only training that drew on the strength of an institution could sustain Merrill and Fisher's gains. As New England's established colleges were either unequipped or outright hostile to the training of evangelical pastors, Fisher and Merrill chose to found their own.

Founding of New Institutions

In his seminal study, *After Virtue*, Alasdair McIntyre commented that, "no practices can survive any length of time unsustained by institutions."[10] In the case of Fisher and Merrill, transmitting the knowledge and practices of the spirituality forged in the fires of revival was a worthwhile investment. These pastors were neither the first, nor the last to establish educational institutions whose original mission was training preachers and missionaries. In the mid-eighteenth century, New Light Presbyterians founded the College of New Jersey, later Princeton University, in large part because of Yale's hostility to New Lights. Jonathan Edwards, the Great Awakening's chief apologist, served a short tenure as the institution's second president. Like Edwards, Fisher and Merrill rightly determined that their respective alma maters had lost an earlier pastoral and missional vision.

Bangor Theological Seminary and Colby College were originally tasked to equip pastors. Fisher called Bangor the "school of the prophets," an allusion to the respective ministries of the

---

[10] Alasdair Macintyre, *After Virtue: A Study in Moral Theory*, 3rd ed. (New York: Bloomsbury, 2021), 226.

biblical prophets Elijah and Elisha. The label, which evokes char-
ismatic and mystical connotations, did not mean that the curriculum for these institutions was sparse or impoverished. Arguably
more rigorous than that of elite universities and most seminaries
today, candidates for ministry at these institutions were required
to complete coursework that included knowledge of classical languages and literature prior to exclusive study in theology. Jonathan Fisher's evangelical instincts did not entail sacrificing intellectual development. Prayer meetings for revival and hours-long
recitation of Virgil in Latin happened in the same residence. Merrill served as the president of the first library in Hancock county,
saw that its shelves were supplied with works of the foremost
thinkers and literary minds of the times, and insisted upon successful completion of a broad and deep literary education for the
young ministers under his tutelage. Both pastors served as committed trustees to their respective institutions in the latter half of
their lives.[11]

In the early nineteenth century, Bangor Seminary and Colby
were not liberal arts colleges in the modern sense. Drawing from
the western intellectual tradition, the schools were principally ecclesial institutions. As with their churches, this mission was sustained in so far as the colleges maintained confessional standards
among faculty and students. Originally called the Maine Literary
and Theological Institution, Colby College, like the majority of
schools in America, bears little resemblance to its founders'

---

[11] Note the following description of Merrill's commitment to Colby, "Rev. Daniel
Merrill. This latter gentleman, as we have seen, was one of the original corporators of
the Institution, and he remained a Trustee through all its vicissitudes till the year 1833,
the sixty-eighth year of his age. During all this period he was rarely absent from any
meeting of the Board, and always active and efficient when present. Besides raising the
funds for the Manual Labor Department, already referred to, he was frequently engaged in raising funds for the general purposes of the· Institution, and generally with
good success. On the whole, perhaps there was no more useful Trustee on the Board."
Cited in T. Champlin, *Historical Discourse Delivered at the Fiftieth Anniversary of Colby
University*, 22.

visions and values. Yet when considering the scope of Christian history, this phenomenon is not extraordinary, for Christianity has had, from its beginnings, an ambiguous relationship to learning. The church is responsible for founding virtually all institutions of higher learning in the west, institutions which have produced luminous saints alongside arch skeptics. The judgment of whether ecclesial bodies have cultivated or hindered intellectual progress depends on a variety of considerations, and scholars continue to debate this subject to the present.

Of course, institutions, as important as they are, possess what McIntyre calls, "corrupting power."[12] This power arises from competitiveness, principally, the desire for academic and cultural prestige. Confessional boundaries, if they constitute the fabric of the school, generally must be stretched for the purpose of gaining more students and higher-quality faculty. Professors will teach what they believe is true, and students will become—to varying degrees—disciples of their thought. But corruption is not attributable to the system alone. It extends to the practices, that is the virtues, of the students themselves. The moral and spiritual quality of the men and women who attend a given school matters. An institution must, to some degree, accommodate the persons whose presence and money are requisite for its survival. A college cannot, however, sustain a meaningful confessional identity apart from the support of local churches. When congregations produce the kind of young persons whose worldview accords with a school's vision and values, education is substantively *Christian*. But what if one or two of these elements is missing?

Prosaic as the observation may be, Fisher and Merrill's example is a reminder that formation is the only viable option when *reformation* is not. Change on a systemic level takes herculean

---

[12] Macintyre, *After Virtue*, 226

efforts. Jonathan Fisher had no illusions of Harvard returning to its Puritan roots. Thus, he spent much of his ministerial service as a trustee for Bangor Seminary, a school which, though it fulfilled its original mission for several generations, would eventually resemble Harvard in its embrace of theological liberalism. The school officially closed in May of 2013. Colby College is today one of the most selective liberal arts colleges in America and was ranked 11th by U.S. News and World Report for 2020.[13] Admirable as that attainment may be, Colby is not training pastors or missionaries—Baptist or otherwise. Those seeking training for the pastorate must look elsewhere. And while it is tempting to muse over the shock and disappointment that Fisher and Merrill might express if they beheld Bangor and Colby in the twenty-first century, such a judgment is premature, perhaps even naïve.

If their lives provide any insight for modern admirers, Jonathan Fisher and Daniel Merrill's decision to found new schools proved to be a wise pursuit. For contemporary evangelicals sympathetic to their theology, their example is a reminder that new colleges and seminaries are necessary to instill future generations with the knowledge and passion made possible under a unified spiritual vision. The state of their theological health is no mere abstraction, but remains crucial for the flourishing of Christianity on a national level. The twin possibility of losing or rejecting a tradition—in the sense of a body of teachings—constituted what Tocqueville called "the two great dangers" to religion. In *Democracy in America* he wrote, "In ages of fervent devotion, men sometimes abandon their religion, but they only shake it off in order to adopt another." The object of one's faith changes, but the fervor remains. Partisanship can inflict damage, but faith retains its importance. The latter danger, if less apparent, is more insidious.

---

[13] "Colby College Overall Rankings" https://www.usnews.com/best-colleges/colby-college-2039/overall-rankings (accessed on December 20, 2021). Calby was tied for #25 for the year 2023.

194

The truth of doctrine is undermined, claims Tocqueville, but "without affirming that of any other." In such cases,

> Prodigious revolutions take place in the human mind, without the apparent cooperation of the passions of man, and almost without his knowledge. Men then lose the object of their fondest hopes, as if through forgetfulness.[14]

Tocqueville's prophetic warning is perhaps a fitting conclusion to this study. In a nation that defeated the totalitarian powers of the 20th century, whose ideologies stood as sworn enemies to Christianity; a country that consistently polls high when the label "evangelical," is employed; with a government that robustly defends religious liberty, there remains the specter of unbelief—not a militant atheism, but that which consists of lethargy and indifference. Here we do find parallels between New England's religious condition after the American Revolution and our own day. The National Period witnessed a major portion of the American population having a nominal Christian identity joined to a heightened political consciousness. It is not hard to envision how a secularized America could have pursued a path similar to that of revolutionary France, a course that was averted in part, because of revival. Fisher and Merrill did not labor by prayer, preaching and proselytizing, principally that a spiritual awakening would bestow civic stability. That was a consequence. In any case, the country has been uniquely shaped, even bettered, by evangelical revival, notably what transpired in the years 1800–1820, particularly in Hancock County Maine.

---

[14]Alexis de Tocqueville, *Democracy in America*, trans. Henry Reeve (New York: Bantam Dell, 2004), 362–363.

Evangelical Exemplars: Moses Merrill, Thomas Merrill, Daniel David Merrill, and Jonathan Fisher Crossette

With an expansive lineage that included deacons, pastors, civic figures, the list of Merrill descendants who served the church, and New England communities broadly, is large. But Daniel's influence extended to America's expanding westward borders. Space does not permit treatment for each of Merrill's children, much less his grandchildren, yet one son, Thomas Ward Merrill, stands above the rest. Thomas' life and ministry encapsulate, or more properly fulfill, the evangelical vision of his father, notably for its theology and activism. The younger Merrill was a graduate of Colby College who studied under George Dana Boardman Sr., and then at Newton Theological Seminary.[15] As noted earlier, Thomas served as a pastor in Maine, New Hampshire, and Michigan. He later helped to found the Michigan and Huron Institute, a Baptist school that would eventually become Kalamazoo College. Thomas served as a college trustee and left a ten-thousand-dollar endowment. Coe Hayne describes Thomas Merrill's move from New England to the Michigan Territory and his early experiences as a "Gospel Ranger," like his father in the following:

> After a brief period as a teacher in Amherst College, he felt that he must respond to the call of the wilderness. Accordingly he secured the right to secure subscriptions for *Mrs. Judson's Memoirs* and the *American Baptist Magazine* and started west, the destitute Michigan 'backwoods' being his destination. He arrived in Detroit May 23, 1829, with seven dollars in his pocket. The first six months of his residence in Michigan Territory, Merrill spent in visiting, on foot and horseback, settlements remote from Detroit where the gospel seldom or never had been heard. T.W. Merrill was

---

[15] Merrill was the chairman of the committee that resulted by its action in the organization of The Northern Baptist Education Society, and the Newton Theological Seminary, the second institution his son attended.

ordained at Detroit, February 6, 1831. To visit one settlement containing nearly one hundred people and give them 'one Lord's day services,' he rode horseback one hundred miles, and to make a house-to-house visitation in the district, twenty miles more. He declared afterwards that he did not regret the exertion. During this time he made an excursion into Canada and visited some of the brave little churches near the Detroit River as well as an African settlement for fugitive slaves. Running short of funds, he opened a Select School in the village of Ann Arbor, November 23, 1829, having as an assistant his brother Moses. Through friends he petitioned the Territorial Legislative Council for a charter for a school that should be under Baptist control with a theological as well as an academic department. The petition was refused, but Merrill's activity resulted in the granting of a charter for an academy to be situated in Ann Arbor with a local board of trustees. This institution in after years became the University of Michigan. Merrill was offered the principalship of the new academy, but refused it. Soon thereafter he severed his relations with the Select School, having taught in Ann Arbor about nine months."[16]

Thomas Merrill's first wife, Sarah, died in 1845 and he married Eliza, the widow of his brother Moses—also a Baptist missionary in Michigan—in 1847.[17] He had six children by his first wife. Their son Daniel David Merrill served as a deacon and a leading Baptist and treasurer of the Minnesota Baptist State Convention. D.D. Merrill's son, George Ernest Merrill, served as a Deacon of the Baptist Church he helped found in Annapolis

---

[16] See Coe Hayne, *Baptist Trail-Makers of Michigan* (Philadelphia, PA : Judson Press, 1936) 72–73 in the chapter titled, appropriately, "Pioneer Gospel Ranger of Western Michigan." See also William D. Green, "Called To Serve," *The Children of Lincoln: White Paternalism and the Limits of Black Opportunity in Minnesota, 1860*-1876 (Minneapolis, MN: University of Minnesota Press, 2018). The University of Michigan was founded in 1817, but officially located in Ann Arbor in 1837.

[17] Moses, like most of his siblings, was converted—at age thirteen—by a sermon his father preached.

Maryland.[18] William D. Green notes that "G.E. Merrill, son of St. Paul's D.D. Merrill, would become a successful businessman like his father, who strengthened 'all manner of Baptist interests' in Annapolis, Maryland."[19]

Rev. Moses Merrill had married Eliza Wilcox and was a teacher in Maine before moving to Michigan, where, along with Thomas, they reopened the "Select School." The Merrill brothers had been commissioned by the American Baptist Missionary Union on April 27, 1832 as missionaries to the Otoe tribe in Nebraska Territory. Their task was to translate parts of the Bible into the Otoe language. The Merrills lived 200 miles from the nearest white settlement and their son is reputed to be the first non-native child born in the Nebraska Territory. Moses died seven years later of tuberculosis at the age of 36.[20] His son, Moses Daniel Merrill was a Baptist choir leader, Sunday School teacher, and Sunday School Superintendent in St. Paul, Minnesota. His other son, Rev. Samuel Pearce Merrill, was a poet and his biography in the Sedgwick Centennial remains an important source of information for Merrill scholars.[21] Samuel was a graduate of Rochester University

---

[18] Merrill, "Rev. Daniel Merrill, An Appreciation," 60. See also *100 Years of Christian Service 1849-1949: Prepared in commemoration of the One-hundredth anniversary of The First Baptist Church St. Paul,* Minnesota (Minnesota: Published and Distributed by The First Baptist Church St. Paul, 1949), 31.

[19] Green, "Called To Serve," 203.

[20] In the spring of 1833, the board ordered them to "a more promising field in the great Indian Territory of the West." In late fall they arrived at Bellevue, now Nebraska, where the Otoe Indians were located, two hundred miles from the nearest white settlement. There they built a school for children, preached through an interpreter until they had learned the language, and provided medical assistance. It would be here that Moses succumbed 'to tubercular troubles' on February 6, 1840, and was buried on the eastern bank of the Missouri River. "He died on February 6, 1840, and was buried on the east bank of the Missouri River opposite Bellevue. The Otoes called him 'The-One-Who-Always-Speaks-The-Truth.'" Addison Erwin Sheldon, *History and Stories of Nebraska* (Chicago: The University Publishing Company, 1913), 75.

[21] Samuel Pearce Merrill, *My Loves and My Lovers* (Jamaica, NY: Marion Press, 1909).

and the Rochester Theological Seminary, where he served as Secretary for more than fourteen years.[22]

As D.T. Magill, a chronicler of the family noted early in the 20th century, "There has, without any doubt, been no family which has had so large and so long-continued an influence in Baptist affairs as the Merrills of Maine, Michigan, Nebraska, Minnesota, New York, and Maryland, from 1805 to 1907."[23]

Daniel David Merrill, the son of Thomas, moved to St. Paul, Minnesota in 1856, and though the citizen of a free state, would face the realities of personal and systemic racism against black Americans—even fellow black Baptists. Along with the members of the First Baptist Church of St. Paul, D. D. Merrill would offer protection and financial support to the freed slaves that founded what would become Pilgrim Baptist Church. William D. Green notes that freedman Robert Hickman and his followers entered the region in the spring of 1863 after traveling northward on a barge from Missouri. Prior to arrival,

> A mob in St. Paul, already agitated by the rumor that this boatload of contraband had been brought to the city to take jobs from white laborers, stoned the boat until the captain ordered that they continue upstream to Fort Snelling, where they could safely disembark.[24]

The group hoped to find safety in the city of St. Paul itself. Though having a tenuous existence, they received hospitality from Caroline Nelson, a black woman who owned a home on Fifth

---

[22] Merrill, "Rev. Daniel Merrill, An Appreciation," 61.

[23] Green, "Called To Serve," 201.

[24] Green, "Called To Serve," 198. "The Reverend Robert T. Hickman, a Negro slave in the South, stole his wife and children from a neighboring plantation and brought them with a group of other Negroes up the river to Minnesota"and started "the Baptist church, which they named Pilgrim Baptist, because they looked upon themselves as pilgrims coming to a new land." *100 Years of Christian Service 1849–1949*, 38.

Street between Washington and Franklin Avenues. "Once or twice a week" these Baptists rented several lodge rooms, but being unable to pay the rent, moved to various locations in the commercial district.[25] In the following year, Hickman and Thomas Scott made a written request for support to the all-white, 162-member First Baptist Church. On behalf of the fifteen "Colored Baptist members of Saint Paul," they said, "we have organized ourselves but we do not feel satisfied without been [*sic*] united to the church and then bee [*sic*] a branch from your church buy [*sic*] a request from the members."[26] J.H. Randall, First Baptist Church's clerk, reported the request that, "a company of col'd people then meeting in the Ancient Hall request[ed] to be a branch of our church." Randall commented that, as Hickman et. al. were fellow Baptists, First Baptist was obliged to "have had them under our watch care and supervision as members with us of the Church of the Living God." In a subsequent entry, he recorded,

> Of the [numbers] rec'd by baptism I were from the Col'd branch and 13 col'd people have been rec'd upon the Christian experience. We have been compelled to exclude 4 of the col' members for grievous sins.[27]

Thus, the mission for the colored Baptists of St. Paul was created, worshipping under the tutelage of First Baptist. The word "pilgrim" had not yet become their formal name.[28] These believers attended services at First Baptist throughout the winter, but soon pursued the founding of an independent congregation. Hickman sent a delegation to First Baptist in October 1866. A petition

---

[25] Green, "Called To Serve," 199.
[26] Green, "Called To Serve," 199.
[27] Green, "Called To Serve," 199.
[28] Pilgrim Baptist Church (www.pilgrimbaptistchurch.org), 732 Central Ave. West Saint Paul, MN.

signed by nine members requesting, "letters of dismission so as to enable them to form a separate organization. On motion the following committee was appointed to meet and confer with them — Deacon Cavender, Bros. Prescott, Sherie, Randall, and Merrill."[29]

The leadership of First Baptist focused on three key issues pertaining to the request: 1. the sincerity of their calling to be an independent church, 2. their commitment to remaining with the small but growing Minnesota Baptist Association, and 3. the acquisition of a permanent place for worship. Hickman explained his long-term vision for the future of Pilgrim Baptist Church, his hope that it would become the center of all manner of religious, social, and educational uplift for the small but growing black community of St. Paul. Green notes that Hickman's "ambitious and enterprising spirit impressed the men from First Baptist, all people of considerable standing within the business community of St. Paul."[30] These men, born as slaves, having only a few years' experience of freedom were, notwithstanding, "highly motivated and best poised to advance their race and larger community all in the service of their Lord and Savior."[31] Merrill and others sought to protect Hickman from unscrupulous prospectors and men of dubious character. Hickman was introduced to prominent realtors and bankers such as Charles Oakes, the senior partner of St. Paul's largest and oldest banking house, Borup and Oakes.[32] Thomas Merrill's son, the thirty-two-year-old Daniel David, would become central to the work. Born in Comstock, Kalamazoo County, Michigan, on February 16, 1834, and educated at Kalamazoo College from 1851 to 1854, Merrill brought a remarkable

---

[29] Green, "Called To Serve," 199.
[30] Green, "Called To Serve," 200.
[31] Green, "Called To Serve," 200.
[32] Green, "Called To Serve," 200. George H. Oakes, Charles' brother, was a member of First Baptist Church.

degree of business acumen and experience to service. Green chronicles the young Merrill's accomplishments in business and politics. Daniel David,

> engaged in real estate before taking office as deputy city treasurer. In 1856 he joined First Baptist Church, by letter, and helped to organize the YMCA in the city, serving as its secretary and treasurer. Meanwhile, his considerable business skills helped him to soon become eminently successful. During the Civil War, Merrill was secretary and treasurer of the United States Christian Commission, and would become treasurer of the Minnesota Baptist State Convention from 1865 to 1890, when he would be elected its president for the next four years. In 1857 he stumped the territory with Carl Schurz, Galusha A. Grow, Schuyler Colfax, and other nationally prominent Republicans of the day. Within a very short time he had impressed powerful men in the financial and political quarters of the city and soon-to-be state.[33]

Merrill was in a prime position to negotiate a property deal on behalf of the black Baptists. D. D.'s service was very much in keeping with his family legacy of religious and educational entrepreneurialism that started in Maine at the turn of the century.[34] Daniel David acquired and held the title to the property in trust for Hickman and his followers for a mutually agreed time. On November 13, Hickman formally requested the trustees of First Baptist to purchase in trust for them the lot on the southwest corner of Thirteenth and Cedar Streets. The trustees approved the deal. One day later, on November 14, the committee reported back to the church membership recommending that they approve the

---

[33] Green, "Called To Serve," 200; Coe Hayne, *Baptist Trail-Makers of Michigan*, 81.

[34] Green, "Called To Serve," 201.

request of Hickman's congregation to form a separate church.[35]

True to their expressed intent of granting Hickman and his congregation autonomy, Trustee Merrill made the following motion on behalf the First Baptist church of St. Paul: 'That the following named Colored Brothers and Sisters be granted the letters of dismission from this church for the purpose of organizing an independent Baptist Church.' The motion was seconded and approved.[36] After congregational singing, the membership departed as the newly formed Pilgrim Baptist Church.

Conscious of the New England tradition of establishing congregations by reason of conviction and the prompting of the Holy Spirit, Pilgrim Baptist's future pastor, the Reverend John Brown, would claim in a sermon delivered during the seventy-fifth anniversary of First Baptist that, "In New England we find entire congregations setting up their light and their churches in the wilderness, having been driven from across the ocean for conscience sake.' "[37] The passage of three-quarters of a century's time had not erased the memory of a worthy—and at the time—rare form of cooperation between black and white churches in America. Black Protestants, noted Reverend Brown, were the authentic descendants of Puritan New Englanders. Merrill's assisting First Baptist's purchase of the property that became Pilgrim Baptist Church was admirable enough. Granting the congregation autonomy in good faith suggests that Merrill and First Baptist believed that Hickman and his followers were, above all else, fellow Baptists.

During the same period, Jonathan Fisher's household, though considerably smaller than Merrill's, was following his evangelical

---

[35] Green, "Called To Serve," 203.

[36] Members of the church present included: Fielding Combs, Adeline Combs, R. Hickman, Matonia Hickman, Henry Moffitt, Charlotte Moffitt, George Chambers, Eliza Chambers, Melvinia Asak, and Giles Crenshaw.

[37] Green, "Called To Serve," 204.

example of taking the gospel to the frontier. Josiah Fisher and his son, James Boorman Fisher, followed a more conservative, yet fruitful path, pastoring congregations as "gospel preachers" in New Jersey, New York, and Pennsylvania.[38] Nancy Fisher Kittredge and Rev. Hosea Kittredge struck out west to serve Presbyterian churches and institutions. Nancy died in New York in 1845— the Kittredge family continued west and Hosea ministered in Michigan at about the same time the Merrill brothers, Thomas and Moses, were working in that field. Dorothea Fisher Crossette and Rev. Robert Crossette, after establishing the Congregational church in Dennysville Maine, ministered to various congregations to the south and west before finally settling in Cincinnati Ohio, in order to be near family. Their son, Jonathan Fisher Crossette and spouse Mary, answered the call to take the gospel once more to the eastern frontier—in latter half of the 19th century, that boundary had extended to the fareast in China.

Most of what we know of Jonathan Fisher Crossette and his spouse, Mary, are taken from mission reports and one account by an American foreign envoy, released by the US State Department upon Jonathan Crossette's death. Jonathan Fisher Crossette graduated in 1869 from Lane Seminary, the Presbyterian theological college in the Walnut Hills neighborhood of Cincinnati and site of important debates during the establishment of the Abolitionist movement in 1834.[39] It was Jonathan's choice of Lane for a

---

[38] Candage, *Historical Sketches of Bluehill, Maine*, 65.

[39] This *Annual Report* is a compilation of annual reports presented by year—page numbers begin again with each new year, noted in the citations. *Annual Report of the Board of Foreign Missions of the Presbyterian Church Relating to China and the Chinese 1871-1882.* Year 1871 (Cleveland: no publisher, 1916), 6. *Lane Seminary Debates,* Walnut Hills Historical Society. https://walnuthillsstories.org/stories/lane-seminary-debates (accessed September 2, 2022). Also, "Jonathan Fisher Crossette, a student at Lane Theological Seminary in Walnut Hills, had recognized the need for young women to have a place to stay while looking for employment in the city, and recruited his sister, Aurelia Fisher, to help. Together they launched the local WCA. (It became the Young Women's Christian Association in 1893.)" Jeff Suess, *Building Enables YWCA to Empower Women*, The Enquirer, February 3, 2015. www.cincinnati.com/story/news/

seminary education that brought his mother and father west in their twilight years. Upon Jonathan's graduation, the couple immediately embarked upon a mission to China and was assigned to the Presbyterian missionary station on the coast at Tungchow, which had been established in 1861.[40]

Their work in China was initially confined to that area until 1872 when, under *The Question of Access to the Interior Cities*, we find this record of Jonathan's first foray inland:

> Rev. Jasper S. McIlvaine, a young unmarried missionary, left Peking in March, 1871, with the heroic purpose of planting the gospel at Tsi-Nan-fou, the capital of the Shantung province. He was wholly unattended, except by a single native Christian, whom he had baptized but a few months before ... Once located, he soon began the arduous work, though with heavy discouragements. He not only maintained a school, with the help of his assistant, but preached daily in a room which he had rented for a chapel. But, the over-work, together with the depressing influence of *loneliness* in such a city, and with none with whom to exchange sympathies or even words in his mother tongue, began to affect both mind and body. His letters excited alarm. Rev. J. Fisher Crossette volunteered to join him, at least for a time; but he found him so reduced in health and strength by eight months of this lonely service as to render it necessary for him to return to Peking.[41]

Another important event impacted the Crossettes when

2015/02/03/building-enables-ywca-to-empower-women/22790155/ (Accessed September 7, 2022).

[40] *Annual Report of the Board of Foreign Missions of the Presbyterian Church.* Year 1871, 68.

[41] *Annual Report of the Board of Foreign Missions of the Presbyterian Church.* Year 1872, 82–83. The account included this insightful note: "The case Illustrates the wisdom of Our Saviour's method, when He sent out His Disciples *by twos*, but never alone. Companionship and mutual help are indispensable to the health of body or mind, and the Church should furnish so adequate a force that no such sacrifices as here recorded shall be necessary."

Jonathan's father, Robert, died after years of poor health. Rev. Bosworth, in his eulogy, rehearsed this moving exchange between Robert and Dorothea Fisher Crossette upon his deathbed, imparting a final testimony to their son, affectionately referred to as "Fisher:"

> Among the last words of his which will be sacredly treasured by those who held him dear, was a message to his missionary son. During the last days, and even weeks, of his life, he spoke with considerable difficulty and pain. 'What message shall I send from you to Fisher?' asked his wife one day as she was writing to him. "Oh! I cant' talk much now," was the reply, thinking doubtless, that there was very much he would like to say, but feeling himself inadequate to the task. "Shall I tell him that Christ is precious to you?" "Oh! yes;" and his eye kindled, and his voice rose to something of its wonted emphasis, as he spoke. "Oh! yes; He is my all in all!"[42]

One is reminded of dying conversations between the Rev. Jonathan Fisher and his family or friends in the days leading up to and in anticipation of their certain death, meticulously detailed in Father Fisher's diaries. The language of deathbed testimony in the remembrance above, along with the exigency of recording ones parting Christian affirmation, displays the evangelical imprint of both mother and father upon Dorothea.

Mary Crossette, along with another female missionary, became very ill and took a furlough to the United States in 1874. That same year, Rev. John Livingston Nevius, who developed what would come to be known as the "Nevius Plan," calling for evangelization through indigenous missionaries and the planting of self-supporting churches, began his legendary trek to China's

---

[42] W.A. Bosworth, *A Discourse Delivered at the Funeral of Rev. Robert Crossette* (Cincinnati, OH: R. Clarke, 1872), 13.

interior.[43] There, he came upon the pioneering work of Rev. McIlvaine and Jonathan Crossette, who had teamed up once more to take the gospel inland.

> The results of the district work of Dr. Nevius were such as to convince him [Nevius] more and more of the importance of preaching the Word and scattering books broadcast in rural districts. The work of Messrs. McIlvaine and Crossette at Chen-nan-fou is an auspicious one. They occupy the capital of the Shantung province, which constitntes [*sic*] one of the best mission-fields in the empire.[44]

The final reference to the work of the Crossettes, as a couple, in Presbyterian foreign missionary reports describe them continuing the Fisher legacy, pushing out into new frontiers in 1876:

> Several changes have occurred in the China Missions during the year. Rev. John Murray and his wife sailed in the early autumn, as missionaries of the Board to Chen-nanfou. They reached their destination in safety, and were warmly welcomed by the missionaries of that remote station, Mrs. Crossette having for the year previous been 'the only white woman' in that city or its vicinity.[45]

The Crossettes returned to the United States in 1881 with "Mr. Crossette's health being so seriously impaired that he ... resigned his connection with the Board."[46] Mary Crossette died in 1919 and lies buried in the Newton New Jersey cemetery alongside

---

[43] Nevius. Helen S. Coan, *The Life of John Livingston Nevius: For Forty Years a Missionary In China* (New York: Fleming H. Revell Company, 1895), 424.

[44] *Annual Report of the Board of Foreign Missions of the Presbyterian.* Year 1874, 63.

[45] *Annual Report of the Board of Foreign Missions of the Presbyterian Church.* Year 1877, 62.

[46] *Annual Report of the Board of Foreign Missions of the Presbyterian Church.* Year 1881, 65.

Jonathan Fisher Crossette. But, their story does not end there. Jonathan died twenty years earlier, on June 21, 1889, aboard a steamer between Shanghai and Tientsen to the north. We do not know if Mary was by his side or not and, after severing ties with the Presbyterian Board eight years earlier, the circumstances surrounding his return to China are unknown. Nevertheless, we have been given a glimpse into the kind of missionary he was, as well as the details of his final moments from what appears to be a dispatch to the western press titled "Death of A Good Man: The Remarkable Work of an Independent American Missionary in China," penned by a diplomat of the US Government:

> In speaking of Mr. Crossett [*sic*], Minister Dinby ... says: "Mr. Crossett's life was devoted to doing good to the poorest classes of the Chinese. He had charge of the winter refuge for the poor at Pekin [*sic*] during several winters. He would go out on the streets on the coldest nights and pick up destitute beggars and convey them to the refuge, providing them with food. He also buried them at his own expense. He visited all the prisons and often procured the privilege of removing the sick to his refuge. The officials had implicit confidence in him and allowed him to us it at pleasure in all prisons and charitable institutions. He slept on a board on the floor, even in his last hours. Being a deck passenger on the El Dorado, he refused to be transferred to the cabin; but the kindly captain, some hours before he died, removed him to a berth where he died, still speaking of going to Heaven, and entreating by-standers to love the Lord.[47]

Conclusion

Providence seems to have smiled upon the legacy of both Jonathan Fisher and Daniel Merrill, when one considers that each had a

---

[47] *Death Of A Good Man. The Remarkable Work of an Independent American Missionary in China.* Piscataquis Observer (August 22, 1889), 2. https://www.findagrave.com/memorial/63379487/j-fisher-crossette (accessed August 24, 2022).

grandson who carried their names and their legacy beyond Sedgwick and Bluehill—two, small, close-knit communities in rural Maine. Crossette and Merrill struck out on divergent paths into new and distant frontiers, yet they shared the same Evangelical message, resolve, and expectation that they, like their grandfathers before them, were not laboring in vain. Those ministers who had been raised in the Fisher and Merrill households, by and large, set aside the advantages, comforts, and prestige that could likely have been theirs in settled New England, in order to seek and to serve the lost, the poor, and the marginalized. Though they could not know the future, Daniel Merrill and Jonathan Fisher's doctrine, piety, and disciplined lives displayed anything but a "a high and dry Calvinism with no unusual notes at all."[48] Rather, theirs was an optimistic, Evangelical conviction that, in the tribute by their mutual friend and fellow minister, James Gilpatrick, "came forth from a heart deeply imbued with the love of Christ ... for the nations.[49]

The faith that informed Jonathan Fisher's larger than life persona within a small coastal village on the Easter Frontier, impacted the wider world in ways that he seemed to discern afar off, though almost endlessly opposed, impeded, and disappointed in his ministry at home in Bluehill. But, as noted above, Jonathan Fisher's diaries and biographers reveal the nature of a man whose life was free of bitterness or pessimism and full of optimism and resolve to see God's Kingdom come. His sanguinity and determination found expression in the exceptional family he raised, along with Dolly, on their hardscrabble farm, subsisting on a country parson's salary. Jonathan Fisher Crossette, though the details are sparse, lived and died a life that, from afar off, bears those same qualities. Like his grandfather before him, Jonathan Fisher

---

[48] Chase, *Maine Parson*, 6

[49] Wilson, "Daniel Merrill," *The Annals of the American Pulpit*, 509–510.

Crossette's life his was characterized by the faith described in the New Testament Letter to the Hebrews:

These all died in faith, not having received the things promised, but having seen them and greeted them from afar, and having acknowledged that they were strangers and exiles on the earth. For people who speak thus make it clear that they are seeking a homeland. If they had been thinking of that land from which they had gone out, they would have had opportunity to return. But as it is, they desire a better country, that is, a heavenly one. Therefore God is not ashamed to be called their God, for he has prepared for them a city. (Hebrews 11:13–16 ESV)

When Rev. Daniel Merrill followed the black pastor, Rev. Thomas Paul, into the pulpit of the Baptist Church at Nottingham West New Hampshire in 1814, the Abolitionist Movement in the United States was incipient and national leaders would not emerge for at least another decade. The ordination of Rev. Paul as clergy among a majority white congregation was not so much a plank in "the Baptist platform" early in the 19th century as it was an Evangelical feature of deeply rooted New England Puritan piety in Maine Baptists like Daniel Merrill, Adam Wilson, Rebekah Pinkham,[50] and James Gilpatrick. Whether slavery or issues regarding injustices committed against indigenous Americans were a matter of frequent or serious discussion among the Merrill household in Sedgwick, we do not yet know.[51] But, Merrill's

---

[50] Edwin William Garrison, *Memoir of Mrs. Rebekah P. Pinkham; Late Consort of Rev. E. Pinkham, of Sedgwick, Me., Containing an Account of Her Conversion, Interesting Letters to Her Friends, Her Writings for the Promotion of Missionary Objects, &c.* (Portland: Office of Zion's Advocate, 1840), 126–132.

[51] There is at least one record of Merrill, the legislator, advocating on behalf of a native American, who was tried and convicted of larceny in 1824. "In Council, July 12, 1824 ... To the Governor and Council of the State of Maine. Your Petitioner asks leave to say, That the petitioner was present, when Mayhew Tecunsy [*sic*], an Indian, was before the Supreme Judicial Court ... He was convicted of the crime, and sentenced to

legacy of preaching freedom in Christ through the gospel to people on the margins, both culturally and geographically, as a Gospel ranger, seemed to animate and inspire many of those in his immediate family and, particularly, his grandson Daniel David—"the Minnesota Merrill."

The actions of Daniel David Merrill and the members of the First Baptist of St. Paul were unusual for the time—and sadly, for the hundred years that followed. Understandably, modern readers can overlook the moral courage of the black and white Baptists in 1860's Minnesota. A large majority of evangelical churches in America today seek cross-racial cooperation. Few would openly advocate segregation. And virtually none would posit a theological or biblical defense of racism. Daniel David Merrill's actions appear today as the most consistent appropriation of evangelical theology—of his grandfather's theology. Those aware of treatment of African Americans—most of whom were (and are) Baptist and Methodist—lament that their (our) ancestors did not follow a path akin to First Baptist of St. Paul. And if it took another century to make the right moral connections, churches like Pilgrim Baptist exist today in part because of D.D. Merrill and others. Black and white alike, these Christians acted upon the knowledge of a unity drawn principally from theology that remains personal, experiential, and centered on Jesus Christ.

---

one month solitary imprisonment, and Eighteen months to hard labor ... Mayhew appears unusually intelligent, and was far from exhibiting the determinate villain; he has rather the appearance of frankness, honesty and good humour. But, being at a certain time, in a state of partial intoxication, he unloosed an horse tied to a post, wrode him a mile, took from the saddle bags, which were upon the horse, a bottle of rum, and a piece of cloth, and turned the horse adrift... Your Petitioner would further say... that the common good would not be endangered by extending pardon to the said Mayhew. Your Petitioner therefore prays the Governor and his honourable Council to take the above into their wise consideration and gratify the benevolence of their hearts in extending mercy in the present case." "Petition of Daniel Merrill for the Pardon pf [*sic*] Mayhew Tecusy" (1824). 1820-1829, 1147. https://digitalmaine.com/arc_executive_council_1820s/1147 (accessed June 26, 2023).

Evangelicalism today, global in its scope, possesses a strikingly diverse racial and ethnic composition, and it continues to grow by revivals akin to America's early awakenings. Even, in the 21st century, its message is taken by preachers who travel from town to town, some on foot, in a manner similar to Jonathan Fisher and Daniel Merrill—Gospel Rangers, ranging "to and fro" across the globe—"fathers of an extensive country." Their ministerial endeavors are yet unknown, the extent of their impact will be felt in years to come, but the story is familiar.

Bibliography

100 Years of Christian Service 1849-1949: Prepared in commemoration of the One-hundredth anniversary of The First Baptist Church St. Paul, Minnesota. Published and Distributed by The First Baptist Church St. Paul, Minnesota, 1949.

The Allens from William Allen (1602–1679) of Manchester England, and of Salem and Manchester, Massachusetts, in the direct line of descent through Nathaniel Allen (1744-1789) of Beverly, Massachusetts and Sedgwick, Maine, to Lt. Raymond Frederick Allen, Jr. (1931-) of Rochester, New York, with certain other descendants and collaterals" (no publisher or date: The State Historical Society of Wisconsin, original copy at the University of Wisconsin.

The American Baptist Magazine, published by the Board of Managers of the Baptist General Convention, Vol. IX. Boston: Lincoln & Edmands, 1829.

The American Baptist Magazine, published by the Board of Managers of the Baptist General Convention, Vol. XI.Boston: Lincoln & Edmands, 1831.

*Annual Reports of the American Bible Society: With An Account of its Organization: Lists of Officers and Managers, of Life Directors and Life Members. Extracts of Correspondence &c. &c..*New York: Daniel Fanshaw, 1838.

Appletons' Cyclopaedia of American Biography, James Grant Wilson and John Fiske, ed., New York: D. Appleton and Company, 1888.

The Baptist Memorial and Monthly Record, vol. 4. New York: John R. Bigelow, 1845.

Bluehill Academy, "GSA Course of Study, 1831" (1831). Blue Hill Documents. https://digitalmaine.com/blue_hill_documents/33

CATALOGUS COLLEGII WATERVILLENSIS M DCCC LXIII. Boston: Johannes-Milton Hewes et soc., 1863.

Colby College Overall Rankings | US News Best Colleges (accessed on December 20, 2021). https://www.usnews.com/best-colleges/colby-college-2039/overall-rankings

Daniel Merrill Estate Inventory, photographic copy of the original and transcript, Sedgwick-Brooklin Historical Society, Sedgwick, Maine.

Eighth Report of the American Bible Society, Presented May 13, 1824. With An Appendix, Containing Extracts of Correspondence, &c. &c. New York: Abraham Paul, 1824.

"First Baptist Church in Epitome," *One Hundredth Anniversary of the First Baptist Church Sedgwick Maine 1805-1905.* Anniversary Program June 11–18, 1905 (no publication information). https://www.sedgwickmaine.org/sargentville-library-historical-archive/library/REL/REL.4%20%20First%20Baptist%20Church%20of%20Sedgwick%20100th%20Anniversary%201905.pdf(accessed March 29, 2022).

Life and Times in a Coastal Village, Sedgwick Maine-1789–1989, commemorative booklet with no publication information produced for the Sedgwick Maine bi-centennial.

Minutes of the Fifteenth Anniversary of Hancock Baptist Association Held with the North Church in Sedgwick, Tuesday, Wednesday, and Thursday, Sept. 4th, 5th, and 6th, 1849. Portland: A. Shirley and Son, Printers, 1849.

Pilgrim Baptist Church, 732 Central Ave. West Saint Paul, MN; https://www.pilgrimbaptistchurch.org

A Record book belonging to the Church of Christ in Sedgwick. 1794.

Sixteenth Annual Report of the American Bible Society. New York: Daniel Fanshaw, 1832.

Traditions and Records of Brooksville, Maine, collected by The Brooksville Historical Society 1935–36. Auburn: Merrill & Webber Company, undated.

Adams, Priscilla. *Versatility Yankee Style.* The Farnsworth Museum. Rockland, Maine: Courier-Gazette, Inc., 1977.

Ahlstrom, Sydney. *A Religious History of the American People.* New Haven, CT: Yale University Press, 1973.

Anderson, Rufus. *An Estimate of Immersion: the Main Principle of Close Communion, as Defended by Rev. Daniel Merrill: Concluded with an Address to Him in Several Discussions, Offered to the Friends of Truth and Peace.* Salem: Joshua Cushing, 1806.

_____. *The Close Communion of the Baptists: In Principle and Practice, Proved to Be Unscriptural, and of a Bad Tendency in the Church of God.* Salem Massachusetts: Joshua Cushing, 1805.

Bibliography

Aquinas, Thomas. *Selected Writings*. Edited and translated by Ralph McInerny. New York: Penguin, 1998.

Armstrong, O. K. and Marjorie Armstrong. *The Baptists in America*. Garden City, NJ: Doubleday, 1979.

Augustine of Hippo. *Homilies on the Gospel of John 1–40*. Edited by Allan D. Fitzgerald. Translated by Edmund Hill. New York: New City Press, 2009.

Austin, Samuel. *An Examination of the Representations and Reasonings Contained in Seven Sermons, Lately Published, by the Rev. Daniel Merrill, on the Mode and Subjects of Baptism: In Several Letters Addressed to the Author, in Which It Is Attempted to Shew, That Those Representations and Reasonings Are Not Founded in Truth*. Worcester, MA: Isaiah Thomas, 1805.

Baines, Ron "Daniel Merrill 1765–1833," *A Noble Company: Biographical Essays on Notable Particular-Regular Baptist in America Vol. 6*, ed. Terry Wolever. Springfield, MI: Particular Baptist Press, 2015.

Baines, Ronald S. *Separating God's Two Kingdoms: Regular Baptists in Maine, Nova Scotia, and New Brunswick, 1780 to 1815*, (2020) Electronic Theses and Dissertations. 3183. University of Maine.

Ban, Joseph D. "Was John Bunyan a Baptist?: A Case Study in Historiography" *Baptist Quarterly*. Volume 30, no. 8. 367–76.

Banks, Ronald F. *Maine Becomes a State: The Movement to Separate Maine from Massachusetts, 1785-1820*. Middletown, CT: Wesleyan University Press.

Baxter, Richard. *A Christian Directory*. Ligonier: Soli Deo Gloria Publications, 1990.

Bebbington, David. *Patterns in History: A Christian Perspective on Historical Thought*. Vancouver, Regent College Publishing, 2000.

———. *Evangelicalism in Modern Britain: A History from the 1730's to the 1980's*. New York: Routledge, 1989.

Benedict, David. *A General History of the Baptist Denomination in America, and other Parts of the World*. Volume 1. Boston: Lincoln and Edmands, 1813.

———. *Fifty Years Among the Baptists*. Boston: Gould & Lincoln, 1860.

———. *The Watery War: or, A Poetical Description of the Existing Controversy Between the Pedobaptists and Baptists, on the Subjects and Mode of Baptism*. Boston: Manning & Loring, 1808.

Bergamasco, Lucia. "Religion, patriotism, and political factionalism during the war of 1812," *Revue française d'études américaines*, No. 139, Wars of 1812 / Guerres de 1812. Paris: Editions Belin, 2014.

Bianco, Jane, *A Wondrous Journey: Jonathan Fisher & the Making of Scripture Animals*. Rockland: Farnsworth Art Museum, 2014.

Bosworth, W.A. *A Discourse Delivered at the Funeral of Rev. Robert Crossette*. Cincinnati, OH: R. Clarke, 1872.

Bowden, Karen, Charles E. Clark, and James S. Leamon, eds. *Maine in The Early Republic*. Hanover, N.H.: University Press of New England, Published for the Maine Historical Society and Maine Humanities Council, 1988.

Burnham, Emily. "Man Leads Effort to Preserve Sedgwick Church," *The Bangor Daily News*, July 19, 2010: https://bangor-dailynews.com/2010/07/19/living/man-leads-effort-to-pre-serve-sedgwick-church (Accessed March 29, 2022).

Burrage, Henry S. *History of the Baptists in Maine*. Portland: Marks Printing House, 1904.

Butterfield, Herbert. *Christianity and History*. New York: Charles Scribners, 1949.

Calvin, John. *Institutes of the Christian Religion*. Edited and translated by Henry Beveridge. Grand Rapids: Eerdman's 1989.

Candage, R. G. F. *Settlement and Progress of the Town of Bluehill, Maine. An Historical Address*. Boston: T. R. Marvin & Son, 1886.

_____. *Historical Sketches of Bluehill, Maine*. Ellsworth: Hancock County Publishing Company, 1905.

Case, Isaac. "Further Account of Rev. Mr. Case's Mission in the District of Maine, extracted from a Letter of his to the Secretary of the Society, dated at Reedfield, January 8th, 1805," in Baldwin, editor. *The Massachusetts Baptist Missionary Magazine*, 1 (Sept. 1803–Jan. 1808), No. 4 (May1805): 107–108.

CATALOGUS COLLEGII WATERVILLENSIS M DCCC LXIII. Boston: Johannes-Milton Hewes et soc., 1863

Carter, Richard. "A Puritan Encounter with the Nineteenth Century: The Mind and Ministry of Jonathan Fisher." Unpublished doctoral thesis. Gordon-Conwell Theological Seminary. South Hamilton, MA, 2004.

Cathey, Brittany P. "Reverend Jonathan Fisher: One Thread in the Web of Early American Education, 1780–1830." Unpublished MA thesis. University of Maine. Orono, ME, 2015.

Chadbourne, Henry. *A History of Education in Maine*. Orno, ME: University Press, 1936.

Chadwick, Jabez. *Four Sermons, on the Mode and Subjects of Christian Baptism. By Jabez Chadwick, Pastor of the First Presbyterian Congregation in Onondaga*. Utica: Seward and Williams, 1811.

Champlin, T. *Historical Discourse Delivered at the Fiftieth Anniversary of Colby University, August 2nd, 1870*. Lewiston: Journal Steam Press, 1870.

Channing, William Ellery, "Likeness to God: Discourse at the Ordination of the Rev. F. A. Farley, Providence, RI., 1828, in *The Works of William E. Channing, DD*.

Chapman, George T. *Sketches of the Alumni of Dartmouth College from the First Graduation in 1771 to the Present Time, with a Brief History of the Institution*. Cambridge: Riverside Press, 1867.

Chase, Mary Ellen. *Jonathan Fisher: Maine Parson, 1747–1815*. New York: The Macmillan Company, 1948.

Chute, Anthony L., Nathan A. Finn, and Michael A. G. Haykin, *The Baptist Story: From English Sect to Global Movement*. Nashville, B&H, 2015.

Clark, Calvin Montague. *History of the Congregational Churches in Maine. Volume 1: History of the Maine Missionary Society 1807-1925*. Portland, ME: The Southworth Press, 1936.

_____. *The Congregational Churches in Maine. Volume 2: History of the Individual Churches 1600-1826*. Portland, ME: The Congregational Christian Conference of Maine, 1935.

_____. *History of Bangor Theological Seminary*. Boston: The Pilgrim Press, 1916.

Clark, Charles E., Leamon, James S. and Bowden, Karen, eds., *Maine in The Early Republic*. Hanover, N.H.: University Press of New England, Published for the Maine Historical Society and Maine Humanities Council, 1988.

Clough, Annie L. *Head of the Bay: Sketches and Pictures of Blue Hill, Maine, 1762-1952*. Printed by Shoreacre Press for Congregational Church of Blue Hill. Woodstock: Elm Tree Press, 1953.

Dillenberger John and Claude Welch, *Protestant Christianity: Interpreted through its Development*. New York: Charles Scribner's, 1954.

Dorrien, Gary. *The Making of American Liberal Theology: Imagining Progressive Religion 1805–1900*. Louisville: Westminster John Knox, 2001.

Emerson, Ralph Waldo. *The Essays of Ralph Waldo Emerson*. Cambridge, MA: Harvard University Press, 1987.

Field, Joseph. *Strictures on Seven Sermons, with an Appendix, by Reverend Daniel Merrill, of Sedgwick Maine. On the Mode and Subjects of Baptism. In Twelve Sections*. Northampton: Thomas M. Pomroy, 1806.

Finn, Nathan A. *History: A Student's Guide*. Wheaton, IL: Crossway, 2016.

Fisher, Jonathan. *The Diaries of Jonathan Fisher: July 1795–January 1835*, Typescript (https://digitalmaine.com/blue_hill_documents).

_____. *Records of the Hancock Association formed at SEDGWICK, Septem. 1, 1797. Bluehill Mar. 29. 1830*, Transcript in a Word doc., Jonathan Fisher Memorial Society, Blue Hill, Maine.

_____. *A Sermon, Preached at Machias, September 3, 1800, at the ordination of Rev. Marshfield Steele: to the pastoral care of the church and society in that town*. Boston, MA: E. Lincoln, For David J. Waters, 1801.

_____. *A Short Essay on Baptism, Designed for the Benefit of Common Readers*. Boston: Samuel T. Armstrong, 1817.

_____. *Sermon 914, February 29, 1806* (Archives, Jonathan Fisher Memorial, Blue Hill, ME, p. 4); transcription from Fisher's shorthand by Michael McVaugh, July 2023.

_____. *Sermon 915, undated* (Archives, Jonathan Fisher Memorial, Blue Hill, ME, p. 1); transcription from Fisher's shorthand by Michael McVaugh, July 2023.

_____. *Sermon 916, March 2, 1806* (Archives, Jonathan Fisher Memorial, Blue Hill, ME, p. 4-5); transcription from Fisher's shorthand by Michael McVaugh, July 2023.

_____. "Sketches from the Life of the Rev. Jonathan Fisher, pastor of the Congregational Church in Bluehill, Maine, interspersed with extracts from his journal written by himself" (*Sketches*). Transcribed by Edith Weren, Blue Hill Library, Blue Hill, Maine, 1812.

Fitzgerald, Allan D. *Homilies on the Gospel of John 1–40* ed., trans., Edmund Hill. New York: New City Press, 2009.

Garrison, Edwin William. *Memoir of Mrs. Rebekah P. Pinkham; Late Consort of Rev. E. Pinkham, of Sedgwick, Me., Containing an Account of Her Conversion, Interesting Letters to Her Friends, Her*

Writings for the Promotion of Missionary Objects, &c. Portland: Office of Zion's Advocate, 1840.

Garrison, William Lloyd. *Thoughts on African Colonization, or, An impartial exhibition of the doctrines, principles and purposes of the American Colonization Society: together with resolutions, addresses and remonstrances of the free people of color.* Boston: Garrison and Knapp, 1832.

Gilmore-Lehne, William J. *Reading Becomes a Necessity of Life: Material and Cultural Life in Rural New England, 1780–1835.* Knoxville: University of Tennessee Press, 1992.

Gilpatrick, James. "Biographical Sketch of the Rev. Daniel Merrill," from the funeral sermon he preached upon the death of Merrill, in *The Baptist Memorial and Monthly Record.* Volume 4. New York: John R. Bigelow, 1845.

_____. *A Sermon Delivered June 5th 1833, at the Funeral of Rev. Daniel Merrill, A.M. Late Pastor of the First Baptist Church in Sedgwick.* Ellsworth, ME: Robert Grant Printer, 1833. (The only extant copy known to the authors resides in the archives of the Jonathan Fisher House, Blue Hill, ME).

_____. *The Annals of the American Pulpit; or Commemorative Notices of Distinguished American Clergymen of Various Denominations, from the Early Settlement of the Country to the Close of the Year Eighteen Hundred and Sixty. With Historical Introductions..* William B. Sprague, D.D., Vol. VI. New York: Robert Carter & Brothers, 1860.

_____. *Transcript of Letter Sent to Moses Merrill from James Gilpatrick dated January 25, 1825.* Acadia Archives, Acadia University. https://archives.acadiau.ca/islandora/object/research%3A4547?search=Merrill (accessed October 16, 2022).

Gleason, Randall, and Kelly Kapic. Editors. *The Devoted Life: An Introduction to the Puritan Classics.* Downer's Grove, IL: Apollos, 2004.

Goetting (née Cathey), Brittany. "'He Has Abundantly Poured out His Holy Spirit in Eden and Mount Desert': The Baptist Connection on Mount Desert Island, 1790-1840," *Chebacco: The Magazine of the Mount Desert Island Historical Society*, vol. XX, 2019, ed. Tim Garrity. Newcastle: Lincoln County Publishing, Co., 2019.

_____. "Bound by Print: The Baptist Borderlands of Maine and the Canadian Maritimes, 1770-1840" (2022). Unpublished doctoral thesis. Electronic Theses and Dissertations. 3571. https://digitalcommons.library.umaine.edu/etd/3571

Green, James Benjamin. *A Harmony of the Westminster Presbyterian Standards with Explanatory Notes*. Richmond: John Knox Press, 1951.

Green, Samuel L. "Thomas Lord, Joiner and Housewright," *Magazine of Art: A National Magazine Relating the Arts to Contemporary Life*. Edited by John D. Morse, Volume 40, Number 6, October, 1947. New York, New York.

Green, William D. "Called To Serve," in *The Children of Lincoln: White Paternalism and the Limits of Black Opportunity in Minnesota, 1860–1876*. Minneapolis: University of Minnesota Press, 2018.

Hall, Gaylord Crosette. *Supplement to the Biographical Sketch Of The Rev. Jonathan Fisher of Blue Hill, Maine*. New York: Gaylord C. Hall, 1946.

Handy, Robert. *A History of the Churches in United States and Canada*. New York: Oxford University Press, 1977.

Hatch, Nathan O. *The Democratization of American Christianity*. New Haven, CT: Yale University Press, 1989.

Hayne, Coe. *Baptist Trail-Makers of Michigan*. Philadelphia: Judson Press, 1936.

Hindmarsh, Bruce. *The Evangelical Conversion Narrative: Spiritual Autobiography in Early Modern England*. Oxford: Oxford University Press, 2005.

_____. *John Newton and The English Evangelical Tradition*. Grand Rapids: Eerdmans, 1996.

Hudson, Winthrop. *Religion in America: An historical account of the development of American Religious Life* 2nd edition. New York: Charles Scribner's, 1973.

Historical Memorial: Presbyterian Church of Succasunna, N.J. 1765-1895. Dover: Press of the Iron Era, 1895.

Jackson, Andrew. State of the Union Address. 6 December, 1831
_____. State of the Union Address. 3 December, 1833.

Kidd, Thomas. *George Whitefield: America's Spiritual Founding Father*. New Haven, CT: Yale University Press, 2017.

_____. "The Bebbington Quadrilateral and the Work of the Holy Spirit," *Evangelicals: Who They Have Been, Are Now, and Could Be*, Mark Noll, editor. Grand Rapids: William B. Eerdmans Publishing Company, 2019

Klein, Joshua A. *Hands Employed Aright: The Furniture Making of Jonathan Fisher (1768-1847)*. Fort Mitchell, KY: Lost Art Press, 2018.

Leonard, Bill J. *Baptist Ways: A History*. Valley Forge, PA: Judson Press, 2003.

Lewis, C. S. "On the Reading of Old Books," in *God in the Dock: Essays on Theology and Ethics*, Edited by Walter Hooper. Grand Rapids, MI: Eerdmans's, 1970.

Lloyd Jones, Martin. *Revival* 5th edition. Wheaton, IL: Crossway, 1997.

Macintyre, Alasdair. *After Virtue: A Study in Moral Theory* 3rd edition. New York: Bloomsbury, 2021.

Marini, Stephen. "Religious Revolution in the District of Maine 1780-1820." In *Maine in the Early Republic*. Charles E. Clark, James S. Leamon & Karen Bowden, editors. Hanover, NH: University of New England Press, 1988.

Marinner, Ernest Cummings. *The History of Colby College*. Waterville: Colby College Press, 1963.

McLoughlin, William. *Soul Liberty: Baptists' Struggle in New England 1630–1833*. Hanover, N. H.: University of New England Press, 1991.

Merrill, Daniel. *Autobiography of Rev. Daniel Merrill*. Philadelphia: Baptist General Tract Society, 1833.

_____. *A Sermon Preached at the Ordination of Rev. PHINEAS BOND, PASTOR OF THE FIRST BAPTIST CHURCH IN STEUBEN, May 25, 1825*. Waterville: Wm. Hastings, 1825.

_____. *Balaam Disappointed a Thanksgiving Sermon, Delivered at Nottingham-West, April 13, 1815 a Day Recommended by the National Government*. Concord, New Hampshire: Isaac & W.R. Hill, 1815.

_____. *The Constitution of a Society for Promoting the Education of Religious Young Men for the Ministry, and Also for Sending the Gospel to the Destitute*. Salem, MA: Joshua Cushing, 1803.

_____. *The Gospel Church, Vindicated by the Scriptures. From the Severe Accusations; the Ingenious but Very Mischievous, Sophistry of Nathaniel S. Prime, Pastor of the Presbyterian Church, in Cambridge, N.Y.* Concord: Hill & Moore, 1819.

_____. *The Gospel Rangers. A Sermon Delivered at the Ordination of Elder Henry Hale*. Second Edition. Springfield, MA: Henry Brewer, 1807.

_____. *The Kingdom of Heaven, Distinguished from Babylon, a Sermon Delivered at the Introduction of the Lincoln Association, Sept. 21–22, 1808.* Buckstown, Maine: William W. Clapp, 1810.

_____. *The Mode and Subjects of Baptism Examined, in Seven Sermons; to Which Is Added, a Brief History of the Baptists.* Salem, Massachusetts: Joshua Cushing, 1804.

_____. *Letters Occasioned by Rev. Samuel Worcester's Two Discourses* published in 1807 and *The Second Exposition of Some of the false Arguments, Mistakes, and Errors of the Rev. Samuel Austin, Published for the Benefit of the Public.* Boston: Manning & Loring, Boston: Manning & Loring, 1807.

_____. *Dr. Merrill's Answer to the Christians, and Other Inhabitants of Sedgwick; also the Confession and Covenant of the Church of Christ in that place.* Newburyport, Massachusetts: Edmund M. Blunt, 1801.

_____. *Open Communion with All Who Keep the Ordinances as Christ Delivered Them to the Saints. Eight Letters on Open Communion Addressed to Rufus Anderson, A.M.* Boston: Manning & Loring, 1805.

_____. "Revival in Sedgwick, Extract of A Letter From Rev. D. Merrill to One of the Editors," *American Baptist Magazine and Missionary Intelligencer.* Volume 3. Boston: James Loring, and Lincoln & Edmands, 1822.

_____. *The Second Exposition of Some of the false Arguments, Mistakes, and Errors of the Rev. Samuel Austin, Published for the Benefit of the Public*, 1807.

Merrill, Samuel Pearce. "Rev. Daniel Merrill, An Appreciation," *Centennial of the First Baptist Church, Sedgwick, Maine, June 11–18, 1905* (1905) 59. Sargentville Library Historical Archive online.

_____. *My Loves and My Lovers.* Jamaica, N.Y: Marion Press, 1909.

Millet, Joshua. *A History of the Baptists in Maine; Together with Brief Notices of Societies and Institutions.* Portland, Maine: Charles Day & Co., 1845.

Moore, Susan Hardman. *Pilgrims: New World Settler and the Call of Home.* New Haven: Yale University Press, 2007.

Morison, Samuel Eliot. *Three Centuries of Harvard.* Cambridge, MA: Harvard University Press, 1936.

Morril, David Lawrence. *A Concise Letter Written to Rev. Daniel Merrill, A.M., of Sedgwick Containing Strictures and Remarks on*

Several Letters by Him, Addressed to Rev. R. Anderson, A.M., Entitled, Open Communion with All Who Keep the Ordinances as Christ Delivered Them to the Saints: In Which the Fallacy of His Propositions and Arguments Is Illustrated. Amherst: Joseph Cushing, 1806.

Murphy, Kevin D. *Jonathan Fisher of Blue Hill, Maine: Commerce, Culture, and Community on the Eastern Frontier.* Boston: University of Massachusetts Press, 2010.

Nevius. Helen S. Coan, *The Life of John Livingston Nevius: For Forty Years a Missionary In China.* New York: Fleming H. Revell Company, 1895.

Niebuhr, Reinhold. *The Irony of American History.* Chicago: University of Chicago Press, 2008.

Olds, R.L., *THE HISTORY OF THE FIRST BAPTIST CHURCH in BLUEHILL.* Typescript copy of the manuscript for a presentation at the centennial celebration of the First Baptist Church. First Baptist Church of Blue Hill in Maine, archives.

Payne, Roger M. *The Self and the Sacred: Conversion and Autobiography in Early American Protestantism.* Knoxville: University of Tennessee Press, 1998.

Pelt, Owen, and Ralph Lee Smith. *The Story of the National Baptists.* New York: Vantage Press, 1960.

Pinkham, Rebekah P., *Narrative of the Life of Miss Lucy Cole, of Sedgwick, Maine. In Which is Exhibited the Controlling Power of Piety in Early Life.* Boston: James Loring, 1830.

_____. *Memoir of Simeon J. Milliken, Esq. Of Mount Desert, Maine, with a Short Sketch of the Last Hours and Dying Scene of His Two Beloved Brothers.* Boston: James Loring, 1836.

Pomeroy, Swan. "Jonathan Fisher," *The Annals of the American Pulpit; or Commemorative Notices of Distinguished American Clergymen of Various Denominations, from the Early Settlement of the Country to the Close of the Year Eighteen Fifty-Five. With Historical Introductions*, Vol. II. William B. Sprague, ed.. New York: Robert Carter and Bros., 1857.

Powers, Peter. *A Brief Account of the Late Revivals of Religion in a Number of Towns in the New-England States, and Also in Nova-Scotia. Extracted Chiefly from Letters Written by Several Gentlemen of Unquestionable Veracity. To Which is added, A Very Interesting Letter, From a Minister in London to His Friend in Massachusetts.* Boston: Manning & Loring, 1799.

Powicke, Frederick J. *The Reverend Richard Baxter Under the Cross (1662–1691)*. London: Jonathan Cape Ltd., 1927.

Pratt, Dura D., *The Baptist Encyclopaedia. A Dictionary of The Doctrines, Ordinances, Usages, Confessions of Faith, Sufferings, Labors, and Successes, and of the General History of the Baptist Denomination in All Lands, with Numerous Biogrpahical Sketches of Distinguished American and Foreign Baptists, and a Supplement.* Edited by William Cathcart, D.D. Philadlelphia: Louis H. Everts, 1883.

Prime, Nathaniel S. *A Familiar Illustration of Christian Baptism: In Which the Proper Subjects of that Ordinance and the Mode of Administration are Ascertained from the Word of God and the History of the Church; and Defended from the Objections Usually Urged by the Opposers of Infant Baptism, and the Advocates of Immersion: In the Form of a Dialogue.* Salem, (N.Y.): Dodd & Stevenson, 1818.

Reed, John. *An Apology for the Rite of Infant Baptism and for the Usual Modes of Baptizing in Which an Attempt Is Made to State Fairly and Clearly the Arguments in Proof of These Doctrines, and Also to Refute the Objections and Reasonings Alleged against Them by the Rev. Daniel Merrill and by the Baptists in General.* Providence: Heaton & Williams, 1806.

Rorabaugh, William. *The Alcoholic Republic.* New York: Oxford University Press, 1981.

Ryrie, Alec. *Protestants: The Radicals Who Made the Modern World.* London: William Collins, 2017.

Saint Pierre, Jacques-Henri Bernardine. *Paul et Virginie.*

Sassi, Jonathan D. *A Republic of Righteousness: The Public Christianity of the Post-Revolutionary New England Clergy.* New York: Oxford University Press, 2001.

Sewall, Jonathan. *A Memoir of Rev. Jotham Sewall, of Chesterville, Maine.* Bangor: E. F. Duren, 1853.

Sheldon, Addison Erwin. *History and Stories of Nebraska.* Chicago, IL: The University Publishing Company, 1913.

Smith, Raoul. "The Language of Jonathan Fisher (1768–1847)," *Publication of the American Dialect Society* 72 (1985).

Smith, Arthur Warren. *Historical Sketch of the Town of Sedgwick.* "Centennial of the First Baptist Church Sedgwick, Maine: June 11–18, 1905, Two Historical Papers." (no publication date or publisher, bound 64 pages).

_____. *A Baptist Factor In A Critical Decade Of New Hampshire History: a paper setting forth the contribution of Daniel Merrill, as pastor of Nottingham-West Baptist church, to New Hampshire history; read before the annual meeting of the New Hampshire Baptist Historical Society at Dover, October 7, 1908.* Typed manuscript, New Hampshire Historical Society archives.

Sprague, William B. Editor. *Annals of the American Pulpit*, Volume 2. New York: Robert Carter and Bros., 1857.

Spring, Samuel. *Mr. Spring's Sermon. A Sermon Preached at the Ordination of the Rev. Daniel Merrill in Sedgwick. Sept. 17, 1793.* Newburyport: Edmund M. Blunt, 1794.

Stevens, George. "George Stevens' Will" (1851). Blue Hill Documents. 32. https://digitalmaine.com/blue_hill_documents/32

Taylor, Alan. "From Fathers to Friends of the People: Political Personas in the Early Republic," *Journal of the Early Republic,* Vol. 11, No. 4, Winter, 1991.

_____. *Liberty Men and Great Proprietors: The Revolutionary Settlement on the Maine Frontier, 1760-1820.* Williamsburg: Published for the Institute of Early American History and Culture, University of North Carolina Press, 1990.

Thurston, Brown. *Thurston Genealogies Compiled by Brown Thurston, Portland, Maine.* Portland: Brown Thurston, 1892.

Thurston, David. *1635–1880 Thurston Genealogies Compiled by Brown Thurston, Portland, Maine.* Portland: Brown Thurston and Hoyt, Fogg and Donham, 1880.

Tocqueville, Alexis. *Democracy in America.* Translated by Henry Reeve. New York: Bantam Dell, 2004.

Turner, John G. *They Knew They Were Pilgrims: Plymouth Colony and the Contest for Religious Liberty.* New Haven: Yale University Press, 2020.

Walker, Williston, *The Creeds and Platforms of Congregationalism.* New York: Charles Scribners, Sons, 1893.

Ward, Nathaniel. *The Simple Cobbler of Aggawam in America* 4th edition. London, 1647.

Whitefield, George. *George Whitefield's Journals (1737–1741).* Edited by William V. David. Edinburgh: Banner of Truth Trust, 1986.

Wilbur, E. M. *A History of Unitarianism in Transylvania, England, and America.* Boston, MA: Beacon Press, 1945.

Willison, John. *The Afflicted Man's Companion, or, a directory for persons and families afflicted with sickness or any other distress: with directions to the sick.* New York: Evert Duyckinck, 1806.

Wilson, Adam. "Daniel Merrill," in *The Annals of the American Pulpit; or Commemorative Notices of Distinguished American Clergymen of Various Denominations, from the Early Settlement of the Country to the Close of the Year Eighteen Hundred and Sixty. With Historical Introductions..* William B. Sprague, D.D., Vol. VI. New York: Robert Carter & Brothers, 1860.

Wolever, Terry. Editor. *A Noble Company: Biographical Essays on Notable Particular-Regular Baptist in America Vol. 6.* Springfield, Missouri: Particular Baptist Press, 2015.

Wood, Esther. *A History of George Stevens Academy* https://www.georgestevensacademy.org/Page/5 (accessed March 19, 2022).

_____. "George Stevens, Village Squire," in *Deep Roots: A Maine Legacy.* Camden: Yankee Books, 1990.

_____. *SKETCH OF THE BLUE HILL BAPTIST CHURCH Given in June of 1956.* Typescript copy of the manuscript for a presentation at 150th anniversary of the First Baptist Church. First Baptist Church of Blue Hill in Maine, archives.

Worcester, Samuel. *Two Discourses, on the Perpetuity and Provision of God's Gracious Covenant with Abraham and His Seed.* Salem: Haven Pool, 1805.

Worcester, Noah. *Impartial Inquiries concerning the progress of the Baptist Denomination* (1794).

Wright, Conrad. *The Beginnings of Unitarianism in America.* Boston: Beacon Press, 1957.

Index

Index

Index